# Jewish Life in America

# Jewish Life in America

Edited by THEODORE FRIEDMAN AND

ROBERT GORDIS

HORIZON PRESS    NEW YORK    1955

Copyright, 1955, by Horizon Press inc.
L. C. Catalog Card Number 55–11462
Manufactured in the United States of America

# Contents

         5

## THE COMMUNITY

# Preface

This volume had its genesis in the special issue
of the quarterly magazine *Judaism* published in
the fall of 1954 on the occasion of the Tercen-
tenary celebration of the American Jewish community. The warm
reception afforded the special issue and the enthusiastic comments
of its readers led the editors to believe that both in scope and in
approach it met a perceptible, continuing need. Its scope, here
extended to include significant areas untouched in the magazine,
embraces the whole range of Jewish spiritual and cultural creativity in America; the movements and forces—religious, intellectual, social and esthetic—that bid fair to give shape and
substance to the life of the American Jewish community of tomorrow. In each instance these are viewed by the contributors
to this volume against the background of the American environment and its interplay with the tradition. Again, in almost every
instance, the contributors, while assessing the past contributions
and plotting the course of development of a particular movement,
tendency or form of Jewish expression, have sought to give some

8

indication of its prospective place in the totality of the future of American Jewish life. Finally, the whole is viewed within the context of the present and putative situation in the domain of church-state and interfaith relationships: the permanent framework of all forms of Jewish activities on the American locale.

Comprehensiveness of scope was but one of the twin goals the editors aimed to achieve in the projection of the present volume. Of no less moment was their unmitigated desire for a judicious, evaluative approach. Party and institutional publications bring the American Jewish reader a surfeit of self-encomium and a loud trumpeting of achievements. Our contributors, though personally aligned and deeply committed to the movements and ideologies they analyze, display, in the editors' opinion, a remarkable ability to approach their respective themes with critical objectivity; achievements are contrasted with deficiencies, solid gains with ambiguities, consolidations with setbacks. Here too, then, the reader will meet with the kind of tempered appraisal of the mainstreams of American Jewish creativity rarely to be found in contemporary writing. The latter falls either into the category of bland and blind self-congratulation or subtle, or not so subtle, devaluation. Objectivity and personal commitment are not mutually exclusive; of their happy union, this book is solid evidence. It is a mark of Jewish maturity that a group of writers and scholars could be found who see the creative aspects of American Jewish life steadily and whole.

It remains but to record our deep sense of indebtedness to the American Jewish Congress, whose generous and understanding sponsorship has made possible the publication of the quarterly *Judaism*. We are indebted, too, to its distinguished Executive Director, Dr. David Petegorsky, without whose encouragement and counsel this volume would not have been possible. Our gratitude is expressed to Mr. Ben Raeburn, President of the Horizon Press, whose counsel and assistance have been of inestimable value. We are thankful, too, to Rabbi Abraham I. Shinedling for his meticulous preparation of the index.

ROBERT GORDIS and THEODORE FRIEDMAN

# American Jewry: Fourth Century

## ROBERT GORDIS

It was three centuries ago in September, 1654, that the American Jewish community was born.

The event took place in true traditional fashion—with the arrival of a group of refugees in New Amsterdam, fleeing from Brazil. The town which was later to become New York was their fourth home in recent memory, the third lap in their apparently endless quest for safety from religious persecution. For their trek had begun in Spain and Portugal, from which they had fled, seeking refuge from the rigors of the Inquisition. They had come to Holland and thence to Brazil, originally a Dutch possession. Now Portugal had captured Brazil, bringing the Inquisition into the New World, and so the Jews had taken the wanderer's staff in hand again. Their reception in New Amsterdam was somewhat less than cordial at the hands of the Dutch governor, Peter Stuyvesant. Yet from the beginning, such was the spirit of this new land, that they and their successors saw in it a measure of opportunity and a degree of liberty without parallel in the millennial history of their people.

Today, that score of fugitives has grown to five and a half million souls, the largest and freest Jewish community in the world. With the exception of Russian Jewry in the days of the Czars, American Israel constitutes the single largest aggregation of Jewish population in history. Palestine, the homeland of the Jewish people, never counted so large a number.

In every conceivable way, the manifold Jewish contributions to American life have been surveyed, assessed, and praised. The saga of patriotism and heroism written by Jewish fighting men in all the wars of the Republic from Revolutionary days to our own day has been glorified. The historian and the journalist have been hard put to do justice to all that American Jewry has contributed to the welfare and progress of the country in peace. In the fields of government and public affairs, commerce and industry, science and literature, music and art, American Jewry has played a distinguished role. Men of genius and talent have made a major impact upon every section of American life and untold numbers of lesser men have played creditable roles. Haym Salomon and Mordecai M. Noah, Jacob H. Schiff and Julius Rosenwald, Louis D. Brandeis and Benjamin Cardozo, Albert Michelson and Albert Einstein, Emma Lazarus and Edna Ferber, Henrietta Szold and Lillian Wald, Samuel Gompers and Sidney Hillman—this roster of names, chosen almost at random, could be matched by others of equal stature in many other areas of achievement.

For good or for ill, America is essentially a practical civilization. Being American to the core, American Jews have responded to the same stimuli as their fellow-citizens. Hence the contribution of American Jewry to Jewish life has been expressed largely in practical terms. The doer has been more noticeable than the thinker. Countless tributes, largely deserved, have been paid to the magnificent achievements in philanthropy by American Jews since the outbreak of the First World War to the middle of this century. Funds for the relief of pogrom victims, for migration and rehabilitation, for physical care, for religious education and vocational training—all have been poured forth by American Jews with prodigal generosity. American Jews have been in the forefront of the defense of Jewish rights the world over, beginning with the battle for minority rights in the Treaty of Versailles and culminating in the emergence of the State of Israel as a viable entity in the family of nations. They supplied a large part of the cost of weapons of defense for the young state against its bellicose neighbors, and thus helped to frustrate the five-pronged invasion that threatened to drive Israel into the sea. During the years of Israeli independence, American Jews have made available much of their technical know-how, the skill and efficiency characteristic of American industry for the upbuilding and defense of the new State.

## II

All these aspects of the creative activity of American Jewry both on behalf of America and the Jewish people have within recent years received their due. But neither the defenders of American Jewry nor its detractors—and there are both—have paid much attention to the spiritual and cultural achievements of American Jewry. By all but universal consent, American Israel, like America itself, is regarded as the land of the Rule of Gold, not the Golden Rule. American Jewry is commonly charged with materialism and with a lack of concern for the spirit. Now undoubtedly no period in American Jewish history rivals the contribution of Spanish Jewry to the vast treasure-house of Jewish culture. American Jewry has produced no such massive and enduring monument to the Jewish spirit as the Babylonian Talmud, nor, truth to tell, is there a likely prospect. One may even doubt whether American Jewish achievements are relatively as significant as the contributions of Hellenistic Jewry in ancient Alexandria, which produced the first translation of the Bible in history, the famed Septuagint, and much of the Apocryphal and Pseudepigraphical literature. No Jewish philosopher has yet arisen in American Jewry to rival Philo of Alexandria in stature and significance.

That American Jewry is a young community, to be treated with the indulgence granted to youth, is an alibi which has grown threadbare with the years. The three hundredth anniversary of American Jewish settlement on this continent has made us wary of taking refuge in this excuse. America as a whole has come of age and so has American Jewry, and heavy responsibilities have been thrust upon both. The ills of American Jewry, its vast shapelessness, the incredibly low level of Jewish knowledge, its consequently easy surrender to vulgarity and emptiness, its abandonment of the prophetic tradition in favor of conformity and "inconspicuousness," all these have persisted too long to be discounted as signs of immaturity or as mere growing pains. There is far too much that is unsatisfactory in the situation that cries out for wise and energetic action.

Nonetheless, it is not true that American Jewry has been spiritually sterile. The twentieth century has produced an imposing array of scholars in all schools of thought, who have enriched every branch of Jewish literature, history and thought. Outstanding religious leaders have come to the fore, who have exerted a valuable and powerful influence upon America as a whole and upon the Jewish community in particular. The deep-seated literary gifts of the People of the Book have expressed themselves in increasing measure in English, but there have been outstanding achievements in Yiddish literature, and some creditable work in the field of Hebrew. The last few decades have shown a renaissance of interest in Jewish art and music. Much of this cultural activity is still in the rudimentary stage, yet the future historian may find in it more than a little of the permanent, or at least of the promising.

III

In all these respects, American Jewry is building upon the foundation of the past, developing branches of culture that have long been traditional in earlier Jewish communities. Naturally these manifestations of the Jewish spirit have taken on forms reflecting the American environment. It has, however, not been adequately recognized that American Jewry has produced several specific contributions to the vitality of Judaism which are characteristically American, and not merely a replica of older forms.

The first of these, curiously enough, is actually the oldest living institution in the world today, the Synagogue. The novelty of the American synagogue has been obscured by being confused with the synagogue building in earlier communities. In the past, the synagogue structure always served a variety of communal purposes, conventionally subsumed under the three headings of the *Beth Hamidrash,* "the house of study," the *Beth Haknesseth,* "the house of assembly" and the *Beth Hatefillah,* "the house of prayer." But these activities of public worship, community deliberation and group study were only physically centered in the synagogue structure. There was no organic unity underlying them all. Undoubtedly, the intense Jewish life of the traditional East European Jewish community made the creation of a formal organizational pattern unnecessary. Not so in the West. There the pulse of Jewish life beat far more weakly and fitfully. In Western Europe the congregation did make its appearance in modern times as a *Kultusgemeinde* "worship-fellowship," which maintained certain auxiliary activities. Neither pattern could serve the needs of the dynamic American environment, with its limitless challenges to Jewish survival. It was here that the synagogue-building became transformed into an institution, stimulating and ministering to all the spiritual needs of the community in the broadest sense, making provision for group worship, community organization and education. This far-reaching change is reflected in the appearance of a new name for the institution, which represents a new concept, the Synagogue-center.

Another specifically American institution is the Community Center. Until very recently, the community center stressed the recreational and social aspects of its program to the virtual exclusion of specific Jewish content. In particular, it avoided any religious emphasis, on the ground that it sought to escape the pitfalls of sectarianism. The past two decades, however, have seen a steady growth of the Jewish values and activities in most community centers, in spite of the absence of an underlying philosophy of Judaism that would reckon with the centrality of religion. The community center is another American contribution to the armamentarium of Jewish group survival.

Both institutions may well supply the answer to pressing social, cultural and moral problems confronting Jewish communities in South America, South Africa and Western Europe. The synagogue-center in particular may ultimately prove of the highest value in revitalizing religion for youth in the State of Israel.

Equally characteristic of the American scene is the tremendous proliferation of youth activities, principally social and philanthropic, but also cultural and religious. One has only to contrast this phase of American Jewish life with the feeble efforts in this area being put forth elsewhere in the world to recognize another important American note. The vast network of national youth organizations affiliated with B'nai B'rith, the Zionist organizations and the synagogue unions are far less culturally active and intellectually mature than their published programs would lead one to suppose. But, together with the Hillel Foundations on hundreds of college campuses, they represent a reservoir from which may be drawn a conscious and loyal leadership and an informed Jewish laity in the next generation unparallelled anywhere else in the Diaspora. Moreover, recent discussions in Israel suggest that the problems of building future leadership from the ranks of youth are by no means being solved automatically even in the Jewish State.

Closely associated with the appearance of the synagogue in a new form in America has been the transformation of the function and significance of the rabbi. It is true that in the process much of great value was lost, or at least submerged. The traditional *rav* was a venerable figure, the symbol of scholarship and piety in the community. He spent his days principally in the study of Torah and performed judicial functions upon request. Jewish life was so deeply rooted in each community that it was not dependent upon him for stimulation or even for direction— it sufficed that he was its crowning glory, the living symbol of Torah.

But America was different, radically, bewilderingly, painfully different. In an environment where there were no long centuries of traditional practice, no educated laity, where every Jewish practice ran counter to the prevailing *mores* of a non-Jewish society of which Jews were members, Jewish life could not afford the "luxury" of the *rav* merely as a symbol, however exalted. The rabbi in America had to become the dynamo about whom most forms of positive Jewish values cluster and from whom most Jewish activities derive their impetus and direction.

The decline in scholarly attainment and personal piety of the rabbi cannot, of course, be compensated for by concrete practical achievements; they belong to different levels of being. Yet the change has not been a total loss. There has been a broadening of cultural outlook and not merely a lowering of the level of Jewish learning in the transformation of the rabbinical calling. Creative scholarship and serious philosophic and theological thought, which had largely been absent from the life of the traditional East European rabbi, have emerged once more in the pattern of activity and thought of some American rabbis. To be sure, they are a minority, but their number is growing.

Here nostalgia for the past is not merely useless; it may prove positively harmful, if it prevents a realistic appraisal of the situation. The metamorphosis of the rabbi's role from passive contemplation to active leadership in the community was absolutely called for by the conditions of modern life. Whoever doubts the need for this transformation has only to observe the situation in the State of Israel, where the old rabbinic pattern has been retained in the face of a new and dynamic situation. In Israel the rabbi has sunk to a position of relative insignificance, being little more than a state functionary for registering vital statistics, possessing no vital connection with a congregation of men, women and children. In Israel the synagogue serves only as a prayer house, playing no dynamic role in the fashioning of Jewish personality or in the solution of the manifold spiritual and ethical problems of a nation in travail.

There are strong grounds for believing, with countless observers, that if religion in Israel is to become a vital force and prove an influence for good in the life of the people as a whole, it will come to pass only through the medium of a revitalized synagogue and an active rabbinate. Both can learn more than a little from American synagogues and rabbis at their best.

IV

  In no area of Jewish life has greater disappointment been registered than in the field of Jewish education. Here, too, it is easy to paint a tragic contrast between the intensive schooling of the traditional Yeshivah or Academy in Eastern Europe and the low level of Jewish knowledge in America. Due allowance should of course be made for the roseate effect of nostalgia playing upon the memories of a dear, dead past beyond recall. The '*am ha'aretz* (the Jewishly illiterate) has always existed in Jewish life, even in the halcyon days of East European Jewry. Jewish ignorance is neither an American invention nor its monopoly.

  At the same time, it is undeniable that the low status of Jewish knowledge in American Jewry is a major peril to meaningful and rewarding Jewish living. But here again, it is important to note the direction of the process as well as its precise status at the moment. In Eastern Europe, the Jewish child could attend no other school except the Heder and the Yeshivah and no culture beckoned to him except that of Judaism.

  The closest analogy, therefore, to the problem of American Jewry is to be found in Western Europe, where a rich, general culture, Christian in orientation, and propagated by a general educational system, competed successfully for the time, interest and loyalty of Jewish youth. Having noted the parallels, we should observe the significant differences. The educational institutions created by West European Jewry for its youth showed a consistent decline in Jewish content and achievement from the first schools opened by Israel Jacobsohn, David Friedlander, Samuel Meir Ehrenberg and their contemporaries to their successors in the pre-Nazi period. In America, on the other hand, the trend has been upward. The Sunday School, an ill-considered imitation of the Protestant institution, is far from spent in Jewish circles, but it is increasingly being recognized as a failure. Hence it is giving way to a more intensive and ambitious program of weekday instruction. With the breakdown of the old Jewish ghettos in the large cities, many first-rate afternoon Talmud Torahs, under communal auspices, declined and perished. The congregational schools which came in their stead in new neighborhoods and suburbs were considerably inferior to the older schools, in respect to the quantity and the quality of instruction, administration and achievement. But signs are multiplying that the congregational school is developing increased seriousness in its attitude toward its obligations, and a corresponding rise in the character of its goals and accomplishments is already noticeable.

The most striking phenomenon of recent years has been the rise of day-schools, the most significant achievement of Orthodox Jewry, but now no longer limited to their circle. This trend offers hope that a significant minority of thoroughly well-educated Jewish leaders, both lay and professional, will emerge in the next generation. The modern day-school, as thoroughly American as it is Jewish, has few prototypes in other communities. It is essentially an American achievement. The Colleges of Jewish Studies in a dozen American cities, the growing numbers of courses on Judaism on college campuses, all these are indigenous developments. They affect only a minority to be sure, but Israel is the people of the "Saving Remnant."

In sum, even a cursory glance backward indicates that American Jewry, over and above its many-sided contributions to American life, has not been altogether without influence or creativity within the confines of Judaism. It has not only carried forward the traditional concerns of the Jewish spirit, but has brought into being new incorporations of traditional institutions in the fields of religion, philanthropy, education and group-defense. The instruments for a renaissance of Judaism, in the days to come, are at hand.

# RELIGION

# American

# Orthodoxy:

# Retrospect and

# Prospect

## EMANUEL RACKMAN

The earliest Jewish settlers on American soil
brought with them the only Judaism they knew—
Orthodox Judaism. Two centuries later Reform
Judaism took root and fifty years thereafter Conservative Judaism was born. Under the circumstances, one would have expected that Orthodox Judaism would be the first to meet the
challenge of the American scene, both ideologically and institu-
tionally. In fact, it was the last to do so. Paradoxically enough, it
is only in the last few decades that Orthodoxy seriously came to
grips with the problem of its own future.

For too long a time Orthodoxy relied upon the fact that the
preponderant number of American Jews professed to be its adherents. Majorities supporting the status quo in many social situations often rely upon the force of their numbers and their inertia, while well organized and dedicated minorities make gains
for change. The Orthodox Jewish community once was such a
majority. It was slow to realize the extent to which it was losing

23

its numerical advantage. Also, the ranks of American Orthodoxy were constantly replenished with thousands of immigrants from abroad. The new arrivals more than compensated for the defections to other groups. Now the loss of the European reservoir of Jews has caused American Orthodoxy to become concerned. It had to find the way to command the loyalty of American-born Jews. Finally, Orthodoxy by its very nature compromises less easily with new environments and new philosophies, so that it could not avail itself of that flexibility which aided the growth of the Reform and Conservative movements. The challenge of the American scene had to be met differently and the solution came later. Nonetheless, the contributions of Orthodoxy to our dual heritage as Americans and as Jews were many and significant.

It fell to the lot of Orthodoxy to establish the legal status of Jews and Judaism in American democracy. To the everlasting credit of our pioneering forbears it must be said that they were not content with second-class citizenship in the United States. George Washington confirmed this attitude in his now famous letter to the Orthodox congregation in Newport, Rhode Island. However, the false dictum that America is a "Christian state" must be challenged again and again, even in the twentieth century, and while the battle is now waged by all Jews, and especially by the defense agencies, it is usually one Orthodox Jew or another who creates the issue. The right of Sabbath observers to special consideration where "Blue Sunday" laws are in effect; their right to special treatment in the armed forces; their right to unemployment insurance benefits when they decline employment because of religious scruples—these are typical of many problems that Orthodox Jews raise in the hope that their resolution will insure maximum expansion of the American concept of equality before the law. In many instances, bearded Orthodox Jews who retain their Eastern European dress are also a challenge to the sincerity of most Americans who boast that their way of life spells respect for differences. The resistance of many of our co-religionists to the levelling character of American mores, and its inevitable discouragement of diversity, is a healthy contribution to our understanding and practice of democracy.

Altogether too often American Jews require the reminder even more than American Christians.

In the same spirit it was American Orthodoxy that bore, and still bears, the burden of resistance to world-wide calendar reform. Though all Jewish groups have cooperated, it is Orthodoxy alone that regards any tampering with the inviolability of the Sabbath day fixed at Creation as a mortal blow to Judaism and in the name of the religious freedom of minorities it seeks to alert the American conscience to desist from prejudicial action.

It was, however, in the establishment and construction of thousands of synagogues throughout the country that Orthodox Jews made manifest not only their loyalty to their ancestral heritage but their appreciation of their grand opportunity in this blessed land of freedom. How truly pauperized immigrants managed, in cities large and small, to rear beautiful edifices for worship is a saga worthy of more attention than it has heretofore received. What is particularly noteworthy is that no central agency guided or financed the movement. In every case it was individual Jews who banded together and performed the feat, a remarkable tribute to the effectiveness of our tradition in inducing in individual Jews the capacity to act on their own initiative for the greater glory of God. Even today no central body guides or directs the establishment of Orthodox synagogues. Orthodoxy's synagogue organization—the Union of Orthodox Jewish Congregations of America—is still totally ineffective in this kind of work. The initiative must always come from Jews who desire an Orthodox synagogue, and not from any resourceful missionary, national or international, body. In part, this is also one of the weaknesses of Orthodox Judaism which its leaders want to correct on the threshold of its fourth century on the American scene. However, it remains to be seen whether it will be the Union of Orthodox Jewish Congregations or Yeshiva University that will blaze the new path.

The extent to which Orthodox Jews gave of their worldly goods for the establishment and construction of synagogues was exceeded only by their willingness to sacrifice for the cause of Jewish education. Their first venture in this direction, even before the era of the public school, was a Jewish all-day school under the auspices of Congregation Shearith Israel in New York. The usual approach to the problem, however, was via the Talmud Torah, the afternoon school in which children spent from five to ten hours weekly. In some instances the Talmud Torahs were successful, and many distinguished American Rabbis and scholars received their earliest instruction in Judaica in such schools. Yet altogether too often because of incompetent instructors, bizarre methods, and inadequate facilities, the Talmud Torahs failed to induce either a love or an understanding of Judaism. In the twentieth century, therefore, Orthodox Judaism countered with the Yeshiva movement. This movement has enjoyed a phenomenal growth. In the ranks of Conservative Judaism, too, it is receiving sympathetic attention and support, and even among Liberal Jews one occasionally hears suggestions that the all-day school is the most effective answer to Jewish illiteracy.

Three organizations of Orthodox Jewry now propagate the Yeshiva program and supervise the establishment of new schools. The Vaad Hachinuch Hacharedi of the Mizrachi Organization of America also deals with Talmud Torahs, while Torah Umesorah whose program and goal were conceived by the saintly Rabbi Faivel Mendelowitz, is concerned with Yeshivoth alone. The Lubavitscher Hasidim have their own unit for identical work. The Vaad Hachinuch Hacharedi is more Zionist in its outlook than the latter two groups, which even regard the knowledge of Yiddish as important for the survival of Torah. Together, however, they stress the importance of a thorough background in the Bible and Talmud at the same time that secular studies more than meet the standards of the American public schools. With the increase in the number of schools on the elementary level, there came also an increase in the number of schools on the secondary level. Beyond the high school level there was also established a network of schools which ordain Rabbis. At one time the Rabbi Isaac Elchanan Theological Seminary in New York (still the largest) and the Hebrew Theological College, founded by the late Rabbi Saul Silber of Chicago, were the only two Orthodox seminaries in America. Now there are at least a dozen. Unfortunately, however, these schools are not even federated with each other; there is no joint action whatever. Even their graduates are not affiliated with one Rabbinic body, although the Rabbinical Council of America has the largest percentage of all the graduates, while the Rabbinical Alliance of America, and the oldest of all, the Union of Orthodox Rabbis of the United States and Canada, get a fair measure as well. These three Rabbinic groups have recently sought some areas for joint action but as yet the results are meagre. And this is perhaps the greatest weakness of Orthodox Jewry—its inability to consolidate, or even coordinate, its educational institutions and their alumni.

Nonetheless, the enrollment of about thirty thousand Jewish boys and girls in the all-day schools constitutes Orthodox Jewry's proud achievement at the close of the third century of American Jewish history. The financial burden has been great, and the financial problem will be insoluble in times of economic depression. For that reason many supporters of the Yeshiva movement hope for state support of parochial schools. Heretofore Jews have been quite unanimous in their support of the defense agencies' position on the complete separation of church and state in America. However, with most welfare funds denying aid to the Yeshivoth of their own communities, or at best making niggardly allocations, one can predict that in the not too distant future, the sponsors of the Yeshivoth will be desperate enough to join with representatives of the Roman Catholic Church in an effort to obtain state or federal aid. Such a move may make for a further cleavage between Orthodox and non-Orthodox Jews. But Orthodox Jews feel that the growing movement for the organization of Jewish day-schools (*Yeshivot*) may be justly hailed as a major contribution to the survival of Judaism in America and that the time has come for welfare funds to abandon their hostility to the cause. New York City's Federation of Jewish Philanthropies, for example, has already begun to see the light.

One interesting by-product of the Yeshiva movement has been the remarkable financial success that publishers have enjoyed in their republication of classics in Judaica. The Union of Orthodox Rabbis republished the Babylonian Talmud about thirty-five years ago. Since, commercial publishers have done it profitably several times, and added many other works. Orthodox Judaism does not yet adequately subsidize its scholars nor provide for the publication of their original contributions to scholarship. Yet enough of a demand for books has been stimulated to make many a reprinting financially worthwhile.

Another interesting by-product of the Yeshiva movement has been the effect of the presence of a Yeshiva in many a midwestern city upon the Orthodox group within that city itself. Within the Orthodox community, where only chaos and anarchy reigned before, the Yeshiva became the great cohesive force, and the Yeshiva leadership inspired greater control over *kashrut* (preparation in accordance with Jewish dietary laws) supervision, the construction of better facilities required by Orthodox Jews for all ritualistic observances, and even more cooperation in fund-raising for local and overseas religious needs.

How the Yeshiva movement served more than the cause of Torah, narrowly conceived, can be gleaned from the fact that it was a Yeshiva, led by the brilliant and visionary Dr. Bernard Revel, that established on American soil the first Jewish college of arts and science, later to become America's first Jewish University. More recently it undertook the construction of a medical and dental school. Furthermore, that Orthodoxy in America was prepared to abandon its historic indifference to the education of women, was made manifest not only by the fact that a large percentage of the children enrolled in the Yeshivoth are girls, but that Yeshiva University headed by the resourceful Dr. Samuel Belkin, now has a secondary school and college for them.

In the area of overseas relief Orthodoxy was always impatient with the general agencies because of their neglect of religious institutions, and as a result during and after World War I the Central Jewish Relief Committee and Ezrath Torah Fund were organized to bring aid to European Yeshivoth. The Union of Orthodox Rabbis deserves special commendation for this achievement. With regard to Palestine, too, Orthodoxy was preoccupied with religious development. Within the framework of the World Zionist Organization, American Orthodoxy advanced the program of the Mizrachi and Hapoel Hamizrachi parties. Rabbi Meyer Berlin (Bar-Ilan), who was also the founder of the Teachers' Institute which became affiliated with the Rabbi Isaac Elchanan Theological Seminary and later was one of the larger schools of Yeshiva University, was the ideological spokesman and administrative head of every phase of the work. With the new wave of immigration immediately prior to and after World War II, the separatist Agudath Yisrael party gained an appreciable following in the American Jewish community and created a marked cleavage between the traditionalists who hoped for some synthesis of western thought with our ancestral heritage and the traditionalists who hoped to establish on American soil replicas of Eastern European Jewish communities. The former are also more cooperative with non-Orthodox Jewish groups and participate in the work of the Synagogue Council of America even as they are represented in the Commission on Jewish Chaplaincy of the National Jewish Welfare Board and organizations like the New York Board of Rabbis. The profound ideological differences between the two groups came to the fore with respect to the issue of the conscription of women in Israel. However, the same lack of unity that has weakened Orthodoxy's achievement in the fields of synagogue and Yeshiva organization has also undermined the esteem in which Orthodoxy's significant achievements for Israel ought to be held. Nonetheless, it is American Orthodoxy that has always borne the brunt of the responsibility for the preservation of almost all of Israel's religious life.

Orthodox Judaism has maximal objectives not only for religious education in America and abroad but also with regard to religious observances. In this area, too, it has failed to achieve any measure of unity or coordination. Kashrut supervision for example, is under the aegis of no central body, and even the cooperation of states that have laws on the subject has not eliminated the anarchy that prevails. The most progressive step forward was taken by the Union of Orthodox Jewish Congregations, in cooperation with the Rabbinical Council of America, when it registered its "U" as a guarantee of kashrut and made the label available to firms that meet the strictest requirements. This helped to popularize kashrut and the Union not only advertised the products it endorsed but published brochures on the significance of the dietary laws generally. The ultimate hope is to divest individual Rabbis of the right to act on their own for personal gain. The resistance of members of the Union of Orthodox Rabbis is great and even the Rabbinical Council of America had to pass resolutions censuring its members who flout the policy and give *Hechsherim* (Rabbinical attestation that a food product has been prepared in accordance with the requirements of the Jewish dietary laws) as individuals. In the area of Sabbath observance there has been less success although the number of professional and business firms that observe the Sabbath has been increasing. The Young Israel movement has helped to find employment for Sabbath observers but as yet the future of the Sabbath depends principally upon the elimination of Saturday as a work day. The Young Israel movement, on the whole, not only helped to dignify orthodox religious services, and create social and economic opportunities for observant youth, but also made a magnificent contribution to Jewish adult education all over the country. Modern Mikvehs are being built in many communities and though the laws pertaining to *Taharat Hamishpacha* (requirement of ritual immersion after the menses) have suffered the greatest neglect, Orthodox Judaism has sought to improve the situation by constructing more attractive and inviting facilities for their observance and by publishing literature on the subject in English.

In the area of English publications and public relations generally, Orthodox Judaism must meet new challenges. Its *Halakhic* (relating to Jewish Law) and scholarly journals, such as *Talpioth*, of Yeshiva University, have a limited circle of readers while most American Jews have only the vaguest notions of the nature of Orthodoxy and its spiritual and intellectual vitality. Too often they regard Orthodox Judaism as a petrified survivor of the past, entirely oblivious to the winds of modern doctrine and the needs of present-day Jewish experience. They do not know that Orthodoxy grapples with all the problems and all the ideologies of our day. It does not exclude Halakhic creativity or changes, flexibility, and growth in concept and method to meet the most perplexing of the problems that trouble religious minds. But it insists that such evolution must be organic, i.e., it must be a further unfolding of historical continuity and develop authentically out of tradition. Orthodoxy may not be paving the way for certain basic changes in the Law that many American Jews want. Unfortunately the clamor for change in the Law too often expresses simply a desire to substitute new values for old ones—to make the Sabbath the occasion for a good time instead of a day of holiness, to make the table a gourmet's delight instead of an altar, to make sexual relations open to lust instead of disciplined for love. That is why Orthodox Jews move slowly in their Halakhic creativity—with the same turmoil of soul that characterizes the authentic religious experience, but with the firm faith that where the basic values of Judaism still live, the Law will suffice to meet the requirements of life.

True, within the ranks of Orthodox Judaism there are many to whom the modern scene and western thought constitute no challenge. These elements are to be found principally among the recent immigrants to the United States. And they often intimidate the more progressive Orthodox elements who recognize that Jewish law was always dynamic and that Judaism never required an ostrich-like indifference to currents of thought. A sad illustration of the dangers of such intolerance was recently afforded Orthodox Jews when an Orthodox Rabbinic Journal—which was never noted for its progressive approach, and even delighted in attacking the younger Rabbis of the Rabbinical Council of America—found itself under attack by an even more "rightist" journal because it published an article suggesting that the redactors of the Babylonian Talmud did not see the Palestinian Talmud! The tendency to canonize each and every view of the past with absolutely no critical or historical evaluation is strong among these "rightists." Some of them even favor the social and economic isolation of Orthodox Jews. They propose the establishment of Orthodox Jewish communities with Sabbath-observing vendors of the necessities of life, Sabbath-observing professional and service personnel, etc.

The position of these "rightists," however, is not typical. Most American Orthodox Rabbis are not isolationists. They admit that for at least another generation or two most American Jews will not be observant. Nevertheless, they want these Jews to appreciate their moral obligation to support the totality of their ancestral heritage as Jews that it may be transmitted intact to later generations whose knowledge of Judaism and whose spiritual climate may be more conducive to the development of Judaism in consonance with its historic philosophy and pattern rather than as a compromise with Jewish illiteracy and the materialistic, "sensate" values of the present era. The prevailing values of our day are antithetical to most of the values of Judaism. They, therefore, believe that to adjust Judaism to the values of today is to forfeit the role of religion as a goal and aspiration for a more spiritual tomorrow. Our posterity should not be prejudiced by us and receive from us only truncated conceptions or patterns of Jewish thought and practice. With this approach, most Orthodox Rabbis are urging even the non-observant to identify themselves with Orthodox synagogues and send their children to Yeshivoth. Serious problems do arise when such children are confronted with the contrast between what they are taught in school and what they see at home. However, the leaders of the day-school movement are trying to solve these problems through their publications, their conferences with parents, and their day-by-day contact with the children.

Most Orthodox synagogues now have English-speaking Rabbis who preach in English. Prayer books and copies of the Pentateuch with English translations are the rule, not the exception. Especially noteworthy among the English translations of the traditional prayer book is Dr. David de Sola Pool's edition, recently sponsored by the Rabbinical Council of America. Under the auspices of the Union of Orthodox Jewish Congregations, Dr. Leo Jung edited a number of excellent volumes on Jewish information. Several of the essays have become classical expositions of Orthodox Judaism. At least one, "Study as a Form of Worship," by Professor Nathan Isaacs of Harvard University, has gained a world-wide currency among Jews. Rabbi Herbert S. Goldstein translated selections from Rashi's commentary on the Pentateuch for family use on the Sabbath, and more recently a linear translation was made available by a commercial publisher.

Orthodox Judaism is endeavoring to recapture the loyalty of American Jews. It cannot, however, "adjust" to the American scene. The term "adjust" too often implies man's right to trim religion to meet his personal desires. Such a right Orthodoxy denies any Jew, and notwithstanding even Dr. Kinsey, the seventh commandment of the Decalogue is binding no matter how high the percentage of spouses who flout it. Nonetheless, most American Orthodox Rabbis recognize that there has always been, and still are, different modes of Orthodox Jewish thought and practice, and that Orthodoxy has always admitted a great measure of innovation. The innovation, however, is always within the Halakhic process and pursuant to its revealed norms. The result, therefore, is organic development of God's will, not man's. Orthodoxy regards any rejection of the revealed character of both the Written and the Oral Law as a negation of the very essence of the Halakhah. Jews who thus reject would do better to regard their interest in the Halakhah as comparable to the antiquarian's interest in antiquity. They may become historians of the Halakhah or borrowers from it but not creators within its tradition.

In order to communicate this point of view to American Jews, Orthodoxy must have leaders who are not only articulate in English but also masters of western thought and its temper. That is why Yeshiva University and the Hebrew Theological College advocate the mastering of all western thought in order to create an ultimate synthesis with Jewish learning. This goal will be achieved as more of the graduates of these schools and other Yeshivoth become expert in the natural and social sciences.

There already exists a society of Orthodox Jewish scientists which is dedicating itself to the solution of problems created for Orthodoxy by modern technology. Many a Halakhic point of view is receiving support from the natural sciences, and what is

more important, these scientists are demonstrating that there is
no conflict between natural science—which has abandoned the
notion that it can attain any absolute truths whatever—and religion which calls for faith in given absolutes. The greater challenges to Orthodoxy, however, come from the social sciences and
an impressive group of Orthodox leaders, lay and Rabbinic, are
coping with them.

Orthodoxy's position vis-à-vis the Higher Criticism of the Bible
is one such area. While Orthodoxy is committed to no one conception of Revelation, all Orthodox Jews regard the Pentateuch
as divinely revealed. Moses wrote it while in direct communion
with God. Moreover, with Moses too, the Oral Law had its beginnings and its process was ordained by God. German Jewish Orthodoxy perhaps made more progress in its defense of this position than has American Jewish Orthodoxy to date. However,
Orthodoxy relies heavily on the fact that modern archaeological
research has bolstered the historicity of the Biblical narrative
and Orthodoxy is confident that further progress in philology
will precipitate the same kind of retreat from anti-Orthodox
viewpoints that the Bible's erstwhile plastic surgeons have suffered. Rabbi Chayim Heller, at Yeshiva University, is stimulating
both the confidence and the type of research necessary to sustain
the Orthodox position. Moreover, many Orthodox thinkers believe that with a retreat from humanism generally, humanism
will no longer be the vantage point from which the revealed
Word of God will be arrogantly evaluated. Man will not be the
measure of God.

The greatest challenge of all, however, lies in the realm of
Halakhah; first, the importance of its study, and second, the
importance of living by its prescriptions. Is the Halakhah viable
in the modern age? Does it enrich our spiritual existence? Is it
relevant to our yearnings and aspirations and can it edify and
fulfill them? Only a small percentage of even Orthodox Jews are
content with the mandate, "The Law is the Law and must,
therefore, be obeyed." Philosophical approaches to Halakhah
and philosophiclal analyses of the Halakhic process must be
articulated. The undisputed leader of the Orthodox Jewish com-

munity in this domain is Dr. Joseph B. Soloveichik, of Yeshiva University, who is now also Chairman of the Halakhah Commission of the Rabbinical Council of America. In addition to his brilliant resolution of many involved Halakhic problems of the modern age, and his equally masterful analyses of Talmudic texts, he is demonstrating the viability of the Halakhah, the relevance of its insights to abundant and adventurous spiritual living, and the intellectual harvests to be reaped from preoccupation with its study. Most of the great Halakhic scholars who adorn the faculties of America's Yeshivoth, and most of the distinguished Orthodox Rabbis who founded and still lead the Union of Orthodox Rabbis of the United States and Canada, deserve credit for their benign influence upon the loyalty of thousands of American Jews to our ancestral heritage. But they have done little more than transplant the Orthodoxy of Eastern Europe on American soil. It is to Dr. Soloveichik, his co-workers and students, that American Orthodoxy looks for the ideological content, the techniques and the conclusions required to stem the tide of defections to other groups by making it abundantly clear that Halakhic Judaism is eternal and has naught to fear from the challenges of Western thought, present and future.

First, however, it wants to stimulate a renascence of Torah learning on American soil. Orthodoxy feels that until Jews are learned they cannot be pious. It insists that it suffered its greatest set-back in America because of *Am ha-Arazuth,* Torah illiteracy. For more than two and a half centuries America could not boast a score of men learned in the Law. How then could Orthodoxy achieve here that synthesis that was once the glory of Spanish Judaism? The first task, therefore, is to spread the knowledge of Torah. As tens of thousands become masters of the Halakhah, the Halakhah will have a new birth in the new world.

Second, Orthodoxy does not believe that the modern contribution to progressive revelation can come until the modern age recaptures basic religious experience. The commitment of our age to material values has deadened our capacity for religious experience. Yet, there is evidence, as we face the atomic era in human history, that there will be a resurgence of religious values

and a reawakening of religious experience. In such an atmosphere, Judaism will thrive. Particularly will Halakhic Judaism
thrive as more and more Jews seek to apprehend God's will
rather than merely indulging their own.

# Jewish Tradition in 20th Century America: The Conservative Approach

## THEODORE FRIEDMAN

One searches in vain through the vastness and variety of Jewish history for a convincing precedent for the Jewish experience in America. Here, a totally new constellation of forces, social, economic and intellectual, swirled around the Jewish immigrant. The full potential of their impact on the forms, concepts and organizational expressions of Judaism cannot as yet be fully judged if only for the fact that the majority of American Jews stands but one generation removed from their immigrant forebears. Another generation, at least, must elapse before the process of integration will have worked itself out with any degree of finality. That is not to reduce the rise and growth of Conservative Judaism in America to a resultant of sociological forces. The American environment, for all its massive, determinative character, embodies but one factor in the equation to be solved. The other, and no

less potent factor, is the body of ideas, loyalties and practices
with which the leaders and ideologues of Conservatism confront
the environment in their efforts to perpetuate and advance an
historic faith. It would be fatuous, however, to deny that the
impress of the American milieu, inclusive of Reform Judaism,
lies deep on both the thinking and practice currently obtaining
in Conservative Judaism, and for that matter, on other schools of
thought. It would, however, be equally blind not to see the roots
of the Conservative interpretation of Judaism in ideas and tendencies whose rise is not to be attributed to the American experience, and which, indeed, long antedate it. In sum, the law of
multiple causes operates here as elsewhere.

It has long been customary to locate the genesis of the Conservative interpretation of Judaism within the context of the
Historical School of Jewish Scholarship of the nineteenth century. The influence on the rise of Conservative Judaism of that
galaxy of Jewish scholars who for the first time turned the re-
vealing light of modern historical methodology on the Jewish
past is clearly decisive; decisive enough to warrant the somewhat
extended analysis to which we shall presently subject it. For all
its pervasiveness, still at work, one would miss the essential tim-
bre of Conservatism if one did not recognize that, in almost
every instance, it was an influence that played on personalities
originally steeped in and stamped by the traditional Jewish life
and learning then prevailing in Eastern Europe. Solomon
Schechter, Louis Ginzberg, Israel Friedlander and, "to divide between the living and the living," Mordecai M. Kaplan, were all
surrounded by traditional piety and learning long before they
made contact with either secular learning or the Juedische
Wissenschaft of Western Europe. The fact is central in character
and helps to explain the catholicity, which has been all but
raised to the status of a "dogma" of Conservatism by Solomon
Schechter. In a characteristic passage he writes:

. . . is it not time that the new theology should consist in the best
that all the men of Israel, including Geiger, gave us, but should
modify and qualify his views, dating from a rationalistic age, by
the loyalty to the law of Rabbi Akiba Eger and Rabbi Mordecai

Baneth, by the deep insight into Jewish History of a Zunz and a Krochmal, by the mysticism of a Baal Shem Tov and some of his best followers, and by the love of Israel's nationality and its perpetuation of Herzl or Ahad Haam.[1]

Schechter's own appreciation of historic personalities and trends in Judaism extended to such diverse phenomena and figures in Judaism as the Hasidim, the Safed School of Mystics, Abraham Geiger and Nachmanides. In this he was followed by Louis Ginzberg whose volume of popular essays *Students, Scholars and Saints* contains appreciations of Elijah, Gaon of Vilna, Rabbi Israel Salanter and Zachariah Frankel. Is this a mere eclecticism, a charge often laid at the door of Conservatism? Such a conclusion is premature and fails to reckon with Schechter's and his colleagues' understanding of Judaism.

It was a native appreciation risen to the level of recognition and conscious affirmation, thanks to training in the methods of *Juedische Wissenschaft,* that almost from its inception Judaism contained within itself a variety of trends and emphases. To isolate one phase of Jewish spiritual creativity and to denominate it as the essence of Judaism to the derogation of all else is to force Judaism into some preconceived procrustean bed. So classical Reform had, in response to the cultural compulsion of its time, fastened upon Prophetic Judaism as the permanent climax of Judaism, a climax far beyond the level of the Written to say nothing of the Oral Law. And so, latterly, had secular nationalists transformed the principle of Israel's nationality into the prime exclusive dogma of Judaism. And so too, had Jewish universalists urged that Judaism, possessing no dogmas, could accommodate itself to virtually any ism or wind of doctrine. These, and kindred schools of thought, Schechter challenged in a series of brilliant addresses and essays in which with a wealth of learning, matched by a virtuosity of style, he demonstrated that the Jewish religion and its institutions were an organic historical development based on "the revealed Bible."

Schechter never attempted either to define or delineate his concept of revelation. Having thoroughly explored Rabbinic

[1] *Studies in Judaism,* Third series, pp. 82-83.

theology, he was aware that the Rabbis permitted themselves
an extraordinarily wide range of opinion in theological matters
on the assumption that there is

"only One who knows the exact truth about the great mystery.
But we may indicate our doubt about one doctrine by putting by
its side another, which we may affirm to be not more absolutely
true, but more probable. This seems to have been the attitude,
too, of the compilers of the ancient Rabbinic literature in which
the most conflicting views about this grave subject (Divine Ret-
ribution) were embodied. Nor did the Synagogue, in general,
feel called upon to decide between these views . . . It refused a
hearing to no theory for fear that it contain some germ of truth but
on the same ground it accepted none to the exclusion of the
other."[2]

Schechter's non-defined postulate of Biblical revelation has
given way latterly in the Conservative School to a variety of
interpretations. These range all the way from outright rejection
of the supernatural origin of the Torah, to a reinterpretation of
the concept with emphasis upon its human, subjective element,
to a reaffirmation, by a leap of faith, of revelation as a divine
incursion into history of whose actual content man can never be
absolutely certain. Until the last decade, actual theological discussion found few participants in the Conservative School.[3] This
comparative neglect of theology, except in its historical phases,
is already adumbrated by the emphases underscored by Schechter,
in consonance with the entire Historical School of Judaism. To
this day these emphases continue to draw the major concern and
interest of the Conservative interpreters of Judaism.

The stage is most quickly and adequately set for our discussion
of the ideological problems that have constituted the agenda of
Conservative Judaism by two quotations; the first from the writ-

[2] *Some Aspects of Rabbinic Theology*, pp. 213-4.
[3] This is not, of course, to overlook the notable exception of Prof. Mordecai
Kaplan. Since, however, his thinking and that of his disciples is extensively
treated by Rabbi Harold Schulweis in the next essay "The Temper of Reconstructionism", we have made no reference to the theological aspects of
his thought.

ings of Schechter and the second from an essay on Zachariah Frankel by Louis Ginzberg.

Its (the Historical School) theological practices may perhaps be thus defined: it is not the mere revealed Bible that is of first importance to the Jew, but the Bible as it repeats itself in history, in other words as it is interpreted by Tradition . . . Since, then, the interpretation of Scriptures or the Secondary Meaning is mainly a product of changing historical influences, it follows that the center of authority is actually removed from the Bible and placed in some living body, which, by reason of its being in touch with the ideal aspirations and the religious needs of the age, is best able to determine the nature of the Secondary Meaning. This living body, however, is not represented by any section of the nation or any corporate priesthood or Rabbinhood, but by the collective conscience of Catholic Israel, as embodied in the Universal Synagogue. This Synagogue, the only true witness to the past, and forming in all ages the sublimest expression of Israel's religious life, must also retain its authority as the sole true guide for the present and the future . . . Another consequence of this conception of Tradition is that it is neither scripture nor primitive Judaism, but general custom which forms the real rule of practice. Holy Writ as well as history, Zunz tells us, teaches that the Law of Moses was never fully and absolutely put into practice. Liberty was always given to the great teachers of every generation to make modifications and innovations in harmony with the spirit of existing institutions . . . The norm as well as the sanction of Judaism is the practice actually in vogue. Its consecration is the consecration of general use or, in other words, of Catholic Israel . . .[4]

Speaking of the positive-historical school,[5] a position he clearly shares, the late Professor Ginzberg writes:

[4] *Studies in Judaism*, First Series, pp. XVII-XIX.
[5] For a brilliant concise specimen of the methodological approach of the Historical School to the Oral Law, the interested reader is referred to Louis Ginzberg's essay "The Significance of the Halachah for Jewish History," pages 77-124 in *Jewish Law and Lore*, Phila., 1955. The reader is referred likewise to Professor Ginzberg's English introduction to his *Commentary on the Palestinian Talmud*, New York, 1941, reprinted in the volume referred to above.

For an adherent of this school, the sanctity of the Sabbath reposes not upon the fact that it was proclaimed on Sinai, but on the fact that the Sabbath idea found for thousands of years its expression in Jewish souls. It is the task of the historian to examine into the beginnings and developments of the numerous customs and observances of the Jews; practical Judaism on the other hand is not concerned with origins, but regards the institutions as they have come to be. If we are convinced that Judaism is a religion of deed, expressing itself in observances which are designed to achieve the moral elevation of man and give reality to his religious spirit, we have a principle, in observance of which, reforms in Judaism are possible. From this point of view the evaluation of a law is independent of its origin, and thus the line of demarcation between biblical and rabbinical law almost disappears.[6]

What Schechter expresses in the foregoing in terms of broad generalization and proposes as the norm for contemporary Judaism, had been spelled out in learned and illuminating detail in the researches of the historical school. I. H. Weiss, Graetz and Zachariah Frankel, followed by others, in their studies of the Oral Law, had established beyond argument that what Schechter terms the Secondary Meaning could only be understood in developmental terms. Moreover, that development was ever subject to a variety of historical forces, inner and external. But whatever the past viability of the Oral Law and the degree of sensitivity of its masters and fashioners to the needs, social and spiritual of their time, one thing was crystal clear. *Halakhah* (Jewish Law) was the method par excellence of Judaism. In the millennial sweep of Jewish history, those groups that broke with the Halakhah eventually found that they had thereby severed themselves from the body of *Klal Yisrael*. To assert as much is to merely set the stage for the problem of Halakhah in modern times, not to solve it.

Once the affirmation of Halakhah as indispensable to a continuing, historically grounded Judaism has been granted, what has been and continues to be the Conservative approach to the problems involved in the effort to render the Halakhah norma-

[6] *Students, Scholars and Saints*, Philadelphia, Pa. 1928, pp. 206-207.

tive in the life of the Jew in the twentieth century? Actually, there have been two concurrent methods at work; methods that have always characterized the history of the Halakhah.

The first has been that of a common consensus arrived at not by formal deliberation and decision based on the Halakhah, but rather by a natural unconscious process into which there have entered in varying proportions the force of tradition and the influence of the environment. Thus, virtually all Conservative congregations maintain family pews though the history of the Conservative movement reveals no official decision permitting such practice, a decision which could hardly be warranted by even the most liberal interpretation of the Halakhah. By a similar consensus, no Conservative congregation has ever even discussed the question of worshiping bare-headed unless it was preparing to leave the ranks of Conservatism. Yet, even from the strictest Halakhic viewpoint, a convincing case could be made for the legitimacy of worshiping bare-headed. Other examples might be adduced of this process of common consensus which has given a fairly uniform character to the Conservative Synagogue and its practices.[7]

The other method of meeting the problems of Halakhah in a technological society, has been the two-fold process of deliberate interpretation and enactment (*Takkanah*), the "classic" methods of the Halakhah. This has been the province of the Committee on Jewish Law and Standards of the Rabbinical Assembly of America.

As an indication of the spirit animating the approach of the Committee to the contemporary problems of Jewish religious observance, one aspect of its decisions should be noted. Where the Committee, counting twenty-three members, is unanimous in a decision, such a decision is considered binding on all members of the Rabbinical Assembly. Where a minority and majority decision are reported a member may follow either opinion.

Several factors, all worthy of consideration, coincided to bring

[7] The examples cited have been deliberately restricted to synagogue practice. The category Conservative Jews—or, for that matter, Orthodox or Reform Jews—is much too loosely defined and shifting to serve as a source for normative practice. The corporate expression can, however, serve as a norm.

about this unique practice of permitting members an option between two conflicting opinions. Historically, it is a conscious return to the method and practice of the ancient Halakhic literature.[8] Again, it is a recognition that certainly today, if indeed
ever in the past, Jewish religious practice in its detail cannot
possess a universally uniform character.[9]

Equally determinative in the adoption of the above described
practice was the implicit recognition that if its decisions were to
genuinely represent the thinking of present-day Conservatism,
then in certain areas, mostly peripheral in nature, the Committee could not speak authoritatively with a single voice. For
truth to tell, within Conservatism three tendencies in regard to
the application of the Halakhah to modern life are discernible.
That their respective advocates have shown no inclination to
turn these tendencies into schismatic lines is proof of the power
and centrality of the ideological commitments held in common,
despite diversity of viewpoint on certain specifics.

One group may be said to oppose any approach to the
Halakhah that would yield decisions that would depart from
what is commonly regarded as the Orthodox norm. Any change
in religious practice, it is argued, must be initiated by bodies
or individuals whose authority is recognized by all Jews professing loyalty to the tradition. Otherwise, Conservatism is certain
to become a sect and ultimately go the way of all sects in the
history of Judaism. In practice, this group has refused to make
few, if any, of the adjustments commonly found in the preponderant majority of Conservative congregations. At the other end
of the ideological arc, are those who while favoring most of the
traditional practices would regard them not as Halakhah and

---

[8] One classic instance, in summary form, may be offered. Rabbi Elazar said:
Even though the School of Shammai disagreed with the School of Hillel in
certain aspects of the laws of marriage and divorce that would affect the
legality of some marriages and divorces, the School of Shammai did not refuse to marry a woman whose legal marital status had been determined according to the views of the School of Hillel. *Tosefta Yeb.* Chapter 1.

[9] The late Professor Ginzberg in the Introduction to his *Commentary on
the Palestinian Talmud* (and throughout that work) points to the differences
in practice between Palestinian and Babylonian Jewry, differences he traces
to the contrasting environments that surrounded these two centers of Jewry.

hence subject to modification and adaptation by the accepted canons of Jewish law, but rather as sanctified religious folkways. The forms of these observances, it is maintained, must ultimately be determined by the people themselves in consultation with their spiritual leaders; presuming, of course, that the former are committed to Judaism and are anxious to employ its resources to the maximum in spiritually enhancing their lives and expressing themselves Jewishly.[10]

Midway between these two schools of thought, though by no means a compromise between the two—a quite inconceivable ideological construction—there stands a third group which may be said to constitute a majority. It regards the traditional Halakhah as an instrument viable enough to meet the changed situation of the modern world in which the American Jew lives. The fact that it has not, on the whole, been so adapted to date does not argue for its inherent intractability but reveals rather the spiritual outlook of those who have been its prime authorities and exponents. That outlook and mood were marked by a natural suspicion of the modern world as inherently subversive of Judaism. Every added constriction of the area of the permissible, it considered a manifestation of piety. Primarily, however, it was its refusal to employ the broad powers implied in the method of *Takkanah* that led to the inertness of the Halakhah in the face of radically altered conditions. In its truly creative periods, the Halakhah, in the hands of a Rabbi Yochanan ben Zakkai, for example, had proven itself capable of meeting the challenge of the cataclysmic changes in the life of the Jewish people that followed the destruction of the Second Temple and the loss of national autonomy. Similarly, it is held that the power of Takkanah, wisely used, could re-align traditional Jewish law with the social realities of our times and, at the same time, set realistic standards of observances that would render the tradition capable of becoming a living force in the daily life of the American Jew.

This approximate three-fold division in the Conservative at-

---

[10] This point of view is expressed in Rabbi Jack J. Cohen's essay, "The End of Halakhah?", *Conservative Judaism*, vol. XIII, No. 2, January 1952, pp. 9-15.

titude toward the Halakhah is a continuation, on another level,
of ideological differences that existed in Conservatism from its
very inception. Even among the handful of original sponsors of
the Jewish Theological Seminary, one notes a distinct variety of
approach and practice. Rabbis Benjamin Szold and Marcus Jastrow edited prayer books that departed from the traditional text
and ministered to congregations that had adopted family pews,
etc. Rabbis H. Pereira Mendes and Bernard Drachman represented Orthodoxy in English garb. Rabbis Sabato Morais and
Alexander Kohut, particularly the latter, took what may be described as an intermediate position.

With the foregoing in mind, a few examples of the Committee
on Jewish Law and Standards' more recent decisions will serve
to illustrate its general approach to some of the contemporary
problems of law and observances. In 1950 the Committee issued a
Responsum on Sabbath Observance,[11] and proposed a program
of Sabbath Observance as the minimum incumbent upon members of Conservative congregations. The program envisaged,
among other activities, the attendance at synagogue at least once
on the Sabbath. Recognizing that the present growing diffusion
of population would make such attendance impossible for a very
considerable proportion of a synagogue's membership, if the
traditional interdiction of riding on the Sabbath were to be maintained, the majority of the Committee moved that "where a
family resides beyond reasonable walking distance from the synagogue, the use of a motor vehicle for the purpose of a synagogue attendance shall in no wise be construed as a violation of
the Sabbath. . . ." It moved further—and here the Committee
was unanimous—that the use of electricity on the Sabbath for
purposes of illumination and the "delight of the Sabbath" should
not be construed as a violation of the Sabbath. At the same time,
the Responsum set forth a program of "basic indispensable elements of Sabbath Observance." These included the cessation on
the Sabbath of "all such activities that are not made absolutely

[11] *Proceedings of the Rabbinical Assembly of America,* Vol. XIV, New
York, 1950, pp. 112-17.

necessary by the unavoidable pressures of life and that are not
in keeping with the Sabbath spirit, such as shopping, household
work, sewing, strenuous physical exercise, etc." The ultimate goal
envisaged in the program is the abstention from one's occupa-
tional duties on the Sabbath and the devotion of the entire day
to spiritual and moral edification.

Latterly, in cooperation with the Faculty of the Jewish Theological Seminary, the Rabbinical Assembly has enacted a *Takkanah* proposed by Prof. Saul Lieberman that is certain to have
far-reaching effects on the execution of the Jewish law of divorce.
The traditional Ketubbah (Jewish marriage contract) has been
revised so as to include a clause in which both bride and groom
agree at the time of marriage to abide by the decision of the
Court of Jewish Domestic Relations (*Beth Din*) should questions
of Jewish marital status arise between them. The clause is aimed
at preventing the occurrence of *iggun* (a situation in which the
woman is unable to obtain a Jewish writ of divorce and hence,
according to Jewish law, unable to remarry even though she
may possess a decree of civil divorce). Obviously, this is an additional forward step in the process already apparent in the history
of the Halakhah, of achieving full equality in matters of marriage
and divorce for the Jewish woman.

To the student of Halakhah it is clear that both methods
described above—that of the common consensus and the deliberative, interpretive and Takkanah making-process—have ever
characterized the history of the Oral Law. In numerous instances,
innovation and adaptations instituted by the people were, at first,
strongly opposed by Halakhic authorities. But once they were
widely practiced, official opposition faded and they came to be
regarded as completely normative even by rigid Halakhists.[12] The
process of growth in Jewish law need not detain us here. It has

[12] The introduction of the wearing of the wig (sheitel) by women in the
seventeenth century was violently opposed as contrary to Jewish Law by so
eminent a Halakhist as Rabbi Jacob Emden. Subsequently, it came to be
regarded as a requirement of both law and custom. The failure of a woman
to shear her hair and don a wig at marriage was considered a sign of wanton
disregard for Jewish law.

been brilliantly illuminated by scholars of the Historical School.[13]

The examples described above of Conservative practices and method in adjusting the Halakhah to the social and moral exigencies of our day reveal, at the same time, the scope of Judaism as conceived in Conservative circles. The boundaries of that scope coincide with the needs, spiritual, moral and social, of the Jewish people in its efforts to maintain and enhance its group life in keeping with its historic character. Denying the existence of any sharp permanent historic break in the character of the Jewish people—such as its presumed transformation at the time of the loss of national sovereignty from the status of nation to that of sect—the leaders of Conservatism as well as the rank and file, have sought in their ideology and program to preserve the "organic" character of Judaism. While, for example, Reform, fairly early in its career, readily abandoned the sphere of Jewish domestic relations (divorce) to the civil authorities, Conservatism has consistently retained this area within the orbit of Judaism. Such insistence is based as much on the desire to have Jewish ideals and practices guide and influence Jewish family relationships as it is grounded on the Halakhah. Similarly, though certain ideological adjustments have been made in the text of the official Conservative prayer book and a variety of English prayers has been introduced as supplemental material, the traditional liturgy has been retained almost in toto. Of no less significance is the retention of Hebrew as the predominant language of the service. Here, Halakhic considerations could readily have provided ample warrant for recasting the service into English. But other considerations, strong and uncompromising, operate to cause the leaders of Conservatism to insist upon both the traditional framework of the liturgy as well as its Hebraic character. Indeed it was on this immediate issue that Issac Leeser, a forerunner of Conservatism, broke with Isaac Mayer Wise.[14] In similar vein,

[13] The interested reader is referred to Boaz Cohen's "Towards a Philosophy of Jewish Law," Conservative Judaism, Oct. 1949, vol. VI, No. 1, pp. 1-31. An interpretation of the meaning of Halakhah for our day and a plea for the setting of acceptable standards for Jewish observance are put forth in Jacob Agus' essay, "Laws as Standards," ibid., May, 1950, Vol. VI, No. 4, pp. 8-26.

[14] Moshe Davis, Yahaduth America Behitpatchutah, New York, 1951, p. 172.

Sabato Morais, a prime mover in the organization of the Jewish Theological Seminary, repeatedly voiced his opposition to a Jewish service in the vernacular on the grounds of "a deep feeling of obligation (solidarity) towards our brethren through the Diaspora." [15]

With an unbroken consistency, indeed, with a deepening emphasis, Conservatism has maintained the indispensable need for retaining the essentially Hebraic mold of the service. With no less insistence it has emphasized, in the face of rival and seemingly more practical philosophies, the centrality of Hebrew in Jewish education. This emphasis is to be traced to its affirmation of the peoplehood of Israel, no new doctrine to be sure, but rather a direct consequence of its loyalty to the integral nature of the tradition in which God, Israel and Torah are conceived as inseverably linked. This loyalty, as we have seen, expresses itself in Conservatism in a variety of ways, not the least of which has been its espousal of the cause of Zionism.

After some initial hesitation, Schechter joined the Zionist movement in 1905. In a letter explaining his former reluctance to align himself officially and his subsequent decision, he wrote: "Theological reasons kept me from joining the movement, but I see that it is a genuine manifestation of the deeper Jewish consciousness; deeper perhaps than several of its leaders realize." [16]

Once having committed himself, he took an active part in the cause, proving a particularly able champion against the attacks of Reform anti-Zionists. He could, on occasion, be equally caustic of those elements in the Zionist leadership, both here and abroad, that viewed the aims and spirit of the movement in purely secular terms. A few years after assuming the Presidency of the Jewish Theological Seminary, Schechter added to its faculty Israel Friedlander, an outstanding exponent of the teachings of Ahad Haam. Friedlander, too, played a leading role in the intellectual leadership of American Zionism. To this day, Conservatism in its leadership, as well as its rank and file, remains committed to the advancement of the welfare of our brethren in Israel and is even

[15] Davis, op. cit., p. 194.
[16] Norman Bentwich, *Solomon Schechter*, Philadelphia, Pa., 1940, page 316.

now engaged in an Israel project designed to promote cultural
and spiritual interchange between Israel and American Jewry.

This conception of the integral organic nature of Judaism has
found expression in the emergence on the American scene, under
the aegis of Conservatism, of an institution unique in Jewish
history—the Synagogue Center. The appropriateness to the
American environment of the philosophy it embodies is attested
to by its rapid spread. Today it is no longer exclusively distinctive of the Conservative group but is sponsored by both Reform
and Orthodox groups. Yet, it must be granted that in its programmatic scope which seeks to embrace the many-faceted aspects of Jewish living, it stems directly from the Conservative
conception of the nature of Judaism and Jewish living.

Conservatism, as an organized movement, is now approaching
the close of its seventh decade. Its institutional and programmatic
growth during these approximately seventy years is evidence of
both its wide appeal and the vision and initiative of its leaders.
This growth is all the more remarkable in view of the fact that
its emergence as a "third force" on the American scene post-dates
that of Reform and Orthodoxy. Isaac Mayer Wise's dream of a
single united American Judaism enjoyed but the briefest existence. His Conservative-minded collaborators, Isaac Leeser and
Sabato Morais, faced with Wise's growing religious radicalism,
soon realized that unbridgeable gaps stood between them and
their Reform colleagues.

The promulgation of the Pittsburgh Platform in 1885, with its
outspoken classical Reform theses galvanized a group of Conservative-minded rabbis and laymen into action. Led by Rabbi
Sabato Morais, in association with Rabbis Marcus Jastrow, Alexander Kohut, Benjamin Szold, H. Pereira Mendes and Bernard
Drachman, they organized the Association of the Jewish Theological Seminary of America in 1886. Sabato Morais was named
President of the Seminary, which opened its first sessions in
1887. Ten congregations in all, and these of diverse character,
affiliated themselves with the new rabbinical school. The student
body was pitifully small and received its instruction from men
whose teaching and scholarly labors were but an adjunct to their

duties as rabbis in their respective congregations. By the turn of the century, an even more unpromising development had occured. With the demise of their Conservative-minded rabbis, the most influential congregations that had heretofore supported the Seminary went over to the Reform camp. Far from stemming the tide of Reform, the institution had failed to make any significant impress on American Jewry. Its existence was at ebb tide when Cyrus Adler, who had been associated with the Seminary from its very inception, succeeded in interesting a small group of influential laymen in the struggling institution. Moved by a variety of motives, they generously provided an endowment fund for the Seminary and made provisions for a new building to be erected in the heart of New York's academic center. The Association was reorganized into a chartered corporation and given the right to grant degrees. The reorganized institution now received new leadership, lay and rabbinic, the former in the person of Louis Marshall, who became Chairman of its Board of Trustees, and the latter in the person of Solomon Schechter, who became President of its faculty.

The coming of Schechter, perhaps the most distinguished Jewish scholar of his generation, marked a new era in the history of the institution. To the faculty of the Seminary, he brought men who were destined to make lasting contributions to Jewish scholarship and rear a small but significant group of disciples. In 1909, the actual scope of the Seminary was expanded by the establishment of the Teachers Institute to head which Schechter invited Professor Mordecai Kaplan. Today, the Teachers Institute maintains, in addition to its Teachers Training Program, extension classes and a Seminary College of Jewish Studies. The latter now offers in cooperation with the School of General Studies of Columbia University a combined curricular program. In 1913, at Schechter's initiative and under his guidance, the United Synagogue of America, the confederation of Conservative congregations, was organized. It now numbers approximately five hundred congregations, ministered to by members of the Rabbinical Assembly.

A clause in the preamble of its Constitution reflects the inclusive character Schechter intended for the organization: "It shall be the aim of the United Synagogue, while not endorsing the innovations introduced by any of its constitutional bodies to embrace all elements essentially loyal to traditional Judaism . . ." Following Schechter's death, the Presidency was held by Cyrus Adler, who had in the meantime assumed the Acting Presidency of the Seminary. As the number of affiliated congregations grew, from an initial group of thirty, the activities of the United Synagogue began to proliferate. Today, these include a National Women's League, a National Federation of Jewish Men's Clubs, a Young People's League, a Leaders' Training Fellowship and a recently organized United Synagogue Youth for teenagers. Among the notable aspects of the present program of the United Synagogue is a chain of summer camps (Ramah) for children and adolescents in which the program is conducted in Hebrew, and Jewish study is an important element.

Within the past decade and a half, under the leadership of its President, Louis Finkelstein, the Seminary has broadened its program far beyond the limits of a school for the training of rabbis and teachers and the promotion of Jewish scholarship. Most aspects of the program are too well known to require more than mere enumeration: The Eternal Light (radio and television program); the Institute of Religious and Social Studies; the Israel-Seminary Institute, the Jewish Museum, the University of Judaism in Los Angeles.

Any contemplation of even this brief historical sketch of the institutional history of the movement must inevitably provoke a question. Is Conservatism, viewed in historical perspective, merely a stopover for Jews on the way from Orthodoxy to Reform and thence to whatever lies beyond? To borrow Emerson's wittily descriptive phrase of Unitarianism—"a featherbed for falling Christians"—is Conservatism a featherbed for falling Orthodox Jews? To put it directly: will Conservatism be able to reproduce itself once the reservoir of human material reared in an Orthodox environment has vanished? No conclusive answer is possible at present. And yet, certain signs on the contemporary horizon offer an indication, even if tentative, that Conservatism is no passing phenomenon.

The days when Santayana could write, "Americans don't ignore tradition, they simply forget it" are fast disappearing. Without attempting to explain the fact, there can be no gainsaying that we are witnessing today a deliberate search for tradition in American life. We see the revival of interest in American writers of the nineteenth century who had hitherto been completely neglected. Of more decisive significance, and widely commented on latterly, has been the radical effort of various intellectual groups to achieve a realignment with religion. The traditional resources of religion long spurned as beyond the intellectual pale are being re-examined with a view to their relevance for the moral and intellectual predicaments that confront our generation. It is inevitable that in the process, the resources of Judaism will fall within the purview of this search and prove irresistible to some spirits.

On both the religious left and right, profound reorientations are taking place. The recent changes within American Orthodoxy, in practice if not in theory, are quite apparent. Within Reform, ideological shifts have long been at work. These are unmistakable signs that the mood and the current of ideas abroad in the American Jewish community seem to be veering towards a Conservative position. If such should prove to be the case, then Solomon Schechter's oft repeated claim and hope that Conservatism represented not a sect, but rather the mainstream of Judaism, will have been validated and fulfilled. If not, Conservatism will have made its contribution in the form of creative personalities, ideas, scholarship and institutions to the American Judaism of the future.

# The Temper

# of Reconstructionism

## HAROLD M. SCHULWEIS

More than twenty years have elapsed since the publication of Mordecai M. Kaplan's classic presentation of the Reconstructionist ideology in his *Judaism As a Civilization*. Reconstructionist activity is a recent arrival. Nevertheless, during these past twenty years, American Jewry has witnessed an amazingly prolific production of religious literature by Dr. Kaplan and his associates, Ira Eisenstein, Eugene Kohn, Jack J. Cohen, and the late Milton Steinberg among others.

Stimulated by the publication of its bi-weekly magazine, *The Reconstructionist* (1934), and the subsequent formation of the Jewish Reconstructionist Foundation (1940), this group of dedicated men pioneered in the creation of a whole body of creative religious literature: A new Hagadah (1942), a thought-provoking essay, "Toward a Guide to Ritual Usage" (1942), a reconstructed Sabbath Prayer Book (1945), followed by a High Holiday Prayer Book (1948), a host of pamphlets, study aids, syllabi, cantatas, and the first publication by the new Reconstructionist Press (1953) of Eugene Kohn's *Religion and Humanity*. However, Reconstructionism remains "in every essential feature the creation of a single thinker." [1] Many of Dr. Kaplan's major concepts have been absorbed into the basic vocabulary of contemporary Jewish thinking, frequently without benefit of "*b'shem omro*" (authorship). The anonymity of the source of many of these seminal ideas has encouraged the association of Reconstructionism exclusively with the unadopted aspects of its program. This in turn has lead to the caricature of its platform as contentious and as essentially negative in nature.

Not everything labelled "Reconstructionist" is subject for polemic or meant to be unique or novel. Much of its provocative genius lies in its skillful resurrection of problems and attitudes prematurely pronounced dead or lazily relegated to partisan affiliates of other ideologies or movements.

It is exceedingly difficult to single out the basic philosophic trait of Reconstructionism. Its orientation has been variously assigned to naturalism, pragmatism, idealism, humanism, experimentalism. This variety of philosophic characterization, resulting in the critics' cry against Kaplan's "pragmatism" alongside the critique of his "intellectualism," is due in large measure to the eclectic character of Kaplan's synoptic approach.

## Theology

Above all, organicity, an almost Spinozistic passion for unity and integration, characterizes most correctly the dominant temper of Reconstructionist thinking. This unified view of the universe finds its most recent theological expression in Kaplan's identification of God, the Power that makes for salvation, with the "cosmic process of organicity which, in subhuman creatures, synthesizes individuation and interaction on an unconscious level, and in men, on a conscious level." [2]

Based upon a temperate naturalism, Reconstructionism has from the start, reacted with discomfiture to the theologically or-

[1] Milton Steinberg, *A Partisan Guide to Judaism*, Bobbs-Merrill, New York, 1945, p. 174.
[2] M. Kaplan, "What is our Human Destiny?" *Judaism*, Vol. 2, No. 3, July, 1953, p. 199.

thodox approach which appears to rupture the universe into unbridgeable realms of natural and supernatural phenomena.
Reconstructionist Holism seeks a more comprehensive interpretation of reality in which events achieve relatedness; and it welcomes a continuity of inquiry which is not paralyzed by the
supernaturalist's indignation whenever religious sancta are subjected to examination. The perspective of a single, monistic universe of natural events, Reconstructionism insists, need not blur
the empirical distinctions of "higher" and "lower" values of existence. But "higher" values have natural histories and do not
require the mystification of *ad hoc* supernatural explanation
which makes of religion "a refuge of ignorance."

God and the world, God and man, live in one world. God is
not the estranged, "totally other" of rekindled neo-orthodoxy,
dwelling with "cosmic snobbishness" beyond man's reach. The
approach to an understanding of God is through God's highest
creature, endowed with His image. The beginning of the knowledge of God is the knowledge of man, his aspirations and dreams
and needs. In this regard, Reconstructionist theology accepts
man's ego-involved predicament as a blessing, not as an obstacle
in man's urge to reach out and touch the face of God. Unless
the anthropocentrism of our theology is made conscious, our fal-
libility will be disguised for indisputable revelation. To speak
the word of God without being aware that it is man who speaks,
is to attempt to jump out of one's own skin.

One of the discomforts of Kaplan's theology may be attributed
to his lack of concern with the traditional methods of talking
God into existence through professional arguments. Assuming an
unfathomable and ineffable Deity, supernaturalists yet seek "the
proof" in a worn logic which either begs the question (e.g., cos-
mological, ontological, *ex gradibus*) or demands an anxious leap
from partial analogy (e.g., teleological). Kaplan's initial theological question is not, "How can I prove that God exists" but
"What do I want my God-idea to be like." "What will I worship,
and for what values will I be willing to lay my life down" is
prior, in Kaplan's approach to theology, to the search for proof
of an assumed revelation. In Wieman's language, our task is "so

to formulate the idea of God that the question of God's existence becomes a dead issue." [3] While God cannot be pointed to
and thereby exhausted, He is still in this world and knowable.
We must however seek Divinity not as one seeks material substance but through the predicates attributed to God. We learn of
God through discovery of Goodness and Holiness which are then
properly ascribed to Divinity.

The critics protest: if God be conceived as a "power which en-
dorses what *we* believe ought to be and that guarantees that it
will be," [4] is not God a mere intra-psychic projection, an hypos-
tatized image of the human self? Milton Steinberg states it
bluntly. "Does God really exist or is He only man's notion? Is
there anything objective which corresponds to the subjective conception?" [5] And Jacob Agus regards Kaplan's theological position as anomalous since "the 'force of life' which causes plants to
grow and flowers to bloom is not divine in itself, but when human beings are around, that 'force' of a sudden, becomes a part
of God." [6] The criticism is not entirely unanticipated. To appreciate Kaplan's position we must look at the God-idea afresh.
God is not an isolable object which may be given ostensive definition. God is witnessed in process, in the context of the constant
*transactions* which take place between man and the *compulsive*
forces in the environment; divinity is discovered in the *interaction* between man's needs, wants, ideals, and the possibilities for
their this-worldly fulfillment. God, then, is not a humanistic
"work of human imagination and will" (Dewey), but remains as
real as "a stone-wall or a toothache." [7] Man's ideals may be made
of whimsy and caprice, but they will soon crumble when placed
before obstinate reality. Man, if he is to live creatively, *must* adjust himself to the compulsive factors of life which often disregard his will. The universe is not as flexible nor are human aspi-

[3] Henry Wieman, et al., *Is There a God?* Willet, Clark & Co., 1932, p. 276.
[4] M. Kaplan, *The Meaning of God in Modern Jewish Religion*, Jewish Reconstructionist Foundation, New York, 1947, p. 324; italics mine.
[5] Milton Steinberg, "Theological Problems of the Hour," *ibid.*, p. 380.
[6] Jacob Agus, *Modern Philosophies of Judaism*, Behrman, New York, 1941,
p. 309.
[7] Henry Wieman, *The Wrestle of Religion with Truth*, Macmillan, New
York, 1929, p. 2.

rations as quickly assured for man to live unconscious of Powers
"operating in ways over and above the plans and purposes of
men, bringing forth values men cannot foresee and often developing connections of mutual support and mutual meaning in
spite of or contrary to the efforts of men." [8]

Neither must the universe be accepted quietistically as in aesthetic naturalism. Much of what was once considered hostile, un-
alterable fact has been turned into an instrument for man's advancement. God is *discovered* neither through a passive reception
of Revelation plunging down through the heavens nor through
shallow humanism granted theological poetic license. Constant
changes in man's ideals and the modification of the energies of
the environment is the lot of man's struggle to utter God's name
more clearly. In his creative responses to the obdurate demands
of his self and his environment, man experiences "the force of a
controlling datum . . . (an) awareness of an ordered cosmos, in
which we, and all whom we recognize as human are presented
with conditions which must be met and laws which must
be obeyed as a prerequisite to our salvation or human self-
fulfilment." [9] The proper study of man and his quest for this
worldly salvation (soterics) turns out to be the ground of Kaplan's empirical theology. In this sense the "nearer we get to
knowing the actual conditions essential to genuine salvation, the
truer is bound to be our concept of God." [10]

There is much faith in Kaplan's concept of a universe which
is an organic totality, conditioning man's choice, yet responsive
to his efforts. In Kaplan's soterics there is a faith-presupposition
that each event somehow carries within it its own natural and
ideal realization. The world is congenial to the human quest for
stable and secure elements which illumine man's life. Belief in
such Power "predisposing man to his ultimate good" is frankly

[8] Wieman & Wieman, *The Normative Psychology of Religion,* Thomas Y.
Crowell, New York, 1935, p. 5.
[9] M. M. Kaplan, "Towards a Philosophy of Cultural Integration" in *Approaches to Group Understanding,* ed. Bryson *et al,* Harper & Bros., New
York, 1947, p. 612.
[10] M. M. Kaplan, *The Future of the American Jew,* Macmillan Co., New
York, 1948, p. 175.

not "a reasoned faith but a willed faith." [11] It plays the role of a pragmatic working hypothesis, as indispensable to human progress as the principles of induction or the uniformity of nature are for the scientist, and as undogmatic as both.

But, Kaplan's critics demand: "Can a belief so provisional and tentative support a faith to die for?" If this alone be the criterion of true faith, the critics' argument stands unopposed. Kaplan's religious temper will certainly not test truth "with the sacrifice of man's life . . . or by staking the lives of all the generations." [12]

But the value of a religion which inhibits man from such fanatic zeal is not negligible. And it is questionable whether the ability to call upon men to sacrifice their lives and their society is to be valued more than the restraint which undogmatic faith places upon man.

The faith in Powers which are said to "endorse what we believe ought to be and that guarantee that it will" and which make cosmos out of chaos raises a query as to the metaphysical status of these forces. Granted our interactional view of Divinity in Process, are the nonhuman forces purposive, conscious agents for human salvation? Or, as the question is put more often, is Kaplan's God personal?

In regard to the problem of the Power's consciousness, the answer must be predicated upon Kaplan's concept of God viewed not isolated but within the context of the natural order; with man taken seriously as a "partner with God," created with an aspect of divinity. "Insofar as consciousness and purpose are indispensable to man's salvation, they are veritable manifestations of God as the Power that makes for salvation." [13] Here again is illustrated Kaplan's theological method of inverting the place of the subject with that of its predicate.

But may not the criticism be turned about? Is not the ascription of consciousness or personality a most blatant form of anthropomorphism? And does not the supernaturalist when put to

[11] M. M. Kaplan, *The Future of the American Jew*, ibid, p. 182.

[12] Will Herberg, quoting from Rosenzweig in the former's *Judaism and Modern Man*, Farrar, Straus and Young, New York, 1952, p. 36.

[13] M. M. Kaplan, "Know How to Answer," *The Reconstructionist*, Vol. XIX, No. 14, Nov. 20, 1953, p. 31.

test to explain his concept of God as "Mind," "Spirit," or "Person," invariably take cover behind the Maimonidean apologia of negative attributes—Wieman pursues the counterattack. He insists that eliminating "personality" from God makes religion more truly theocentric since the attribution of personality to God is argued either on the anthropocentric grounds that without it "man can find no satisfaction of his needs" or that "personality is the highest form of existence that we know." [14]

Many critics have questioned: is Kaplan's God-idea Jewish; is his concept of salvation Jewish? Few arguments are felt to be as devasting as those doubting the "Jewishness" of an ideology or characterizing it as *Chukas Ha-Goi* (the way of the non-Jew). "How fantastic," writes Agus, "to compare the living God of Israel with the name given to those processes and relationships that make for human welfare." [15]

Despite the emotive charge behind the outcry, the history of Jewish thought itself testifies to the fact that the Aristotelianism of Maimonides, the neo-Platonism of Gabirol, the Hegelian spirit of Krochmal, the Kantianism of Cohen, or the existentialism of Rosenzweig and Buber, were all challenged as to their Jewishness. Yet, whom do we call upon to exhibit Jewish theology or philosophy if not these?

Judaism is what Jews believe and practice, and the test of the Jewishness of an idea remains ultimately its acceptance by Jews. Kaplan, like many Jewish theologians in their own day, attempts to reconcile and integrate the inherited tradition with the worthwhile spirit of the contemporary environment and this method of "non-imitative assimilation" has traditionally enriched Judaism.

[14] Wieman et al, *Contemporary American Theology*, Vol. I, Round Table Press.
[15] Agus, *op. cit.*, p. 313, p. 346, 349.

II

*Worship and Ritual*

For Reconstructionists, theology and the domain of worship are interdependent. Therefore, they are especially sensitive to the question: can one pray to an impersonal God? "There are," David Polish writes, "anxieties which man cannot share with man, not even with a cosmic process, but only with the Living Compassionate God. . . ." [16] And Abraham Joshua Heschel adds forcefully: "If God is a what, a power, the sum total of values, how could we pray to it? An 'I' does not pray to an 'it'. Unless therefore, *God is at least as real as my own self; unless I am sure that God has at least as much life as I do,* how could I pray?" [17] It is not entirely clear whether the critics are attacking the intellectual competence of Kaplan's God-idea or are doubting its ability to be psychologically satisfying. And it is of vast importance to the direction of our efforts to know which is the problem to solve.

But precisely what is meant by this "Thou" which is appealed to in traditionalist prayer? It would appear that those theological traditionalists who presumably do conceive of God as "totally other" relapse into an idea of God built upon the attributes of man. It may be questioned whether God is to be compared to man in terms of a difference of degree: man is a person, God is a person; man is living, God is living. Or is God a being really different in kind from man? If the usage of "Thou" emerges out of man's urge to personalize his relations with Divine forces, then it may be a profound, poetic expression. But the need to so address a "Thou," no matter how deeply experienced, is no argument for the existence of the "Thou" as personality. Nothing is wrong with the poetic "Thou" but its reification. Buber, for example, possesses the poetic religious sensitivity to gaze at a

[16] David Polish, "Current Trends in Jewish Theology," *CCAR Yearbook,* Vol. LXIII, 1953, p. 419.
[17] Abraham Joshua Heschel, "The Spirit of Jewish Prayer," *R. A. Proceedings,* Vol. XVII, 1953, p. 162.

mountain or a tree and call it "Thou"; but for anyone therefore to ascribe consciousness or personality to the inanimate object would be to revert to primitive animism.

Reconstructionism's problem with regard to prayer is not an intellectual one but a pragmatic one; a matter of psychology, not truth or logic. Nor is it a question of actually being able to translate the allegedly dispassionate intellectualistic theology of Dr. Kaplan's into the language of prayer, once distinction is drawn between analysis of the God-idea and *belief* in God. Admittedly, the semantics of theology is not that of worship. The supernaturalist's conception of God when read through the "Guide" or the "Summa" is at least as dry and intellectualistic. The Reconstructionist prayer book does not sound the analytic language of its theological treatises.

The serious pragmatic problem which does face the group is two-fold. Will men be willing to pray though the love expressed be not requited from above, and the reverence shown not heard and weighed in the balance of Divine decision?

And if men do come to pray, does it demand too great a mental dexterity from them to shift from the special language and symbolism of prayer to the sophistication and literal exactitude of theology? Is it too strenuous a task to *daven* (pray) "Thou" and think "It"?

Who will utter prayer knowing "it will prevent no misfortune"? Once told it will "relieve some sorrow by expressing it," does not the entire act of devotion appear contrived, almost self-deceptive? Told that prayer "may cultivate hope and resignation," [18] does the telling suffice and will not the worshiper halt in his prayer inhibited? Reconstructionism has these challenges to face. To be sure, the mounting pressures from ritual disuse and abandonment of prayer, has in recent years challenged the traditionalist as well. But his problem is more one of intellectual justification than pragmatics.

[18] All quotations are from Santayana's *Reason in Religion*.

### Reinterpreting Ritual

To the traditionalist, the community of worship is not only prior to the community of belief, but the two are ripped asunder as if each is of no consequence to the other. He has cultivated a begrudging theological liberalism: "Think as you please, as long as you keep the mitzvos intact!" And when rationale is required to be offered up to a recalcitrant people who have rejected the simplicity of the argument from authoritarian scripture and rabbinic judgment, theology is invoked as a handmaiden to ritual practice. Rationale is multiplied and even contradictory vindications for observance accepted—all to restore ritual *status quo ante*. The traditionalist appears blinded to the fact that change in rationale will invariably produce change in observance—if only in the degree, intensity, and manner of its performance.

Pragmatically, the neo-orthodox method proves abortive since either the change in rationale is unreflected in the mode of ritual behavior or the rationale lacks profundity in appreciating the radical change in religious orientation of the modern Jew.

Some of the most theologically neo-orthodox write nostalgic poetry about the choreography of ritual without ever feeling the pressure of the tefilin against the naked arm, the smell of *besamim* (spices used in the ritual marking the conclusion of the Sabbath), the glimpse of a *havdalah* candle (used in ritual concluding the Sabbath), the taste of *Kiddush* (prayer of sanctification over the wine on the eve of Sabbath) wine, or the sound of *zmirot* (Sabbath table songs). Talking *about* ritual has proven more inspiring and uplifting than the practice of ritual itself. Say much and do little.

The organic approach of Reconstructionism is distrustful of such *ad hoc* rationale, conjured up to exorcise the demons of Sabbath apathy or sporadic synagogue attendance. Such piecemeal *takanoth* (rabbinic enactments), at best, postpone the issue, lulling the Jewish world into a false sense of security that something is being done. Reconstructionism interprets the mean-

ing of ritual disuse as symptomatic of more than mere lay leth-
argy or rabbinic indolence. It is seen as symptomatic of a deeper
discontent with the irrelevance of the rationale and the uncon-
vincing theology which mean to vindicate observance. Not that
the layman seeks out convenience or is incapable of sacrifice, but
that the inconvenience and sacrifice do not seem to him worthwhile.

Viewing the sinking forms of worship, traditionalism has
caught upon the straw of "transvaluation." "Transvaluation consists in ascribing meanings to the traditional content of a religious or social heritage, which could neither have been contem-
plated nor implied by the authors of that content." [19]

Reconstructionist "revaluation," as opposed to "transvaluation," seeks a genuine and complete reappraisal of content and
form not alone in the light of tradition, but by contemporary
standards of truth, beauty, and the good. It means adopting in
practice the practical implications of the position which acknowl-
edge ritual sancta as "subject to the laws and limitations of the
human mind and spirit." [20]

One of the employed modes of "transvaluation" is the liberal
use of metaphor and symbol in the treatment of religious ideology. Whether in Bible homiletics or explanation of practiced
liturgy, resort is made to the mythification of theological doctrine. The theological issue of the resurrection of the dead, the
God who "returns souls to dead corpses" is poeticized away into
the ambidextrous "restoration of life to mortal creatures" or
"called to everlasting life"; and the concept of "immortality" is
confounded with the distinctive notion of "resurrection" through
subtler translation. References to the restoration of Temple sacrifices on its ancient site are prayed for—but only as historical allu-
sion, or punned with as meaning the sacrifice of work (i.e.,
avodah) or service of philanthropy. Liturgical pieces reciting the
hope that the "shoot shall come forth from the House of Jesse,"
are chanted with vocal flourish by the Cantor, but left loosely

[19] M. M. Kaplan, *The Meaning of God*, The Jewish Reconstructionist Foundation, New York, 1947, p. 3.
[20] M. M. Kaplan, "Unity in Diversity in the Conservative Movement,"
United Synagogue of America, New York, 1947, p. 14.

interpreted. Is this "shoot" a personal Messiah, the symbol of a messianic people, or the poetic expression of a messianic era to be gained through mankind's efforts?

The flexibility of symbol or poetry is apparently to be used as an instrument to dodge religious controversy. Prayer stands as a halfway house between poetic eloquence and dogma: the prayer flabby enough to substitute literary phrases for uncertain ideological conviction whenever the going is too rough. The slipperiness of symbolism applied to liturgical theology is panacea for the timid. For the sake of "continuity" of worship, the past is sanctified as eternal; for the sake of "change," only the verbalized rationale is altered. Moreover, in many cases, reinterpretation of ritual has become more compelling than the form and content of the ritual themselves. Ritual has become verbalized and, as a consequence, the reinterpretations have produced not more devoted *practice* of ritual but an inspirational meta-language of rite and ceremony, transformed into a satisfying end-in-itself.

Reconstructionism's own traditionalism is evident in its recognition of the indispensability of ritual for religious expression. To transmit a religious heritage without the peculiar ritual idiom of its people is as hopeless as the "attempt to speak without speaking any particular language" (Santayana). Abstract religious ideology needs the intimacy and warmth of everyday ritual enactment.

But neither orthodoxy's stringent ritual legalism, relevant in a different age and social climate, nor classic reform's ritual antinomianism could appreciate the natural piety of ritual. With the former, the charm of reverent devotion is lost behind the authoritarian imperative; and with the latter, the ethical convictions of man stand strained beneath the directionless "intention of the good heart."

Reconstructionism has attempted a third alternative: the development of an autonomous, self-legislating standard of ritual behavior which in time will naturally converge into group patterns. No one questions the values of shared ritual experience, but no one should confuse the privacy of religious commitment with the method of civic jurisprudence. The personal involvement between man and God cannot tolerate ritual as *law* heteronomously administered. The decision to observe ultimately must come from within, without coercion. Religious voluntarism is an acknowledgment of fact. "There is no law and there is no *Beth Din*" (Rabbinic Court). Each community, each synagogue, must therefore after study and research with its spiritual advisers, adopt for itself minimum standards and guides for ritual and ethical behavior. The self-imposed discipline of social groups then becomes more natural and effective than the pronouncements of *issur and heter* (the forbidden and the permitted) from rabbinic bodies. The community must gain respect for itself before it can gain respect for law. Many forms of ritual practices will be transferred to the area of public sanction. In that sense "some minimum cessation from work on the Sabbath and Festivals, observance of the rite of circumcision, and the Jewish validation of marriage should constitute part of Jewish civil law." [21]

The critics have raised the cry of *hefkeruth* (religious anarchy). Yet anarchy does not exist because of the sanction of ritual experimentation, but is an inheritance of an unbending orthodoxy. There are, it cannot be denied, many who have exploited Reconstructionist liberalism as justification of their own ritual *hefkeruth*. But to condemn Reconstructionist ideology because of what some insincere do with it is no saner than the judgment of traditionalism solely on the merits of some of its congregants' behavior.

Rejected, in Reconstructionist thinking, is the indiscriminate adoration of the past. There is no reason for the apostate's rationalization that he cannot find enough in Judaism. For if he "fails to find that kind of stimulus in his Jewish affiliation, the only rational thing for him to do is to reconstruct the conditions of Jewish life with a view to supplying the incentive that it lacks." [22]

This sanction to change is not to be taken lightly. The shift from a set of *beliefs* inherited to an awareness of *wants* to be met

[21] M. M. Kaplan, "Unity in Diversity in the Conservative Movement," *op. cit.*, p. 16.
[22] M. M. Kaplan, *Judaism in Transition*, Behrman, New York, 1941, p. 33.

encourages a religious activism which frustrates the worn excuse of those who contend that Judaism is a matter of "all or nothing at all" and thereby hopelessly static.

The temper of Reconstructionism calls for a large degree of self-reliance and demands a deep concern with Jewish living. The individual must call upon his inner religious and intellectual resources. His freedom unquestionably implies the kind of responsibility which is frightening. He is forever challenged by the Grand Inquisitor's cynical taunt, "Didst thou forget that man prefers peace and even death to freedom of choice in the knowledge of good and evil? Nothing is more seductive than his freedom of conscience, but nothing is a greater cause of his suffering."

### III

### *Peoplehood and Community*

In consonance with Reconstructionism's organic grasp of things, Judaism is not treated in isolation from the other civilizations with which it coexists. In the case of the American Jew, Reconstructionist thinkers have been most candid in recognizing the ancillary character of Judaism to that of the dominant American civilization. Such frankness admits the pointlessness of maintaining an overreaching aspirational level for the American Jew in utter conflict with the obstinate pressures placed upon a religio-cultural minority by the environment of an overwhelming majority. At best Judaism in America may flourish as "secondary to the general American civilization . . . an additional supplementary tradition." [23] The primacy of Jewish civilizational life in America, piously preached, is pretentious. The American Jew cannot go back to the autonomous ghetto, even if he so desired. He lives inescapably in two civilizations and one, the American, is patently and quite naturally dominant.

As Judaism cannot be analyzed in a vacuum, so Jewish people-

[23] Milton Steinberg, *A Believing Jew,* Harcourt, Brace, New York, 1951, p. 97.

hood cannot be evaluated out of context. Thus, Kaplan's philosophic sense of organicity and his naturalistic disposition com-
pel him to reject the traditionalist and reformist notion of Jewry
as abnormally separate, sociologically inexplicable, a divinely
chosen "trans-empirical phenomenon." [24] Jews are not "totally
others." The spiritual ghettoization of the Jew, conceived of as
transcendently gifted with exclusive religious genius, is not only
empirically questionable but of dubious psychologic value for
Jewish morale. For it may well strain Jewish expectancy to the
breaking point, producing ethnic guilt feelings when natural individual or group failings occur. "The nation of Priests" frequently leads a people to easy disillusionment. No matter how
"chosenness" is twisted to appear as involving special obligations,
at times incurring penalty, it retains the character of the favorite
superior child who "should know better." The uniqueness of
Jewish religious *doctrine*, perverted into the mysterious Divine
election of a *people*, is naturally susceptible to an interpretation
of "racial exclusiveness." [25]

For the organicist, the pieces must all fit together. Within Jewish life itself, the fragments of Jewish experience, multiple and
at times pulling in opposite directions, appear to fit together and
resolve their apparent contradictions in an organic whole, the organic Jewish community. This unit will reflect organizationally
the civilizational complex of Judaism. The parochial elements
are to be transcended, overcome in the comprehensive view of
Judaism as a religious civilization; and each isolated expression
of Jewishness is to be embraced as an aspect of the whole.

This perspective recommends itself on pragmatic grounds as
well. Incontrovertible pluralism demands a widened criterion of
Jewishness. Existent diversity of Jewish identification compels an
appreciation of civilizational Judaism.

The aftermath of the emancipation witnessed a spectrum of

[24] *Vid.*, Ludwig Lewisohn's "transcendent separateness" of the Jewish people and Herberg's "supernatural community." Lewisohn, *The American Jew*,
Farrar, Straus and Young, New York, 1950, p. 26. Will Herberg, *Judaism
and Modern Man*, Farrar, Straus and Young, New York, 1952, p. 271.
   [25] See Karl Stern, *The Pillar of Fire*, Harcourt, Brace, New York, 1951, pp.
172-3.

Jewish marks of affiliation so extended as to break any narrowly restricting definition of a Jew. Unless a Jew is considered as one who considers himself as such, Jewry shrivels into a fossilized decadent remnant. Reconstructionism's minimalist definition, however, is no endorsement of *normative* minimalist Jewish behavior, but a refusal to concede a priori to the *yiush* (despair) of parochial definition.[26] The organic Jewish community must find place for every segment of the Jewish population. Kaplan feels that the synagogue regrettably has today lost the prestige and power to serve as the all-inclusive community. The factionalism of religious movements and the increased complexity of Jewish life has lost for the synagogue its unifying strength. No single synagogue movement can hope to meet the diversity of temperament and ideology within the body of Israel. While each group claims to be the *sum* of Judaism, each can be regarded only as its part. Neo-orthodoxy still fights an obstinate rearguard battle, oblivious to the implications of the emancipation; reform falters yet between an etherealized notion of the "spiritual community" and a hesitant return to older nationalist traditions; conservatism, once promised as a *movement* in transition, is now frozen into middle road permanence; so long accustomed to lean on orthodox and reform crutches, it appears frightened to stand aright on its own two feet.

Despite this analysis, Kaplan confides that "the incentive, the rationale, and the leadership necessary to make our functional and purposive organizations into an instrument of Jewish survival must all come from the Jews who are affiliated with the synagogue." [27] However, Kaplan's position with respect to the organic Jewish community abounds in practical problems:

(a) If the synagogue has lost its primacy, in what sense is American Jewry to be considered a religio-cultural group which should be "analogous to that of the Roman Catholic Church minus its authoritarianism." [28]

---

[26] See Robert Gordis' critique of Reconstructionist minimalism in "Towards a Creative Jewish Community," R. A. Proceedings, 1949, p. 321.

[27] M. M. Kaplan, "A University of Judaism," United Synagogue of America, 1936, p. 7.

[28] M. M. Kaplan, *The Future of the American Jew*, op. cit., p. 121.

(b) How is the synagogue to regain Kaplan's endorsed centrality, and Judaism "religious" civilizational character, if Kaplan's proposed organic community is to be democratically organized while the non-synagogue organizations clearly outnumber and outvote her?

(c) The "synagogue center" is proposed by Kaplan, alongside his endorsed Jewish Community center. Are they not naturally turned into competitive agents? Is the community center not compelled to become an organized body for the service of secular Jewry, serving only a segment of the population, thus forsaking its organic character; or is the "synagogue center" not encouraged to abandon its religious ideology for the sake of a more watered down catholicity?

None of these three questions can be lightly answered. One thing remains clear. Whether with or without the structure of an organic Jewish community, the synagogue must regain its centrality and primacy in Jewish life, and to that end answer the social, cultural, and recreational needs of the community along with its more narrowly defined religious needs. If it yet hopes to unite American Jewry, it must transform itself into a far more comprehensive institution and seek to embrace more than "the remnant."

## iv. *Foreword*

Dr. Kaplan himself has offered the keenest appraisal of the practical and ideological contributions of Reconstructionism. He writes:[29]

1. The growing recognition that Judaism is not merely a religion in the conventional sense but a dynamic religious civilization.

2. The concept of *sancta,* as those elements of a civilization which symbolize its soteriological tendencies and functions, provides the religion of that civilization with constants which allow for change in continuity.

3. The concept of *sancta* permits a revelational religion to be

[29] In a correspondence with the author.

reinterpreted into naturalist terms without losing its identity.

The practical influences of Reconstructionism are the following:

1. It provides a *religious* basis for Jewish unity that is compatible with religious diversity.
2. It calls attention to the fact that "Jews must have other interests in common besides religion if they are to have religion in common." That has brought into being the synagogue centers and the community centers.
3. The fact that the leading professionals in the Jewish Welfare Board, Jewish Center work, and Community Councils fall back upon "Judaism as a Civilization" as a rationale for both the wrong and the right things they do indicates that Reconstructionism exercises a definite influence on American Jewish life. Note, for example, the very nature of the Janowsky report which is gradually judaising most of our community centers.
4. The Zionists who believe in the future of Diaspora Judaism generally refer to "Judaism as a Civilization" for their rationale. That provides them with the slogan of "living in two civilizations."
5. The major influence of Reconstructionism has been with the Conservative group and, of late, with elements within the Reform body. This influence on the former group is to be expected, particularly in so far as Dr. Kaplan has served on the faculty of the Jewish Theological Seminary schools for over forty years and has found in its organization a most natural vehicle for the expression of his philosophy.


## The Future of Reconstructionism

"A movement is endangered when it does not create a body: and a body is endangered when it ceases to grow." [30] Reconstructionism has suffered from indecision as to which of the alternative actions would least endanger the effec-

[30] Herbert W. Schneider, *Religion in the Twentieth Century*, Harvard University Press, Cambridge, 1952, p. 22.

tiveness of its philosophy and program. A minority has toyed with the notion of establishing a separate movement, unconnected with mother institutions. This group deems naive the hopes of those who see a bodiless ideology sustained in organizational limbo.

The majority of Reconstructionist leaders, with Kaplan as their chief ally, point to the inherent contradiction of setting up a partisan movement without abandonment of Reconstructionism's critique of divisive denominationalism. Not only would Reconstructionism's proudly held trans-sectarianism prove a mockery, but its entire spirit of independent thinking might be suspended. Self-perpetuity is not the sole criterion of ideological success. Ideologies institutionalized, more often than not, degenerate into tawdry apologia and crush originality through institutional discipline. Movements are audience conscious, and popularization too frequently entails sterile compromise.

As long as Reconstructionism can function freely among the existent religious groups, it will in all likelihood never break away to set up a separatist movement. As more and more of its concepts penetrate into traditional circles, and as time tempers the initial shock of its earlier presentation, the weaker will appear the arguments for its independent competitive existence.

However, Reconstructionism contains within itself other forms of indecision. For some of its leaders and followers, Reconstructionism is too timid, flirting carelessly with supernaturalist semantics like "cosmic urge" and "transnatural and superfactual" values. This group is disturbed by what it feels to be retreating concession to supernaturalist thinking. For example, the treatment by Kaplan of the democratic values of individual responsibility, the dignity of the individual, and equality of ideals gained "through sound intuition" from "some transcendent Source," and considered "super-empirical values" may be cited.[31]

Yet others seek to restrain the strong humanist tendency

---

[31] See M. M. Kaplan's "The Place of Religion in Democracy" in the *Review of Religion*, p. 179, 181, January 1948, and his *Future of the American Jew*, ibid, p. 183.

which in its violent reaction to neo-orthodoxy's exaggerated concern with man's "sinful pride" neglects, even on naturalist grounds, to deal fairly with the problem of man's self-glorification and idolatrous temptations.

In the religious world around it, Reconstructionism finds itself in a similarly awkward position. It is no easy stand to warn both against the "more than" of supernaturalism and the "nothing but" of reductive naturalism.

These internal problems pale somewhat in the face of Reconstructionism's concern with the generally loosened grip of theological liberalism over the thinking men in our contemporary society. One would suspect, for example, that the Jewish intellectual would be most susceptible of all to the approach and idiom of Reconstructionism. Yet, this perpetually pursued intellectual remains elusive. Those Jewish intellectuals who are returnees to Judaism seem ridden with unbalanced nostalgia for an orthodoxy which not even the traditionalism of the conservative synagogue will satisfy. Witness the penitent cases of Herberg, Lewisohn, and some of the *Commentary* affiliates. Among non-Jews, witness the comparable quests of Tate, Eliot, Auden, Waugh. How many literary intellectuals search religion for "some all-embracing, extra-aesthetic authority," for an "absolute ground of being," for "miracle, mystery and authority." [32] And those scientifically trained seem to seek escape from the rigors of their exacting enterprises in the solace of simple, absolute certitudes; a mental holiday from the constant strain of logic and control to be gained through one grand and total "commitment."

The return to the orthodoxies is general, and Reconstructionism shares the fate of all religious liberalism. As such it may at best take comfort in the pendulum theory which points to the regularity of cyclical swings in religious inclinations. The flourishing liberalism of social gospel (1900-1920) held sway until displaced by the reaction of disillusionment and cynicism following the war (1920-35). The frustration and insecurity of

[32] *Religion and the Intellectuals,* edited by James Agee, *Partisan Review,* 1950, Issue #3; p. 68.

new wars prolonged the Barthian brooding over man's sin. Perhaps the melancholy dirge of "crisis theology" is but one more instance of the "puffs of zeitgeist."

But Reconstructionism, if it is to remain a viable school of thought, cannot rest content with soporific theories of this cast. It must recognize its incontrovertible appeal to the struggling "twice-born": those who at one time experienced orthodoxy and rejected it, together with all things Jewish; and who later feel the need to return but to a tradition nourished by a thoroughgoing intellectual modernity. The voyage home is, however, uncharted. "In sum, those who look to Judaism in its present state to provide them with a ready-made scheme of salvation in this world, or in the next, are bound to be disappointed. The Jew will have to save Judaism before Judaism will be in a position to save the Jew. The Jew is so circumstanced now that the only way he can achieve salvation is by replenishing the 'wells of salvation' which have run dry. He must rediscover, reinterpret and reconstruct the civilization of his people." [33]

[33] M. M. Kaplan, *Judaism As a Civilization,* Macmillan Co., New York, 1934, pp. 521-22.

# Reform

# Judaism in

# America

## SAMUEL S. COHON

The Reform chapter in the history of American
Judaism presents a record of continuous growth
and experimentation in the adjustment of Judaism to the ever changing social and economic conditions of
America. Its beginnings go back to November 21, 1824, at
Charleston, S. C. The Jews of the then prosperous port city and
"cultural capital," numbering some six hundred—about a tenth
of the total Jewish population of the country—formed the most
important Jewish community in the U. S. A. Active in public
life, in the professions, in art, science and literature, their feeling
of pride in their Americanism ran high. Their religious life centered in the *Kahal Kadosh Beth Elohim* (their Synagogue, established in 1750), "practically an offshoot of the old Spanish and
Portuguese community of Bevis Marks, London." Though it contained a considerable number of German and Polish Jews, its
ritual—like that of the other American congregations—was Sephardic "as practiced in London and Amsterdam." The service
was conducted along traditional lines in Hebrew, with a portion
of it in Spanish, which no one understood. The service was long

and unattractive and had to be hurried if the time of worship was not to be unduly protracted. In consequence the decorum was bad. No discourse was delivered, save on special occasions, and thus no instruction was offered to the congregation.

To remedy the situation, a group of progressives convened and petitioned the board of Beth Elohim to institute such changes in the service as had recently been adopted in Holland, Germany and Prussia, and thereby make it more intelligible and attractive to the younger generation. The moderate and earnest petition, signed by forty-seven members of the congregation, was rejected by the president as unconstitutional. Those of the signers who would not permit this high-handed action to go unchallenged, convoked another meeting on January 16, 1825, and resolved to organize the "Reformed Society of Israelites for promoting true principles of Judaism according to its purity and spirit."

The society was organized by twelve members of Beth Elohim. Within a year their numbers increased to fifty, who, with their families included more than two hundred souls. At the time the congregation numbered in all upward of three hundred persons. Their leader could claim that "the Jews of Carolina are mostly of our way of thinking on the subject of worship, and act from a tender regard for the opinions and feelings of their parents in not joining the society." Its meetings were held in a Masonic hall. Instrumental music was introduced, and the congregation worshipped with uncovered heads. David Nunez Carvalho acted as volunteer reader. Other laymen participated in conducting the services and in delivering sermons, which were made part of the Sabbath morning worship.

The "leading spirit and the greatest moral force" in the society was Isaac Harby, an educator, journalist, playwright and drama critic. One of the most intellectual Jews in America during the first decades of the nineteenth century, he acted as the chairman of the society's corresponding committee, as the spokesman on its first anniversary and as its president in 1827. His discourse before the society (1826) set forth its ideas with force, clarity and deep earnestness. While manifesting a genuine liberality of spirit, it is rather empty of theological content. Its ruling principle is expressed in his aphorism: "Prayer, to proceed from the heart, must proceed from the understanding."

One of the principal tasks of the Society was to provide an appropriate ritual for its public worship. The men entrusted with the task were Isaac Harby, Abraham Moise and David Nunez Carvalho. They proceeded first to formulate the "Articles of Faith" deemed "essential to faith in revealed religion" and basic to morality and human happiness. The Articles trailed the Maimonidean Creed, though differing from it in essentials. Each article is prefaced with the formula "I believe with a perfect faith." Their number is reduced to ten. They affirm God as Creator and governor of the universe, as one and unique, as incorporeal and as the sole object of worship. The immortality of the soul replaces the traditional belief in the resurrection of the body. The substance of the Mosaic revelation is limited to the Decalogue. The advent of a personal Messiah is replaced with the hope of the spread of the worship of God over all the earth. The Creator is acknowledged as the only redeemer of all His children. Morality is recognized as essentially connected with religion, and the love of God as man's highest duty. Nothing is said about Israel's distinctive role in the spiritual life of humanity. Its strong unitarian emphasis sharply distinguishes the creed from Christianity.

The Articles of Faith preface "The Sabbath Service and Miscellaneous Prayers adopted by the Reformed Society of Israelites." This slender volume, published in 1830, consists of devotional readings, translated from the Sephardic Hebrew liturgy and of some original compositions. While it omits all references to a return to Palestine, the restoration of the sacrificial cult and bodily resurrection, it closely adheres to tradition and is filled with a genuine Jewish piety. Twenty-eight hymns, drawn from Protestant sources, are included in an appendix. The individual prayers are couched in classical English.

The work was of a provisional character, and was to be followed—as the Preface announces—by a new and enlarged edition of the whole form of prayer, to include the service of the festivals, as well as such selections from the original Hebrew as had been unavoidably omitted. As a whole it lacks the liturgical soundness of the Hamburg *Gebetbuch,* published eleven years earlier, and merits attention only as a first attempt at creating a Reform liturgy in America.

The departure of Isaac Harby for New York (June 1828), where he died a half year later, dealt a severe blow to the Society. Several others, among them D. N. Carvalho, left Charleston. Weakened in leadership, the Society lost some of its original zest under the constant pressure of the orthodox elements of the families of the Reformers. As Elzas observed, "the movement was ahead of time, and the masses were afraid to risk the experiment." Finally, on May 2, 1833, a special meeting was convened to liquidate the affairs of the Society. The monies collected for the building fund were returned with interest, to the subscribers. Most of the members who remained in Charleston reaffiliated with Beth Elohim. They were fined various sums, at the discretion of the board, and were restored to their full rights and privileges.

The Society failed, but its spirit lived on. Its members who rejoined Beth Elohim formed the nucleus of a Reform party, which under new leadership achieved the original aims of the Society. In 1836 Beth Elohim appointed Gustavus Poznanski (born in Storchnest, Poland, 1805; died in New York, 1879) as its Hazzan (cantor), and two years later elected him for life. He had been sponsored by the orthodox party and was recommended, because of his piety, by the Rev. Isaac Leeser, the conservative leader and Hazzan of Mikveh Israel of Philadelphia. However, Poznanski was educated in Hamburg, where he was attracted to the forms and ideas of the Reform temple. As a proficient congregational leader, he gained—as a critic of his testified—general approbation of the Charleston congregation for "producing an evident improvement in the tone, manner, and general arrangement in the service of the synagogue," and for creating a more earnest respect for Judaism in the community. During his incumbency, the building of Beth Elohim was destroyed by the great fire of 1838. As the rebuilding proceeded, a committee, appointed at a regular meeting of the Board, waited on Poznanski to express the wishes of the board and of the congregation "to have English introduced during divine service in synagogue, either by discourses or prayers." Poznanski promised to consider the matter and to endeavor to comply with the request as much as possible. As the building was nearing completion 38 members of the congregation, with the expressed approval of Poznanski, petitioned the Board to install an organ in the new edifice to improve the music and to advance the solemnity of the worship. The president turned down the petition as contrary to the constitution of Beth Elohim, which provided that its ritual be *Minhag Sephardim,* a ritual that does not permit an organ. As a concession to the petitioners, the subject was submitted to the congregation for discussion. The congregational meeting overruled the Board by a vote of 46 to 40. Though lacking the requisite number of votes to effect a change in the constitution of the congregation, "the persons who had voted for the organ . . . persisted in carrying out their resolve." A portion of the defeated minority withdrew, and established a congregation of their own under the name *Kahal Shearith Israel* (1841).

With the withdrawal of most of the orthodox members, Beth Elohim remained in the control of the Reformers. At the service of dedication of the new synagogue, Poznanski delivered a sermon in which he referred to the propriety of the introduction of instrumental music and "the Reformed practice of conducting certain portions of the service in the language of the people, instead of a tongue unintelligible to most of them." Touching on the Damascus affair (in which the false charge of ritual murder brought torture and death to leading Jews of the city), of the previous year, he proceeded to point with pride to conditions of "The House of Israel in this land of liberty and equal rights." The news account of the sermon reports that "he kindled with a noble and generous enthusiasm, and declared, in behalf of himself and all grateful Israel, that 'this synagogue is our *temple,* this city our *Jerusalem,* this happy land our *Palestine.'*"

Leeser correctly noted that the introduction of the organ would lead to further reform measures. In 1843 the congregation published a volume of "Hymns written for Beth Elohim Congregation," largely the work of Penina Moise. The same year Poz-

nanski preached before the congregation on the first day of Passover, declaring that the observance of the second days of festivals
was groundless, and recommended its abolition. Four out of the
seven members of the Board, who happened to be opposed to
Reform, forced through a resolution censuring Poznanski's declaration. A conflict developed in the congregation between the orthodox and reform elements.

Dissension mounted and invaded the families of the community.
Son was arrayed against father, and brother against brother. Poznanski became the target of vilification and persecution. Leeser
and a few of his colleagues in other cities joined in the attacks
against him. In exemplary forbearance, Poznanski made no reply.
At the outbreak of the strife he resigned from the congregation.
When the orthodox element was granted the privilege of using
the synagogue on alternate Sabbaths, he resumed his ministry to
the Reform group without remuneration. The trial dragged
through the courts for three years, ending with the victory of
the Reform party. The orthodox finally withdrew and built a
synagogue of their own (1847). Poznanski's friends were left in
possession of the congregational property. But he was weary of
the struggle, and requested the Board's permission to retire from
office. Yielding to the wishes of his friends, he continued to minister until the election of his successor in 1852.

## The German Phase of Reform

The Charleston experiment, despite its turbu-
lence, was not lost on the evolving Jewish community of America. The innovations introduced in that American congregation
served as an example to elements in Baltimore and in New York
who espoused the cause of Reform. These elements consisted of
immigrants from Germany and other central European lands
who, owing to oppressive political conditions, in ever-increasing
numbers sought liberty and economic betterment in the new
world. Bavaria contributed the largest quota of immigrants due
to its peculiarly harsh marriage laws and commercial restrictions.

Settling in the cities and towns of the land, they found an organizational void. Only a few Ashkenazic congregations existed in Philadelphia and in New York. Many of the newcomers were too much absorbed in establishing themselves economically to pay the necessary attention to their own spiritual needs and to the educational requirements of their children.

Like the other elements that came from England, Holland and Poland, the first German Jews were orthodox. They also included some political liberals and religious reformers who gave new direction to Jewish life in America. What they were unable to achieve in the established communities of Europe, they set out to attain in America, which was free from deeply rooted traditions. The separation of Church and State, the democratic spirit of the land and the friendly relationship between men of different faiths, made America the answer to their prayers. At the same time the freedom of the New World had a dizzying effect on many of them. With the removal of social barriers between Jew and Christian, much of religious observance fell away. The dietary laws, the observance of the Sabbath and the festivals and the religious training of the young steadily deteriorated. Strenuous measures were required to preserve the Jewish people for Judaism. This became the task of Reform Judaism.

The development of Reform among the German Jews in America followed the pattern of *Reform Vereins,* organized for cultural and religious purposes. This was the case in Baltimore, New York, Philadelphia and Chicago. The first German Jewish Reform congregation came into existence in protest against the inflexible orthodoxy of Rabbi Abraham Rice, the spiritual head of Baltimore Jewry. A number of Jews, impelled to dispute the Rabbi's authority, organized the "*Har Sinai Verein Society* of Baltimore for the purpose of cultivating an acquaintance among the Hebrews of said city, and for their mutual improvement in moral and religious knowledge." The Verein commenced to hold services during the Holy Days of 1842 in a hall, conducted by laymen, in Hebrew and in German, from the Hamburg *Gebetbuch* and from its Hymnal. A parlor organ was installed to accompany the singing. While no ordained rabbi was engaged, a "lecturer"

was chosen who performed all the duties of rabbi and reader. Its
form of worship "would today be considered orthodox or very
conservative." The attempt on the part of the more radical members to institute Sunday services on the order of those held in
Germany and in Hungary (in 1854) was dropped after six
months.

In New York a "Cultus Verein" was formed by a number of
liberals, who had come under the influence of Reform in Germany, in 1843. Their aim was (1) to win for Jews a position of
greater respect among their fellow citizens, (2) to enable Jews
to worship with greater dignity, and (3) to attach to themselves
the rising generation. In April, 1845, the Verein with its thirty-
three members set itself up as congregation Emanu-El. Its reforms were limited to a decorous service. In the room, rented in
a private residence for use as a synagogue, the front seats were
reserved for men, who worshipped with covered heads, and those
in the rear for the women. A choir of volunteers rendered the
music on Sabbaths and Holy Days, without instrumental accom-
paniment. The ritual consisted of the traditional prayerbook,
with some German additions. The first rabbi, Dr. Leo Merzbacher (born in Fuerth, Bavaria, 1809; died in New York October 21, 1856), credited with having been "the originator of the
congregation," preached in German. A liturgy committee assisted the rabbi in considering necessary reforms and in deciding
on alterations of the forms and texts in worship. From these efforts evolved his *Seder Tefillah,* The Order of Prayer, in two
parts, with an English translation.

With the acquisition of its first house of worship on Chrystie
Street, the congregation installed an organ to accompany the
Hazzan and choir. The triennial cycle of Torah reading, a memorial service on Yom Kippur and the confirmation of boys and
girls were gradually introduced, while customs deemed obsolete
were abolished. Following Merzbacher's sudden death, Dr. Samuel Adler was brought from Germany as his successor. Since this
distinguished scholar could preach only in German, an English
"lecturer" was appointed to assist him in order to satisfy the
needs of the more Americanized elements. As the lecturer lacked

theological training, the arrangement was discontinued. Not until 1879 was the use of German dropped in Emanu-El.

The rapid economic advance of the German element in New York rendered Temple Emanu-El the most influential congregation in the land. Its name was adopted by numerous congregations from the Atlantic to the Pacific. Its philanthropic activities served as examples to others. By virtue of its position in the great metropolis, it attracted hosts of visitors from all parts of the land and from abroad, who sometimes carried its standards to their own communities. The organization of its women into a Sisterhood (by Dr. Gustav Gottheil) to further tasks of education and benevolence served as a model for women's organizations in synagogues of Orthodox and Conservative as well as of Reform Judaism.

### Isaac M. Wise

In Albany the cause of Reform was linked with the dynamic leadership of Isaac M. Wise (1819-1900). Shortly after his arrival in America (1846), he became the rabbi of Congregation Beth-El of Albany, N. Y. At the same time he accepted membership on a *Beth Din* (religious court), organized by Dr. Max Lilienthal, the newly elected Chief-Rabbi of three German congregations in New York, to serve as authority in religious matters. Wise was entrusted with the task of preparing a ritual for American congregations—a *Minhag America*—that would replace the variety of rituals brought by the different groups of immigrants from the old world and which interfered with the unity of congregational life. While nothing came of the Beth Din, Wise's undertaking marked the beginning of his Reform activities. As he was preparing the draft of his ritual, he came into possession of Salomon Sulzer's *Shir Zion* (anthology of liturgical music), and proceeded to organize a choir in his congregation to render its music in the service. To make room for the music and the sermon, Wise proposed to eliminate the *piyyutim* (liturgical poems regarded as supplemental) from all but

the Rosh Hashanah and Yom Kippur services, to dispense with
the sale of *Aliyot* (honors distributed in the synagogue) and to
reduce the number of *mi sheberachs* (prayers cited for those who
have been accorded an honor) to two. His lectures on the subject
found their way into Leeser's *Occident* and led to the first clash
between the two leaders of American Judaism.

Advocating certain moderate reforms did not interfere with
Wise's insistence on Sabbath observance, on the basis that "one
could not be a Jew unless he kept the Ten Commandments." He
reports that some of his congregants closed their stores on the
Sabbath and many peddlers rested on that day, "so that the Sabbath was observed in the Beth-El congregation in Albany as in
Wilna and Brody." Strangely, his zeal for Sabbath observance antagonized some of his Orthodox members. He was deeply concerned with raising the moral standards of the community, with
the elimination of gambling and perjury, not only for the welfare of the community but also because of the harm being rendered to the Jewish name.

While the *Occident* carried on a controversy concerning the
permissibility of confirmation, Wise prepared a confirmation
class and set the service on Shabuoth. The service met with some
favor, but also brought down upon him the wrath of the Orthodox. Despite the displeasure of the readers of the *Occident* with
Wise's viewpoint, Leeser requested him to take up the fight
against the manifesto of the Presbyterian Church calling for the
conversion of the Jews to Christianity. His response with its
rationalistic view of miracles and the dismissal of the Messiah
idea as "a poetical fiction" pleased Orthodox Jews as little as it
did Orthodox Christians.

Matters came to a head with the arrival of Rev. Morris Jacob
Raphall (1798-1868) as Rabbi of the Ashkenazic congregation
B'nai Jeshurun in New York. The overbearing manner of this
scholarly Orthodox rabbi made him unwelcome to Leeser, who
contrived to have Wise invited to Charleston where Raphall was
due to lecture in defense of Orthodoxy. At a public debate with
Poznanski, Raphall asked the public and then Wise: "Do you
believe in the personal Messiah? Do you believe in the bodily

resurrection?" Wise responded with a loud and decisive "No!"
This ended the debate, but marked the beginning of a series of
attacks on Wise. Together with the officers of the Orthodox congregation of Charleston, Raphall issued a ban against Wise, declaring him "no longer fit to act as rabbi or religious teacher of
a Jewish congregation and hence he should be removed from his
post in Albany as soon as possible."

Wise laughed at this medieval farce but he soon recognized its
serious consequences. Raphall's attacks on him in the columns
of the *Asmonean* and the attacks of the Orthodox of Charleston
had their effect. The president of Beth-El congregation of Albany, a former friend of Wise, who had strong connections in
Charleston, turned against him. An incident was furnished by a
member of the Board of the congregation who opened his store
on the Sabbath. Wise begged him not to set a bad example.
When he refused to listen, Wise asked him to resign from the
Board. To prevent Wise from denouncing the member from the
pulpit at the next service, the president ordered Wise not to
preach. Wise disregarded the order and preached as usual. Dissension arose in the congregation and various charges of "heresy"
were directed against him. Another excommunication appeared
in the *Asmonean* on the ground of his "Deism." In the meantime Rosh Hashanah arrived. Wise appeared in the pulpit as
usual. As he stepped forward to take the scrolls and to offer
prayer, the president stepped in his way and struck him with his
fist. Pandemonium broke loose. Within a few minutes the entire
assembly turned into a struggling mass. The police were called to
restore order. Wise was dragged to the police station as "the
ring-leader of the rebellious mob at public service," but was dismissed on his word of honor.

The Orthodox party seemed to have triumphed, but the following day the Reform element held New Year's services at
Wise's residence. The choir sang and Wise preached a sermon
of comfort and consolation. A new Reform congregation came
into being. By Yom Kippur it was completely organized and incorporated under the name *Anshe Emeth* with Wise as rabbi
(1850). The Yom Kippur service, Wise wrote, was pervaded by

"a spirit of devotion and exaltation such as is rarely met with. . . . A new spirit seemed to possess all. A band of courageous and spirited champions of progressive Judaism, possessed of an inexpressible enthusiasm, had arisen out of the defeat which we had suffered. On that Yom Kippur day I saw American Judaism rise out of the grave, to go forth to ever new triumphs, and it has not deceived me in my expectations." A lecture tour, undertaken by Wise, to Baltimore and to Philadelphia strengthened his "determination to work for light and progress."

Wise's activities in Albany, his propagandistic tours in the interests of Reform and his editorial labors (on the *Asmonean,* which for a period was entrusted to his care) made him the leading figure in American Judaism. Developments in his congregation set the pattern for other congregations throughout the land. One of them was the adoption of family pews. His congregation Anshe Emeth acquired a Baptist church which was equipped with family pews, and, at his advice, decided to retain them, thereby eliminating the separation of the sexes in worship. This innovation subsequently became general in all Reform congregations. Wise became convinced that thorough-going reforms would be possible in Judaism only if there were to be a radical change in the character of its leaders who were for the most part *Hazzanim-Shohtim* (cantor–ritual slaughterer), and whom he regarded incompetent to render a service. He, therefore, abolished the office of Hazzan in his congregation and substituted the plain reading of the prayers and of the Torah, a practice which spread to many other congregations. All singing was done by the choir and the prayers were read by the rabbi. Many of the leading congregations, however, recognized the value of the Hazzan as the exponent of traditional song and would not sacrifice his services in Reform worship.

Wise's aggressive campaign for Reform, which as he himself writes, he conducted "with reckless boldness" roused strong opposition to him from many directions. When his *History of the Israelitish Nation* appeared, it met with the resentment of the entire clergy with the exception of Theodore Parker. The rationalistic treatment of the miracles of the Bible as natural events and the democratic spirit in which the monarchy was condemned as contrary to the laws of Moses—thus undermining the doctrine of the Davidic Messiah—rendered the work objectionable to Orthodox Christian and Jewish readers alike.

After eight years in Albany, Wise moved to Cincinnati, where he became the Rabbi of Congregation B'nai Jeshurun (1854). The forty-six years which this vital personality spent in Cincinnati mark an important chapter in the history of Reform Judaism. As rabbi of his thriving, progressive congregation, vigorous pulpiteer, editor of the *American Israelite* and its German supplement *Deborah*, prolific author of textbooks, controversial tracts and theological works, Wise popularized the cause of Reform and gained for it numerous adherents, particularly in the Middle West and the South.

As in Albany so in Cincinnati, Wise agitated for Sabbath observance and succeeded in inducing the larger business houses of the city to observe the day. His pleas for the promotion of education among the Jews were seconded by his progressive followers, who undertook to organize Zion College. To promote the project, he traveled extensively in the Middle West, planting the seeds of cultural and religious progress. In Philadelphia where he appeared again as guest of the Reform Society, Isaac Leeser and his adherents came to hear him lecture. "Leeser exerted himself from that moment to realize the project in Philadelphia, and succeeded in founding the Jewish school of that city, and later Maimonides College," which existed for six years (1867-1873). Zion College was opened in the fall of 1855 in Cincinnati and was discontinued within the first year for lack of pupils and of support.

Equally premature and abortive was the Cleveland Conference of Rabbis and Congregational Representatives which Wise summoned on October 17-18, 1855. He had agitated for such a meeting since 1848 and at last had won the response of "all the officiating rabbis in America at that time—men of all shades of opinion," without any opposition. The Jewish press devoted numerous articles to the discussion of the issues then confronting the American congregations, such as the use of the organ and mixed choirs, liturgy and liturgic procedure, etc. On the appointed day seven rabbis appeared, among them Dr. Merzbacher of Emanu-El and Isaac Leeser, who was temporarily without congregational affiliation, and lay delegates from congregations in Cincinnati, Chicago, Cleveland and Louisville.

"The debates were violent, the opposing parties obstinate, and no progress toward an agreement had been made at the hour of adjournment, late at night." Not to relinquish the plan of union, Wise and Merzbacher, who "were considered the most radical reformers," and Leeser, the leader of the orthodox, agreed upon the principles of the divine origin of Scripture and the binding authority of the Talmud to serve as the basis of the future synods.

Both parties assumed with certainty that the synod would advance, and not retrogress, and all were perfectly willing for the synod to introduce reforms. All that the Orthodox party demanded was consistent and legal reforms. Wise was certain that the battle was won, that a synod would be instituted to adjust Judaism to the laws of the land, and that provisions would be made for the establishment of a college and congregational schools as well as introduce a common ritual in the American synagogue.

No sooner was the report of the conference made public than a storm of indignation broke loose. From Baltimore, Charleston and New York protests were directed against the "articles of union" and against the proposal to set up a synod that might erect a hierarchy, repugnant to the spirit of Judaism and to the religious liberty of this country. The protests came not from the Orthodox but from the Reform party. The leader of the opposition was Dr. David Einhorn (1809-1879), the new rabbi of Har Sinai Verein of Baltimore. This radical reformer and theologian of distinction had been the victim of the over-zeal of the Orthodox in Germany and in Hungary. In the resolutions of the Cleveland conference, he recognized a reversal of the whole trend of Reform. "The declared legitimacy of Talmudic authority," he protested, "cannot heal, but on the contrary will render permanent our unhealthy religious condition, which consists not in the present conflict of parties, but must be sought for in the demoralizing effects of an antagonism between theory and practice, and in an opposition between prescriptive rules and the unyielding nature of religious and social wants. With the Talmud in hand it is no longer possible to obtain the honorable and efficient means of healing the gaping wounds in the heart of Israel, and reforms bearing on public worship and the general conduct in life, can at best be only smuggled in by a disregard of the law, and a resort to juridical trick and chicanery." While peace in Israel is important, it cannot be bought at so high a price. A few men in the name of collective Israel set up "articles of faith which deny to dissenters a place in the communion of professing Israelites." In the name of peace, American Israel is threatened by "hierarchical movements, which would again forge its chains . . . now in the guise of dogmas—and ere long by a *Minhag America.*"

Einhorn's newly established monthly magazine, *Sinai,* was devoted to the fight on the Articles of Union. The *Asmonean,* now in new hands, was filled with attacks on the conference, its members, officers and resolutions. "Orthodox Judaism was represented as being as offense against reason and morality, and unmercifully scored." Wise and Kalisch were compelled to publish in the *Israelite* several articles in defense of the Talmud and of Orthodox Judaism, which only intensified the bitterness in the camp of the opposition, but won for Wise the confidence of the Orthodox and moderate parties. To this fact, he subsequently attributed the reason for the rapid progress of his Reform ideas in the West and the South.

The efforts of the Cleveland conference came to nothing. "The only monument of the first Cleveland conference," Wise wrote, "was the *Minhag America,*" which he prepared in collaboration with the Rabbis Isidor Kalisch and W. Rothenheim, in 1857. The three volume work, in Hebrew, with English and German versions, closely adhered to the traditional prayerbook, changing only the texts of the prayers which referred to a personal Messiah, a return to Palestine, and restoration of the sacrificial cult, and expressions of lamentation over oppression and persecution and cries for vengeance—which were untrue for American Jews.

It also omitted the Cabalistic portions of the old prayerbook and replaced the belief in the resurrection of the body with that of immortality of the soul. The *Minhag America* won its way into many congregations of the country and subsequently stimulated Drs. Szold and Huebsch to issue similar works to meet the needs of their congregations.

## Einhorn and Hirsch

Einhorn shaped the course of Reform Judaism in the East by means of his great pulpit eloquence and of his monthly *Sinai* (1856-1862), which he devoted to the interpretation of Judaism from the standpoint of Reform. At the outbreak of the Civil War, he was compelled to flee from Baltimore, under the protection of a bodyguard of friends, because of his anti-slavery preaching. Taking up residence in Philadelphia, where he was welcomed by his admirers and elected Rabbi of *Keneseth Israel* congregation (org. in 1847), he at once resumed the publication of his magazine, but discontinued it after a year. As he remarked, "it died in the battle against slavery." His lasting effect on the spirit of Reform was exerted through his *Olath Tamid*. He conceived this prayerbook while still in Europe, and issued the first part of it in Baltimore in 1856 and the complete work in 1858. His progressive compatriots in Baltimore, Philadelphia, and afterwards in Chicago and elsewhere hailed it "as a new revelation." Unlike most of the previous Reform rituals, which limited themselves to the abbreviation of the traditional liturgy and the expurgation from it of antiquated beliefs, the Olath Tamid built out of the old, a modern liturgy infused with the spirit of Reform.

Of his new congregation he demanded not merely "a reformed cult, but a reformed Jewish heart, a reawakened religious consciousness, a reinvigorated belief in God and a restitution of the Sabbath, as Israel's tower of victory and of strength." Under his direction, Keneseth Israel advanced to the forefront of the Reform congregations of the land. He ministered to it until 1866, when he became the Rabbi of *Adath Jeshurun* in New York, which subsequently united with *Anshe Chesed* to form *Beth-El* congregation (now merged with Emanu-El), where he remained until his death in 1879. In Philadelphia, he was succeeded by his friend and co-worker, the Hegelian philosopher, Dr. Samuel Hirsch (1815-1889), formerly rabbi at Dessau and at Luxemburg. For twenty-five years this equally fearless and straightforward champion of radical Reform labored at Keneseth Israel, opposing excessive ritualism, instituting Sunday services to supplement Sabbath worship and extending the philanthropic activities of the congregation at home and abroad. His spirit was continued by his gifted son Emil G. Hirsch (1851-1923) at Sinai Congregation in Chicago.

An attempt to bring together the Reform parties of the East and West was made at the Philadelphia conference of Reform Rabbis in 1869 (November 3-6). The conference was called by Einhorn and Adler and was presided over by Hirsch. Among the participants were: Wise and Lilienthal of Cincinnati, Moses Mielziner of New York, Felsenthal and J. Rolnick of Chicago and Kohler who had newly arrived from Germany. Einhorn submitted a set of principles as the basis of Reform Judaism, defining the distinguishing ideas of the movement as well as its divergent lines of practice. Though a verbal agreement was secured, the rivalry of the leaders persisted. The consolidation of the movement remained a goal to be attained in the future.

### Americanization of Reform Judaism

Wise's conflicts with the leaders of Reform in the East as well as with the orthodox elements led him to the conviction that "there was but one remedy that would prove effective" for the Jews in the New World, and that was their thorough Americanization. As long as they were to continue to be "under German influences as they are now in this country," he maintained, they would become either bigots or atheists. To arouse the Jew to self-consciousness or to independent thought, he "must become an American . . . We must become not only American citizens, but become Americans through and through outside of the synagogue." To counteract the danger of the disappearance of their Judaism in their Americanism, Wise proposed "a better knowledge of Jewish history and Jewish sources." "A Jewish patriotism must be aroused; for this it was that the Jew had lost in the ages of oppression."

It was through his organizational skill that he helped turn Reform from a German into an American movement. After many years of fruitless effort, he resolved to "unite the congregations of the Mississippi Valley," if he could not unite the congregations of the entire country, for the preservation of Judaism. A committee composed of representatives of all the Cincinnati congregations, Orthodox as well as Reform, issued a call to the congregations of the West and South for a convention "to form a 'Union of Congregations' under whose auspices a 'Jewish Theological Institute' shall be established and other methods adopted, which will advance the prosperity of our religion." Thirty-four congregations sent delegates to Cincinnati where, on July 8, 1873, the *Union of American Hebrew Congregations* was organized, with Moritz Loth as president and Lipman Levy as secretary. At the first Council of the U.A.H.C. (1874) with fifty-four congregations represented, a Board of Governors was set up, with Bernhard Bettmann as president, to operate the Hebrew Union College, under the auspices of the Union. Wise was elected president of the College, directing its affairs for nearly twenty-five years. The H.U.C. was formally opened on October 3, 1875, at the Plum Street Temple, with a faculty consisting of Wise and one other full time instructor, and seventeen students, not all of whom planned to take up the rabbinate. Lilienthal, who had worked with Wise for the creation of the Union and the College, soon joined the faculty. Other scholars were added: Moses Mielziner, and later Gotthard Deutsch, etc. An eight-year curriculum was worked out by the faculty in consultation with rabbis and scholars of all shades of religious opinion, consisting of courses in the basic branches of Jewish knowledge and in practical rabbinics. The College was to serve all Jews of the country, Orthodox,

Conservative and Reform, even as the Union ignored all lines of demarcation.

On July 11, 1883, the first class of four rabbis was graduated from the Hebrew Union College. The commencement exercises, addressed by Gustav Gottheil of Temple Emanu-El and by Kaufmann Kohler of Beth-El, New York, were held in connection with the tenth anniversary of the U.A.H.C. which had grown to one hundred twenty-eight congregations. The four graduates— Israel Aaron, Henry Berkowitz, Joseph Krauskopf and David Philipson—embodied the hopes of Dr. Wise and his associates in the Union and the College. They were to justify the confidence of American Jewry in the Hebrew Union College and set standards of an American-trained rabbinate.

Despite all care to hold the different elements together, an unfortunate slip in the arrangement of the menu for the banquet which followed the graduation, broke the artificial unity. "The *trefa* (in violation of dietary laws) banquet" confirmed the lingering distrust of Sabato Morais and other conservatives in "Dr. Wise's College," and reawakened the old antagonisms toward him. The success of the graduates, who were called to the pulpits of some of Wise's former opponents, the consequent progress of the Reform movement, and finally the Pittsburgh conference alarmed the conservatives and prompted them to launch a distinct movement in American Judaism.

### The Pittsburgh Conference

The Pittsburgh Conference was convoked by Dr. Kaufmann Kohler (1843-1924), the son-in-law, disciple and successor to Dr. Einhorn in Temple Beth-El, in response to an attack on Reform by the renowned Talmudic lexicographer Dr. Alexander Kohut, as marking a break with historical Judaism. The conference convened November 16-18, 1885, and was attended by eighteen rabbis (a few of them cantors) from some dozen leading congregations, under the presidency of Dr. Wise. Dr. Kohler placed before them a ten-point program for constructive Reform, the first of which was the adoption of a platform upon which most of the Reform congregations of the country could unite. Its wording was revised in conference and the number of its planks reduced to eight, of which the last dealing with social justice was supplied by Dr. Emil G. Hirsch.

The Declaration of Principles or Platform was motivated by a double purpose. It sought, first, to silence the attacks on Reform from without, and, second, to justify to the rank and file within the movement the departure from traditional belief and observance, and thus compose the conflicting ideas and plans and working at cross purposes, which defeated the best efforts of the reformers. Instead of silencing the opposition, the publication of the platform roused a storm of indignation from the Orthodox and Conservative camps. There was general resentment of the characterization of the Bible as "reflecting the primitive ideas of its own age" and of the statement that the Mosaic legislation was of a provisional character. The renunciation of the Mosaic and rabbinical laws of diet, of priestly purity and dress, as foreign to present thinking and apt to obstruct spiritual progress, appeared to mark a dangerous break with Judaism. The further declaration that "we consider ourselves no longer a nation, but a religious community," etc., antagonized the nationalists, who were growing in numbers and in influence. Dr. Wise's acclamation of the platform, in a moment of enthusiasm, as "a Jewish Declaration of Independence," further enraged his opponents. Their immediate response to the Declaration of Principles was the issuing of a call by Sabato Morais for the creation of a new academic center to uphold the genuine doctrines of traditional Judaism. In vain did Dr. Wise and his associates endeavor to assure the Jewish community that the College and the Union remain unaffected by the Pittsburgh Platform. The die was cast. The conservatives rallied around the *Jewish Theological Seminary*, which was established (1886) in the rapidly growing Jewish community of New York.

The H.U.C. remained the training center and citadel of Reform Judaism. On succeeding Drs. Wise and Mielziner in the presidency of the College (1903), Dr. Kaufmann Kohler made it a condition that "the H.U.C., in addition to being a seat of learning in all its branches, shall forever continue to be the exponent of American Reform Judaism as expounded by its immortal founder I. M. Wise, and his illustrious co-workers." This has continued to be the ideal of his successors, the Drs. Julian Morgenstern (1921) and Nelson Glueck (1947). The scientific character of the College was strengthened, and its curriculum adjusted to changing academic requirements. Scholars of distinction were added to the faculty. The facilities of the College were enlarged by the creation of the spacious campus in Clifton. The library was built up as a vast depository of Jewish literature. Several departments were added: a School of Religious Education (1946) and a School for Sacred Music (1948) in New York, and the American Jewish Archives (1947) and the Museum (1938) in Cincinnati. The H.U.C. Press has issued numerous works, the most important of which are the twenty-five volumes of the H.U.C. Annual. In 1950 the H.U.C. united with the Jewish Institute of Religion, which was founded by the late Dr. Stephen S. Wise in 1922. The two schools are staffed by about forty full and part time professors and instructors. The Cincinnati school has graduated 586 and the New York school 242 rabbis, who have served in all parts of the U.S., in Canada, England, Cuba, Panama, Australia, Union of South Africa, and Israel, as well as all branches of the American armed forces.


## The Union of American Hebrew Congregations

The Reform movement, which was made up predominantly of German Jews, underwent a great change with the flight of East European Jews beginning in the eighties. From Russia, Poland, Rumania, Hungary, etc., millions of Jews fled to America so that by the outbreak of the Second World War the Jewish population grew to about four and a half million. While most of them swelled the ranks of the Orthodox and Conservative congregations, considerable numbers were drawn to Reform Judaism. A survey of Reform Judaism in "The Large Cities" in

1931 showed that the membership of the Reform congregations was about equally divided between members of East European and of German parentage, and the proportion of the former was increasing rapidly as compared with the latter.

In consequence, the lay body of Reform Judaism, the U.A.H.C., registered a remarkable growth. From 136 congregations in 1900, it has increased to 500 in 1955, and the membership within the congregations has multiplied greatly. Its activities, too, have expanded. Three national federations of subsidiary congregational units have been added: the Sisterhoods (1913), the Brotherhoods (1916) and Temple Youth (1939). During Rabbi George Zepin's executive secretaryship, the Union continued to operate from Cincinnati with regional offices in New York, Chicago, etc. Under his successor, Rabbi Maurice N. Eisendrath, the headquarters moved to New York, to the "House of Living Judaism," a gift of Dr. Albert A. Berg and the National Federation of Temple Sisterhoods (1951), and eleven regional offices have been opened in other cities of the land.

The auxiliary bodies operate in semi-independence of the Union. The Council of the Union, forming the highest legislative authority of the organization, is composed of delegates appointed by the member congregations and meets biennially in various cities of the U.S. and Canada. The Council serves as a forum for the discussion of issues affecting Jewish life in the U.S. and abroad. It elects an executive board, which is in charge of the Union, and appoints the boards and commissions which transact its business.

Soon after its organization the Union absorbed the Board of Delegates of American Israelites, which functioned until 1925 as a standing board of the Union. This board issued the first Jewish census in the U.S. (1880) and continuously concerned itself with the protection of the rights of Jews in foreign lands, in Morocco, Rumania, Russia, etc., intervening on their behalf with the State Department. Conditions surrounding immigration were improved through the activities of this board. In 1882 the Union appointed committees in its congregations to receive and to aid immigrants, and later chartered the Hebrew Immigrant

Aid Society (HIAS). From 1876 to 1886 the Union collected funds to settle Jews on farms and to establish colonies. The Union further devoted itself to combating sectarianism in the public schools and various discriminatory measures. In the course of time these tasks were taken over by special agencies of defense and relief.

The primary tasks of the Union consisted in maintaining the H.U.C. (until 1926 when the College was chartered separately) and in furthering Jewish education. At first it pursued its aims through the Hebrew Sabbath School Union (org. 1886), and subsequently through the Commission on Jewish Education. Cooperating with the Central Conference of American Rabbis, the Commission has published a large number of textbooks for the religious schools in history, literature, Judaism and Hebrew, and has engaged in various projects, such as extension courses for teachers, fostering state associations of teachers, teachers' aids, etc.

Another basic activity of the Union has been carried on by the Department of Synagogue Extension, which has aimed to assist in the organization of new congregations. The Commission on Synagogue Activities has engaged in numerous projects designed to enrich congregational life, such as research and information service on congregational problems. The Union has published many tracts on Jewish themes for popular distribution, pamphlets of Holy Day sermons, and several magazines.

## The Central Conference of American Rabbis

The C.C.A.R. forms the companion body of the U.A.H.C. Its members are the ministers of the constituent congregations of the Union. It was called into existence four years after the Pittsburgh meeting. As the numbers of the graduates of the H.U.C. increased, Dr. Wise, who was approaching his seventieth birthday, thought the time opportune to try once more a union of rabbis in America. At his suggestion, Dr. David Philipson called the rabbis in attendance at the Council of the

U.A.H.C. in Detroit to a meeting at which the Central Conference of American Rabbis was organized (1889). Dr. Wise was
elected president, and held the office to the end of his life eleven
years later.

Unlike the preceding conferences of rabbis in Germany and in
the U.S., which failed to achieve permanency, the C.C.A.R. became a continuing assembly, meeting annually and carrying on
its tasks uninterruptedly through its officers and committees. To
create continuity in Reform, the C.C.A.R. took the resolutions of
the preceding Rabbinical conferences as the basis of its activities.
The C.C.A.R. has acted as a deliberative rather than a legislative
body. As a clearing house of Reform Jewish thought and practice
and as a forum for the discussion of the problems of world
Jewry, the Conference has helped shape the patterns of Jewish
life. Learned papers of theoretical and practical character have
been presented at its annual meetings. Committee reports on
religious and social questions of Jewish and of general nature
have been submitted with recommendations for action. The decisions and pronouncements of the Conference are formed by the
free democratic process of open discussion. The majority opinion, while forming the basis of action, does not coerce the minority nor even the individual member. In some instances the Conference has reversed its former position. Former minority
opinions now and then won the recognition of the majority in
consequence of the changed viewpoints of the membership and
the reconsideration of the issues in the light of altered circumstances.

The Conference has helped create a united rabbinate as a
basis for a more unified Reform Jewry. It has operated with the
conviction that its highest function is to continue the chain of
Jewish tradition rather than create a new sect in Judaism. The
devotion of its members to Reform has not remained parochial
but has impelled them to cooperate with other Jewish bodies in
all efforts consistent with intellectual integrity. It has concerned
itself with the spiritual, moral, cultural and material betterment
of the Jewish people in all parts of the world, and it has cooperated with numerous lay organizations and with Conservative

and Orthodox rabbinical bodies in chaplaincy work and in the Synagogue Council, which it helped to create. The Conference and the Union participate in the activities of the World Union for Progressive Judaism.

The Conference has never forgotten its duties to world Jewry; neither has it overlooked its obligations to America and to humanity. Through its Committee on Church and State, it has guarded the liberal heritage of the country against encroachments by either religion or government. Its Commission on Social Justice has sought to apply the prophetic insights of Judaism to the vexing problems affecting the social and industrial relations of the country. The Conference has participated in inter-faith activities to promote good will between Jews and Christians. Many of its members have conducted seminars for the Christian clergy in their communities to present authentic information on Jews and Judaism.

While the attempts of the Conference to establish a central authority for Reform Judaism by means of a Synod have failed due to the fear of setting up an ecclesiastical tyranny, the Conference has striven to arrive at a general agreement on numerous practical issues, such as the admission of proselytes without requiring the rite of circumcision, permitting cremation, recognition of the equality of women in congregational life, coping with the problems of Sabbath observance and Sunday services, disapproval of mixed marriages, etc.

To curb the tendency toward individualism, Dr. Kohler convinced the Conference to set up a committee on *Responsa* to which questions may be submitted by the members who seek guidance; and he served as its chairman for a number of years. The replies have sought to determine the norms of Jewish observance in the light of the Halakhah and of present outlook and need.

The chief contribution of the Conference to the unification of Reform Jewish life has been through the introduction of a common liturgy into the Reform congregations of the country. Prior to the organization of the Conference the practice was fairly general for every prominent rabbi to provide his congregation with a prayerbook of his own. To remove the resulting confusion, the Conference appointed a liturgy committee, with Moses Mielziner as chairman. He was assisted by Kohler, Gottheil, Harris, I. S. Moses, and others, who recast the traditional liturgy for modern use. In creating the *Union Prayer Book*, (1894), the committee built largely upon Einhorn's *Olath Tamid*, making use also of the *Minhag America* and other rituals, and produced a book of devotion for modern men and women, expressed in language and form congenial to their taste and conviction.

The other devotional publications have tended similarly to unify the religious thinking and action of the Reform communities. The *Union Haggadah*, has helped reintroduce the Seder service in Reform homes. The *Rabbi's Manual*, based on the earlier *Minister's Handbook*, has brought Jewish dignity and content to religious occasions requiring the services of a rabbi. So, too, the *Union Hymnal* and the *Union Home Prayerbook*, with varying degrees of success, have sought to restore the spirit of joy and of devotion to private and public worship. These publications have undergone revisions as the need for their improvement has made itself felt in the Conference and in the congregations.

### The Columbus Platform

The need of crystallization of Reform Jewish belief was felt from the very beginning of the movement in America. We noted the earliest attempt at the formulation of Articles of Faith by the Society of Reformed Israelites of Charleston and the subsequent statements of principles by the Cleveland, Philadelphia and Pittsburgh Conferences. With the organization of the C.C.A.R., calls for a clear restatement of the basic doctrines of Judaism were made by Dr. Wise and others, recognizing that all practical innovations and alterations in Jewish religious life are predicated upon definite beliefs. However, the adoption of an official creed was strongly contested.

Not until the fiftieth anniversary of the Pittsburgh Platform were steps taken by the C.C.A.R. to re-think the basic convictions of Reform Judaism. Following a symposium on the Pittsburgh Platform, at its 1935 meeting, the C.C.A.R. appointed a commission to draft a new platform that would express more adequately the position of the movement on the fundamentals of Judaism. In the course of the half century a more realistic conception of the peoplehood of Israel came to possess the minds of the leaders of Reform. In 1885 world conditions permitted the belief that the modern era of universal culture and intellect marked the approach of the realization of Israel's Messianic era. A little over a decade later when Theodor Herzl published his *Judenstaat* and launched the Zionist movement, aiming at the establishment of a legally secure home for the Jewish people in Palestine, strong opposition was raised by the leaders of Reform and Orthodoxy. In his presidential address at the Montreal meeting of the C.C.A.R., Dr. Wise issued a blast against the movement. The Conference recorded its total disapproval of "any attempt for the establishment of a Jewish state" as contrary to Israel's religious mission and injurious to the Jews in lands of persecution by confirming the assertion of anti-Semites that they are aliens in their own homes. The disabilities to which Jews were exposed and their suffering in backward countries, it was believed, would be remedied by the spread of freedom and of democracy to all parts of the world. Instead of improving, conditions deteriorated not only in Eastern but also in Western lands. Following the catastrophic effects of the first World War on East European Jewry, the Balfour Declaration promised new hope for the homeless people. The C.C.A.R., accordingly, welcomed "the decision of the San Remo conference to give Great Britain a mandate over Palestine in line with the Balfour Declaration," without subscribing "to the phrase in the Declaration which says, 'Palestine is to be a national home for *the* Jewish people'" and reiterating that "the Jewish people, like any other religious communion, has the right to live, to be at home, and to assert its message in every part of the world." With the rise of the Nazi menace in the thirties, and the growing restriction upon immigrating to America, it became clear that radical means of

saving the Jewish remnant had to be found. Reform Jews participated in all measures of relief and rehabilitation and cooperated
with the Jewish Agency in directing Jewish immigration to Palestine.

The thinking of Reform Judaism underwent another significant change with regard to its theology and forms of worship.
In 1894 Dr. Kohler himself complained against the trend in
Reform Judaism to foster the intellect and ignore sentiment. In
1907, he took issue with Holdheim's negative attitude toward the
ceremonial law, and urged that ceremonial forms and observances
are indispensable means of expressing religious feeling. Our task
as Reformers, he insisted, is to replace the forms of Judaism that
have grown burdensome with new ones that are more in accord
with the occidental taste of our people and that are vocal with
prophetic truth. These sentiments pervade his work on Jewish
Theology and other writings. Some of his disciples, sharing his
feeling in the matter, have not been as averse to the oriental note
in Judaism as he was. Some of them have stressed the mystic note
in Judaism, which they derived from Hasidism and its modern
interpreters.

The increasing membership of the congregations, too, consisting in large part of East European Jews, brought with them a
nostalgic love for Jewish folkways, Jewish music and Hebrew.
Many of them have sought amid the decorum of Reform worship
a deeper emotional content and a greater regard for traditional
ways. A sizable proportion of them showed a keener appreciation of the problems of world Jewry and a warmer sympathy
with the aims of Zionism. While welcoming the ethical emphasis
in Reform, many of them craved a more positive expression of
their faith and a restoration of some of the forms which they
cherished in the days of their Orthodoxy.

To present these strivings for a richer and fuller Jewish religious life and at the same time to overcome the diversities of
outlook and taste among the members of the Conference was no
easy task. The commission placed a first draft of the *Guiding
Principles of Reform Judaism* before the 1936 meeting of the
Conference. On the basis of the discussion, which followed and

the written comments elicited from the membership, a reformulated statement was submitted to the Columbus meeting (May 27, 1937).

The Columbus Platform was issued "not as a fixed creed but as a guide for the progressive elements of Jewry," and was intended to overcome the negativism which manifested itself in some quarters and the indecision of others, and to meet the challenge of both secular nationalism and of Orthodoxy. The key to the platform is found in the definition of *Judaism as a religion* with a universal message in contradistinction to the attempts to reduce it to a "racial culture," to a "civilization" or to a Jewish variety of "humanism." The specific character of Reform Judaism was taken to consist in the recognition of "the principle of progressive development in religion" and in consciously applying this principle to spiritual as well as to cultural and social life. Against the static view of Judaism, maintained by Orthodoxy, the platform attests that "Judaism welcomes all truth," whether coming from the Bible or from nature. New scientific discoveries, "while replacing the older scientific views underlying our sacred literature, do not conflict with the essential spirit of religion as manifested in the consecration of man's will, heart and mind to the service of God and Humanity."

The atheistic trend in the then current humanism is countered by the reaffirmation of the historical Jewish doctrine of the One, Living God of law and of love, in whom "all existence has its creative source and mankind its ideal of conduct," and who is both transcendent and immanent. Man, instead of being a lost creature, burdened with sin and guilt—as maintained by Pauline Christianity—is "created in the image of God" and possesses an immortal spirit. He is an active co-worker with God.

Authority, the crucial point in every religion, is defined in terms of Torah and Tradition, and charts the way between secularism and Orthodoxy. God's revelation is continuous and universal. "Yet the people of Israel, through its prophets and sages achieved unique insight in the realm of religious truth. The *Torah*, both written and oral, enshrines Israel's ever-growing consciousness of God and of the moral law. Being products of historical processes, certain of its laws have lost their binding force with the passing of the conditions that called them forth. But as a depository of permanent spiritual ideals, the *Torah* remains the dynamic source of the life of Israel. Each age has the obligation to adapt the teachings of the *Torah* to its basic needs in consonance with the genius of Judaism."

The section in the platform which presented the drafting committee with the greatest difficulty and which called forth the most discussion was the one on Israel. The nationalistic and the spiritual interpretations of Israel's role in the world found equally strong champions among the leaders of Reform. Through the earnest efforts of representatives of both groups, the following statement was adopted:

Judaism is the soul of which Israel is the body . . . Living in all parts of the world, Israel has been held together by the ties of a common history, and above all, by the heritage of faith. Though we recognize in the group-loyalty of Jews who have become estranged from our religious tradition a bond which still unites them with us, we maintain that it is by its religion and for its religion that the Jewish people has lived. The non-Jew who accepts our faith is welcomed as a full member of the Jewish community. In all lands where our people live, they assume and seek to share loyally the full duties and responsibilities of citizenship and to create seats of Jewish knowledge and religion. In the rehabilitation of Palestine, the land hallowed by memories and hopes, we behold the promise of renewed life for many of our brethren. We affirm the obligation of all Jewry to aid in its upbuilding as a Jewish homeland by endeavoring to make it not only a haven of refuge for the oppressed, but also a center of Jewish culture and spiritual life.

The section on Ethics stresses the indissoluable union between morality and religion in Judaism. Social service and social justice are not mere luxuries or vagaries that may be dispensed with, but absolute imperatives of Jewish faith. With the war clouds hanging over the world, the platform called for peace based on justice, for "spiritual and physical disarmament" and for "organized international action for disarmament, collective security and world peace."

A novel element in the platform was the emphasis on religious practice. Whereas ceremonies and rituals were disparaged in the Pittsburgh Platform, the Columbus Platform stresses "the preservation of the Sabbath, festivals and Holy Days, the retention and development of such customs, symbols and ceremonies as possess inspirational value, the cultivation of distinctive forms of religious art and music and the use of Hebrew, together with the vernacular, in our worship and instruction."

For the sake of historical continuity, Dr. David Philipson, the only surviving participant in the Pittsburgh Conference, moved the adoption of this "Declaration of Principles." Dr. Abba H. Silver, seconding the motion, stated: "This draft of Principles is, in my judgment, one that the Conference may take a justifiable pride in because it represents not the work of the Commission alone but, in a real sense, it is the work of the entire Conference. It is definitely within the classic channels of Jewish thought. It represents all that is finest and noblest in Jewish life."

The differences within the Conference regarding Israel, Palestine and, to a lesser degree, regarding ceremonial practices, which came to light during the adoption of the Columbus Platform, presaged some of the divergent attitudes that were to emerge in the course of events that followed. The catastrophic conditions of European Jewry under the shadow of Nazism focussed the attention of increasingly large numbers of laymen and rabbis on Palestine as one of the chief havens for Jewish refugees. Zionists recognized in the tragic events a challenge to the realization of their program. The very problems of relief and rehabilitation were subordinated to the main task of creating a permanent Jewish home in Palestine.

The preoccupation with Zionism on the part of a large number of Conference members evoked the opposition of some of their colleagues who feared that Judaism was being transformed from a religion to a type of political nationalism, which was bound to endanger Jewish life and upset the process of Jewish integration in the general American scene. The opposition became particularly vocal in a number of congregations, and took on organized form in the American Council for Judaism, under the leadership of Mr. Lessing J. Rosenwald and Rabbi Elmer Berger (1943). It has maintained its opposition even since the establishment of the State of Israel in 1948. Though avowing its good will toward the Israeli community, the Council stands guard against the recurrent view that Jews everywhere are members of a "collective Jewish nation which has its center in the State of Israel," and insists that Jews outside of Israel are an integral part of the countries of their birth or adoption.

With the positive emphasis of the Council most of the supporters of Zionism in Reform ranks are in complete harmony. They insist, however, that under existing conditions a moral obligation to aid the struggling community in Palestine exists. Consequently the C.C.A.R. hailed with joy the restoration of the State of Israel as "the consummation of the millenial hopes and aspirations of our people" and urged the full recognition of the State by the U. S. government and the adoption of measures by the U.N. to safeguard its existence. The Conference further expressed pride in the fact that its members "have played an important role in the creation of the State of Israel." At the same time it reaffirmed the obligation of American Jews to "continue to build our Jewish life in America and jointly with our neighbors of every faith . . . make our contribution, as Jews and as Americans to the spiritualization of life in this country, to the preservation of democracy."

Another problem which has agitated the Reform Jewish community since the adoption of the platform has concerned itself with the translation of its emphasis on practice into concrete forms. At the annual meetings of the C.C.A.R., and at the biennial conventions of the Union of American Hebrew Congregations, in the pulpits and in the press, the demand has been made for the formulation and adoption of an authoritative code of Reform Jewish observance. Some fear such a venture on the ground that it might turn Reform into a new kind of Orthodoxy and fetter the religious spirit. The proponents of a code argue to the contrary that the Reform Jew is at a disadvantage as compared with his Orthodox brother in that he does not always know what his religious obligations are and how to fulfill them. Judaism has been a religion of law, and its Reform expression cannot wholly dispense with law, if it is to prove effective in the spiritual life of the modern Jew. The new emphasis on psychology in religion has furnished further arguments in favor of a code that would furnish helpful guidance to the individual, and restore something of the normative pattern of historical Judaism.

In line with the emphasis of the Columbus Platform on the need of ritual observances a Joint Committee on Ceremonies, resulting from action taken by the U.A.H.C. and the C.C.A.R. in 1937, has striven to correct the anti-ritualism of the earlier Reformers and to restore "worthwhile old practices, giving them new form wherever necessary to make them consonant with our times, and of creating new practices wherever the need for them has been felt." The effort to invigorate religious observance in the home and in the synagogue and thus produce a richer cultural and spiritual Reform Jewish life in America has not gone without resistance on the part of some laymen and rabbis trained to view Reform as a purely ethical faith unconcerned with externals.

The tasks of Reform have not and never can be finished. Reform is a perennial process of self-renewal, of ever regenerating the creative spirit of Judaism and of carrying forward its goals for the individual and the community. It calls for the constant rethinking of the theological and ethical content of the historic faith and of restating it in terms that are relevant to the advancing generations of American Jews. Reform must stand by its liberal faith despite the obscurantist trends and the waves of reaction in religion. The vast numerical growth of its movement carries the obligation of intensifying its educational efforts, to make its adherents conscious of their obligation as Jews and of the ties that unite them with world Jewry.

Reform has reshaped the externals of Jewish life. In the years ahead it must deepen the Jewish spirit of its followers. It has built beautiful Temples, but it has yet to make the modern Jew worshipful. The Jewish heart has still to be rekindled with the ardor of an abiding faith. The enrichment of the Jewish mind with Jewish knowledge and the strengthening of the Jewish will with loyalty and sacrificial zeal still remain a hope and a prayer. Reform, like all other phases of Judaism, is still looking to the day when the Jew will combine his love of modernity with a sense of eternity and his progressivism with constancy and sanctity.

# Secularism and Religion in the Jewish Labor Movement

## C. BEZALEL SHERMAN

Secularism as a *Weltanschauung* is a much older phenomenon among American Jews than secularism as a Jewish philosophy. Which is to say that American Jews were dedicated to the proposition that church must be separated from the state long before the notion that Jewish survival was not inextricably bound up with the survival of the Jewish faith made any kind of a dent in their thinking.

For half of the three hundred years that Jews have lived in this country there was no Jewish community life outside the synagogue. The oldest Jewish charitable agency in the country cannot claim to be more than 150 years of age. B'nai B'rith, the first national Jewish membership organization, was founded in 1843, while Jewish institutions that were completely divorced from Jewish religion did not appear on the American scene before the end of the 19th century. Prior to that time, all non-congregational Jewish social welfare and cultural agencies recognized the primacy of the synagogue in Jewish collective life. It is no accident that immigration from Germany, which supplied American Jewry with the most effective builders of its institutional edifice, also provided the mass base for classical Reform which, while considering Jews a religious fellowship, rejected the concept of Jewish peoplehood. At the very moment that the German Jews were blanketing the United States with a network of Jewish hospitals, orphanages, homes for the aged and similar institutions, they also produced the Pittsburgh Platform which, among others, contained the following statement:

The modern era heralds the approach of Israel's great messianic hope for the establishment of the Kingdom of Truth, Justice and Peace among all men. We consider ourselves no longer a nation, but a religious community, and therefore expect neither a return to Palestine, nor a restoration of the sacrificial worship under the sons of Aaron, or of any of the laws concerning the Jewish State.

Traveling a different road and moved by a totally different motivation, the founders of the Jewish labor movement practically arrived at the same conclusion as the authors of the Pittsburgh Platform, namely that mankind was on the threshold of Utopia and that Jews did not constitute a people. In a declaration adopted at the first conference of Jewish workers' organizations in the United States and Canada, held in New York in 1890, the view that the Jewish question had ceased to be a national problem found the following formulation:

We have no Jewish question in America. The only question we recognize is the question of how to prevent the emergence of 'Jewish questions' here.

The motto of classical Reform, coined by Gustavus Poznanski at Charleston, South Carolina in 1840, that "America is our Zion and Washington our Jerusalem" found its proletarian paraphrase at the workers' conference, fifty years later, in the slogan: "The world is our fatherland, socialism our religion."

The common ground upon which the two social extremes in American Jewish life—the rising Jewish bourgeoisie as represented by the Reform movement and the rising Jewish labor movement as represented by the socialist groups—met was the denial to Jews of a secular identity. Both hoped to hasten the arrival of human brotherhood by tearing themselves away from their own national roots.

At this point it becomes necessary to delimit the territory we intend to cover in the present essay. A line should be drawn between secularism and secularist ideology. As defined here, secularism is merely an extension of the principle of the separation of Church and State and, hence, not incompatible with the profoundest religious feeling. It marches alongside, rather than in opposition to, religion, and concedes to the latter priority in the sphere of influence which democratic society assigns to faith. Secularist ideology, on the other hand, seeks to eliminate religion from a voice in social relationships. Secularism's quarrel is with the overreaching ambitions of the Church; secularist ideology, in addition to distrusting the Church, is also suspicious of religion itself. This explains why irreligion and atheism flourish in the orbit of secularist ideology.

Both secularism and secularist ideology gave rise to Jewish mass movements at the end of the 19th century. Riding the crest of the surging waves of immigration from Eastern Europe, these mass movements found programatic expression in large organizations, with secularism, as we have defined it, receiving its fullest crystallization in Zionism and secularist ideology in Jewish socialism.

American Zionism, although nonreligious as a movement, except of course for the Mizrachi groups, has always worked closely with the synagogue and has manifested a great loyalty for the tenets of the Jewish faith. Zionism has thus been able to cut across denominational divisions and to enlist the rabbinate as its most effective propagandist, while secularist ideology was sectarian in its very nature. It gained adherents only among certain sections of Jewish labor and, although fairly successful during the formative stages of the Jewish trade unions, proved to be, as will be seen below, no more than a one-generation phenomenon in American Jewish life. It is the main purpose of this article to point out the reasons why secularist ideology failed despite a rather auspicious beginning.

II

To understand why cosmopolitanism was the dominating strain in the ideological fabric of the Jewish labor movement during the first two decades of its existence, it is necessary to remember that that movement was recruited almost exclusively from immigration from Eastern Europe—a part of the world where the Jewish communities constituted states within states as it were. On one end was the political state which held its entire populace in subjugation and denied Jews the few restricted rights other subjects enjoyed; and there was, on the other end, the "State" of the Jewish settlement which regulated every move of its members in matters concerning Jewish belongingness. Organized religion was a factor in each one of the states. The church was one of the pillars which supported the despotic governments of the political state; and the synagogue was the central institution of the Jewish "State" which, resting on religious authority, was not infrequently also bolstered by certain legal prerogatives. The Jewish immigrant, who became a worker for the first time in his life upon arrival in the United States or Canada, thus brought with him the image of government and religion as anti-labor factors.

This is the reason why the founders of the Jewish labor movement, whose social conceptions were fashioned in the school of non-Jewish, primarily German, socialist thought, were able to instill an assimilationist philosophy into the young Jewish trade unions. They won by default because there was no one else at the time to guide the inexperienced Jewish workers on the untrodden path of proletarianization; and because, too, the sudden transplantation of the Jewish immigrant from a ghetto life in a tyrannical, semi-feudal empire to the clear air of an industrial civilization in a political democracy left him in a state of confusion and bewilderment. This was not a gradual transformation, not a planned or systematic growing into new conditions, but a which there was lacking a transitory period. The young Jewish political, socio-economic and psychological upheaval, one in worker had had, as yet, no time to break out of the cobweb of old prejudices and erase the bitter memories that obscured his vision. At the time he first became acquainted with political activity, the image of government and religion he had brought over from abroad still colored his relationships with society. He was mistrustful of all authority, religious or secular.

Lack of a transitory period also marked the religious and communal transformation the new Jewish workers had experienced. Never before had they seen a state or community that was not wedded to organized religion; and there was no bridge to span the gulf that opened up between the total identification of Jewishness with Jewish religion that they had known in their native lands and the system of religious freedom they had found in this country. They had to jump from an all-embracing rigid orthodoxy which regulated all phases of Jewish life for thousands of years to a secular society that made religion a matter of individual conscience. To many this represented a leap into unfaith.

It is this neck-breaking leap that holds the key to some peculiar features in the development of the Jewish labor movement—features that would remain unsolved riddles and inexplicable contradictions but for the use of this key. Uprooted people who never saw a friendly government or a beneficial law would naturally embrace, before finding new moorings, radical programs which called for the complete revamping of the social system. It should, therefore, cause no surprise to find so many of the new Jewish recruits to the industrial working classes accepting, despite their want of a proletarian tradition, the ideology of a militant socialism which advocated the abolition of class society, or of an anarchism which urged the dissolution of the state. Nor

should the fact that so many turned irreligious or atheistic despite recent emergence from a purely religious way of life cause
any wonderment.

This is not to say that all, or even a majority, of the early
Jewish workers were radicals or antagonistic to religion. Quite
the contrary. Most of them remained steadfast in their religious
loyalty, joined Orthodox congregations in large numbers and
went to incredible lengths to safeguard their spiritual heritage.
Countless thousands of Jewish workers were willing to endure
the misery and degradation of the sweatshop merely because it
allowed them to observe the Sabbath; and they also resisted the
efforts of the early union leaders to hoist upon their personal
lives the flag of national nihilism. They resisted in the only way
that was open to them—by dropping out of the labor organizations as soon as strikes were over. The instability of the early
Jewish unions was noted by all students of organized labor; so
much so that John R. Commons, historian of American trade
unionism, was certain in 1906 that Jewish workers, ready for
the greatest sacrifices during economic struggles, were innately
incapable of remaining organized in times of industrial peace.
Commons, who subsequently changed his views, and others failed
to detect in the loss of union interests the reaction on the part
of the rank and file to the irreligious policies of their leaders. A
comparison between those policies and the activities of the synagogues and *landsmanschaften,* whose membership was to a very
large extent also made up of working immigrants, would reveal
how wide was the gap that existed between the social philosophies of the trade unions and the mores of their members.

The average Jewish workers were too raw, too inexperienced,
too bewildered and too immature politically to challenge the
ideologies of the leadership openly. They could only resort to
the passive resistance of abstaining from union activity which
did not relate to matters of immediate economic concern. As for
the leaders, they were united in the conviction that socialism
required the obliteration of national division as well as of class
differentiation. Cosmopolitanism, merely another name for assimilationism, was their answer to the Jewish question. As re-

gards religion, there was agreement among them that it tended to blunt the class consciousness of the Jewish worker. They did not all see eye to eye, however, when choosing methods to "enlighten" those of their followers who clung to timeworn "superstitions."

The anarchists, anti-Marxian in their approach to social issues, accepted as gospel truth the Marxian injunction that religion was the opiate of the working people, and made aggressive atheism an integral part of their program of action. They sent their shock troops to storm the gates of heaven by putting on anti-religious spectacles in the heart of religious neighborhoods. It was the era of the Yom Kippur Ball and the atheistic Haggadah —an era not to recur until a generation later when the Jewish communists produced anti-religious performances which put the action of the early anarchists to shame.

The socialists, the most powerful and most enduring wing of Jewish radicalism, as a rule frowned upon the anti-religious antics of the anarchists. Nevertheless, there were some among them who, like Benjamin Feigenbaum, used whatever Jewish learning they picked up in the Lithuanian or Polish *yeshivoth* (Talmud schools) to point up inconsistencies in the Bible or to dig up passages in the Talmud that could be given an anti-labor twist. The Feigenbaums were decidedly in the minority however. Most of the socialist leaders favored an attitude of respect and tolerance in dealings with professing Jews.

Outstanding among the leaders was Abraham Cahan whose influence on the Jewish labor movement in America is unequalled by any one individual in history. He was the first among the founders of the Jewish Socialist movement to respond to the realities of American life and to be affected by the attitudes toward religion that prevailed in the general community. As early as the 1880's he realized the folly of trying to win over Jewish workers to trade unionism by addressing them in Russian, German and, to a lesser degree, in English. He was the first to employ the Yiddish language in socialist propaganda, and the first to insist on the proposition that relationships between Jewish workers and international labor were not a one-way street. He unfolded the banner of labor solidarity among Jewish workers, but he also missed no opportunity to remind international social-ism that it owed something to the Jewish people.

Illustrative of Cahan's attitude toward anti-religious anarch-ists and socialists is an article, not his first on the subject, which appeared in two installments in the *Forward* on April 22 and 23, 1911. The following lines are worth quoting:

The most comical and at the same time, saddest thing is to see an atheist turn his irreligion into a cold, dry, unfeeling, heartless re-ligion—and this is something most of our unbelievers used to do. One must not sit at a Seder; one must extend no sympathy to the honest, ignorant mother who sheds tears over her prayerbook; one must deeply wound traditional Jews by eating and smoking on Yom Kippur in front of the synagogue. Verily, the former un-believers were, in their way, just as fanatical, just as narrow-minded, just as intolerant as the religious fanatic on whom they warred.

Cahan did not manifest any sympathy for the Zionist cause until late in his very long life. To the end he had very little, if any, faith in the future of the American Jewish community. He never assigned an independent social role to Jewish labor, con-sidering the latter a mere stepping-stone to the American labor movement. Yiddish was to him not an end but a means, one to be employed until such time as the Jewish workers learned to get along in English. First to carry the message of socialism in terms of Jewish conditions, he never had a clear conception of how he wanted those conditions changed.

III

From its inception the Jewish labor movement, as mentioned before, rested on ideological and organizational foundations that were largely borrowed from non-Jewish sources. With no body of experience of their own to draw upon, the Jewish trade unions and socialist groups considered themselves mere props on the stage of international socialism and conceived of their tasks as merely ancillary to those of general labor. Efforts to set up an autonomous Jewish federation in the American Socialist Party were successfully balked until the eve of the First World War. A Yiddish propaganda bureau in the apparatus of the Socialist Party was all that the Jewish workers were entitled to, even though the Jewish districts were at the time the most important strongholds of the socialist movement. The above mentioned conference of 1890 made it clear that it was setting up a Jewish workers' organization in this country not as a permanent institution but only as a stopgap body. It was a matter of expediency rather than principle, as the following statement contained in the declaration adopted by that conference explained:

Because only we, Yiddish-speaking citizens, can be effective among Jewish immigrants; because only we speak their language and are acquainted with their way of life—solely because of this fact do we form this special Jewish body. The Yiddish language is our weapon; to obliterate all lines dividing Jew and non-Jew in the world of labor is one of our goals.

The first protests against the tendency to relegate Jewish workers to an auxiliary position in the general labor movement were raised after 1905 when, following the unsuccessful revolution against the Czar in Russia, there came to this country many thousands of Jewish workers who had been trained in the labor movements of their native lands and had received political schooling in the Jewish socialist parties which had become significant factors in Eastern European life at the turn of the century. Although the first and largest of those parties, the Bund, founded in 1897, still vacillated at the time of the 1905 revolution between neutralism as regards Jewish national continuity and localism as regards Jewish culture, it had nonetheless implanted in its members a loyalty to modern Jewish spiritual values which they were not willing to abandon when they reached American shores. The members of the Labor Zionist and Socialist-Territorialist parties were even more outspoken in their opposition to the policies pertaining to Jewish issues that the official labor leadership was pursuing here. Despite violent conflicts between

Bundists and Poale Zionists (Socialist Zionists) regarding basic problems of Jewish national existence, they had a common denominator in the affirmative evaluation of the part secular Jewish culture played in contemporary Jewish life.

That evaluation has found its classical exposition in the works of the late Dr. Chaim Zhitlovsky, the outstanding theoretician of Jewish nationalism in the camp of socialism. Ideologically close to some Jewish socialist parties and at one time or another a member of others, he was never really fully identified with any one of them although he influenced all. Long before the Bund came into being, he insisted that it was incumbent upon a Jewish socialist to participate energetically in endeavors to rejuvenate Jewish national life. Unlike the Bundists, however, who discarded their theories of Jewish cultural autonomy the minute they struck roots in American soil, Zhitlovsky tried hard for nearly a half century to translate his theories into a program of action which he hoped would strengthen Jewish group life in this country. The fact that that program in no real sense differed from the original platform he proposed for Russian Jewry as early as 1887 is eloquent testimony of his failure to come to grips with the new elements America has introduced into Jewish historical experience.

Zhitlovsky's great contribution to the Jewish renaissance—a contribution that has won for him a prominent place in modern Jewish history—was his relentless struggle against the assimilatory policies and practices which distorted the class conceptions of the early Jewish socialists and made them oblivious of their responsibilities as members of the Jewish community. Mankind, he stressed, was divided into nations as well as into classes. Class interests and national interests intertwined and crossed each other like the black and red squares of a checkerboard. One set of interests could not be ignored without injury being inflicted on the other set of interests. Nations were not created artificially; they were the result of immutable social and cultural processes. These processes cannot be halted, but they can be diverted to either progressive or reactionary channels. Hence, there was nothing intrinsically bad in nationalism. On the contrary, if harnessed to serve liberal causes, nationalism was a creative and constructive force which made for the spiritual and cultural elevation of the human spirit; utilized for reactionary purpose, nationalism inclined to turn into chauvinism and become a menace. It was the mission of the socialist movement to guide nationalism along progressive lines.

With this general theory of the relationships between socialism and nationalism as his point of departure, Zhitlovsky proceeded to spell out a program designed to normalize Jewish national life. He declared war on all ideologies, bourgeois or proletarian, which negated Jewish peoplehood, and devoted himself from the first day he settled in the United States, in 1909, exclusively to the Jewish scene. This brought him into head-on collision with the recognized leaders of the Jewish labor movement who by that time had become firmly intrenched in their organizational prestige and ideological influence.

As against the policy of cosmopolitanism, theoretically envisaging a society in which all national differentiation was obliterated and in its concrete implications fostering assimilationism, Zhitlovsky propounded the principle of internationalism which conceived of mankind as a family of independent nations with each free to develop to the fullest extent the individuality of its national genius. The Jews of the world were entitled to a dignified place at the table of this family of nations.

The creativity of modern nationalism, Zhitlovsky argued, resided in the cultural values of a people rather than in its religious traditions. The Jewish religion which sustained the Jewish people for thousands of years has lost its cementing power. In a sense, it has even become a disintegrating force in that it tended to divide Jews into denominational sects and into professing and non-professing groups. Zhitlovsky summed it all up in the following words:

We reject all religious teaching as a basis for our national existence and productivity, because religious teaching, if it is to be truly religious, cannot be national in character; because it fetters free thought; because it tends to sunder the bonds that tie parents to children and integrate members of a people into one folk;

because it tends to isolate a nation and doom it to stagnation; because constricted religious teaching is a contradiction in terms; because national religious teaching is no safeguard against language assimilation, the most dangerous foe of our normal existence and of our free development as a progressive people among modern nations.

The fallacy of Zhitlovsky's reasoning consisted in his persistent employment, vis-à-vis the Jewish people, of criteria that may have been applicable—even that was questionable—to normal nations of a specific kind, living in certain lands and at certain times. He was schematic in his thinking, inclined to oversimplification, and he overlooked the characteristics that distinguished Jews from other peoples. He insisted that it was theoretically possible, although inconceivable from a practical point of view, for one to be a Christian by faith and a Jew by nationality, even as it was possible for one to be a Frenchman by nationality and Moslem by religion. Should a democratic Jewish community ever be organized in the United States, it would have to provide for the religious requirements of its Christian members out of community funds, as well as for its Jewish religious members. As a matter of principle, such a community would not only have to supply its needy members with matza for Passover, but would have to see to it that none of its Christian members went without pork on Easter.

For it is not religion that weaves Jews from all over the globe into the spiritual pattern of nationhood. Modern Jewish culture, centered about the Yiddish language, is the power that holds Jews together and makes for their creative continuity as a people. The cultivation and spread of Yiddish is, therefore, the cornerstone of Jewish survival. Yiddish is not a tool that is losing its usefulness as the union leaders contend, but a vital instrument for Jewish self-expression and national salvation. Backed by survivalists of all sorts in the ranks of labor, Zhitlovsky initiated a campaign for the establishment of Jewish secularist schools with Yiddish as the language of instruction.

Labor Zionists were the first to embark upon a program of Jewish secular education. They were a small minority in the Jewish labor movement at the time they founded their first school, originally called Nazional-Radicale Shule, in 1910. That they were able to surmount all difficulties and overcome the opposition of the official trade union and socialist leadership was a tribute to the persuasiveness of Zhitlovsky, Joel Entin and other intellectuals in survivalist Jewish socialism, as well as to the determination of the newly arrived Jewish workers who dedicated themselves to the creation of a base of operations for modern Jewish culture in America.

Things were also stirring in the Workmen's Circle, the fraternal order which with the Forward Association and the United Hebrew Trades constituted the trinity that guided the Jewish labor movement in this country. Bundists and non-Zionist or anti-Zionist nationalists joined the Workmen's Circle en masse and bored from within in the direction of a more positive attitude toward Jewish cultural effort. Zhitlovsky also became a member of the Workmen's Circle and attacked that bastion of cosmopolitanism both from within and without. Pivotal in that attack was the demand that the Workmen's Circle enter the field of Jewish education by opening schools of its own. The "Old Guard" fiercely resisted the demand on grounds of practical considerations and ideational consistency. On the practical level the proposition was advanced that the Workmen's Circle, although one hundred percent Jewish in its membership composition, was officially not a Jewish organization. On the ideational level there was the old argument that socialists must not engage in undertakings of a religio-nationalist character. Neither position, however, could be maintained at the time of the First World War with that degree of certainty and finality with which the leadership of the Jewish labor movement brushed aside survivalist demands in previous years. Under pressure by Yiddishist groups inside the Workmen's Circle and the Labor Zionist groups outside it, the "Old Guard" was forced to give ground. It was routed in 1916 when a national convention of the Order decided to promote the establishment of Workmen's Circle afternoon schools based on the Yiddish language and socialist aspiration.

There was for some years still enough opposition to the new

venture to dampen the enthusiasm of its proponents and to give
the Workmen's Circle schools a somewhat negative motivation.
As formulated in the report submitted by the Educational Committee of the National Executive Committee of the Order to the
1916 convention, Workmen's Circle schools were necessary because:

. . . the Talmud Torah cultivates only religion and, more often
than not, also fanaticism of which we would like our children to
be free. And the Nazional-Radicale Shulen give the children an
ultra-nationalist and, for the most part, even openly Zionist education . . .
We do not want our children to receive either a religious or a
Zionist education, but a free Jewish education.

What that "free Jewish education" was to represent was not
stated. That it had very little Jewish substance, judged by present standards, is evidenced by the fact that as late as 1920 a national convention formulated the program of the Workmen's Circle schools in the following terms:

1. To tie the Jewish working child to the Jewish working
   class . . .
2. To inculcate in the Jewish child a sense of justice, love for
   freedom and reverence for the fighters for liberty . . .
3. To develop in the child an appreciation of beauty . . .
4. To stimulate in the child a lofty idealism and a striving for
   great deeds.

Not a word here about strengthening Jewish group life or
about creating conditions for meaningful Jewish survival.

There was still another trend in the secularist school movement, the one known as the Sholem Aleichem Shulen which were
combined into the Sholem Aleichem Folk Institute in 1918. The
leadership of these schools—the first was founded in 1913—came
from the camp of non-Zionist Jewish nationalism. It was strongly
Yiddishist but not nearly as anti-religious as most of the leaders
of the Workmen's Circle. The Sholem Aleichem Schools crystallized their views on Jewish survival in a program adopted in
1927, point three of which read:

The language of our environment is Yiddish; its culture is the modern Yiddish culture. It does not regard religion as the cornerstone of our spiritual life. It sees in the Jewish religious customs only a partial product of our age-long creativeness. Hebrew and those parts of Jewish creativity which are tied up with Hebrew (Aramaic) belong to our national cultural treasure which we evaluate from an objective historical point of view.

The three types of schools which constitute the secularist trend in American Jewish education kept matters of faith out of their curriculum. There were differences of opinion, however, in their assessment of the value of religion to Jewish survival. The divergencies have remained although all schools have since changed their theories and practices and come closer to a consensus on Jewish education than existed at the time they were organized.[1]

IV

The Labor Zionist schools, now known as Folk Shulen and sponsored by the Farband-Labor Zionist Order, Poale Zion Organization, and Pioneer Women, were the first to realize that Jewish education could not be totally severed from Jewish religious tradition. As early as 1914 Hayim Lieberman read a paper at the first national conference of the Nazional-Radicale Shulen in which he insisted that for the schools "to play hide-and-seek with religion was impossible." How, he asked, could we explain to our children Jewish otherness if we do not initiate them into an understanding of Jewish religion? Although roundly scolded by Zhitlovsky, who accused him of introducing reaction into progressive Jewish education, he was not without success in bringing about reforms in the Labor Zionist schools. The 1914 conference passed a resolution which stated in part:

National radical education must instill in the children a sound view on Jewish religion which should be approached from a cul-

---

[1] The schools sponsored for many years by the recently dissolved Jewish People's Fraternal Order are not considered by the writer a part of the Jewish educational system and hence left out of the present analysis.

tural historical standpoint. The teachers should endeavor to present to the children the national-ethical and poetic aspect of Jewish religion.

Today, Labor Zionist schools do not apologize for their affirmative approach to religion. They consider the teaching of the Bible in the original and the observance of certain Jewish religious practices indispensable requisites in Jewish education. The Sholem Aleichem Folk Schools do not go so far, but they too have veered away from their former neutralism and now include a number of Jewish rituals in their curriculum and in the educational program of Camp Boiberik which they sponsor. The new Declaration of Principles, adopted by the Sholem Aleichem Folk Institute at a conference in May of 1953, defines as one of the objectives of the school the stimulation of a "desire to preserve and perpetuate those elements of the Jewish tradition which are in harmony with Jewish life in America."

Even the Workmen's Circle schools have changed with the times. Alongside the Folk Shulen and the Sholem Aleichem schools, they give tangible recognition to Bar Mitzva—something that was excluded from all secular systems at the time they came into being—and celebrate Jewish holidays both in classroom and in adult education programs. They no longer pull their punches or walk on thin ice when speaking of Jewish group continuity as the chief purpose of their teachings.

Thus we see the three school systems arriving at a program of Jewish secularism that has practically abandoned the old secularist ideology which was based on varying degrees of irreligion. Since these schools, more than any other institution, reflect the position of the secularist movement as a whole, it is necessary to examine the reasons which have brought them around to their present conception of Jewish values. These reasons can be grouped under three main headings: 1) sociological factors that have changed the structure of the Jewish community in this country; 2) the growing Americanization of the Jewish population; 3) the bankruptcy of secularist ideology as a philosophy of Jewish living.

V

Technological advancement in this country has wrought havoc with the Marxian prediction, accepted by practically all Jewish socialist groups at the time of their formation, that the middle classes would in time disappear and leave the working class in the majority of the population. In the country as a whole and much more so among American Jewry the exact opposite is taking place. The Jewish community is becoming more middle class and less proletarian every day, and a program based on the slogan "the Jewish working child to the Jewish working class" would be an anachronism—the more so in view of the fact that individual Jewish workers in the United States, of whom there are still hundreds of thousands, no longer form a Jewish labor movement. It would, therefore, be impossible for Jewish schools to continue on a narrow class basis. If they are to exist at all, they must fit into the new socio-economic framework of the Jewish population and flow as a tributary to the general Jewish educational system which has as its aim the perpetuation of the Jewish community. This truth has by this time been recognized by all those who are actively engaged in promoting modern Jewish culture.

One factor should be singled out from among the many that have altered the complexion of the Jewish community, and that is the growing Americanization of the Jewish population. The word "Americanization" is used here in its most literal sense— in the sense that some seventy-five percent of the population of American Jewry is today of native birth. The American-born Jew simply cannot conceive of a Jewish identification in which Jewish religion is completely missing. It is incomprehensible to him first because he cannot separate his Jewishness from some rootedness in the Jewish faith, and second because he sees all other Americans placed in some religious frame of reference. The introduction of various religious rituals into the secular Jewish schools proceeds at a rate that stands in direct proportion to the enrollment of children from native American homes.

It would be wrong, however, to attribute the changed attitudes in the secularist schools solely to considerations of expediency. The fact is that the leaders of Jewish secularism have come to realize that they cannot carry on without the use of some sustaining values from the residue of Jewish religious tradition. Even Zhitlovsky sensed it in his less argumentative moments. In a work titled *The National Poetic Rebirth of Jewish Religion*, published in 1911, he extolled the virtue and beauty of a number of religious institutions which he felt had meaning not alone to the Jew but to others as well. He wrote in that work:

If the branch called 'religion' should ever wither away and fall off the cultural tree of mankind—something I cannot possibly conceive—there will still be left in the possession of man the noblest heritage in the form of the finest and most exalted feelings . . . even the darkest religion has its bright side, to which should be credited the fact that it has taught the human soul to sense holiness and the infinite.

The above lines were written at a time when the ideological struggles between Zionist and anti-Zionist socialists revolved around Palestine and problems of Jewish life in the Diaspora. In relation to America they were practically all Galut-nationalists in that they all ascribed a nationality status to the Jewish community after the fashion of the relationships that existed in Eastern Europe. Again we must turn to Zhitlovsky for elucidation of this view. America, he maintained, was not a melting pot but a chaotic entanglement of various cultural strands of which only one, the Anglo-Saxon, had unrestricted opportunity for normal development and expansion. The principles of democracy required that the other strands, rather than losing their identity or getting into each other's way, also be given *lebensraum*. Jews were entitled to a spot in this arrangement, and it was up to them to equip themselves economically and culturally to occupy and hold the spot. While Zhitlovsky could not gain general acceptance of his autonomist economic notions, he persuaded most nationalist Jewish socialists to follow him in matters pertaining to Jewish culture.

The view that Jews could or would constitute a nationality in the United States with Yiddish as its vernacular and secular Jewish culture as the basis of its group cohesiveness could be maintained only so long as the Jewish immigrant community represented an enclave, as it were, in American society. When this view became shaky, the theory of cultural pluralism was seized as a crutch to support it. But to no avail: the whole ideological superstructure erected by Zhitlovsky and others collapsed beyond repairs after the First World War, pulling down with it the last remnants of secularist ideology. The survivalist elements within the Jewish labor movement have been compelled to come around to a position regarding the relationships between Jewish religion and Jewish peoplehood that approximated the secularism of American democracy. The latter, it should be pointed out again, was based on cooperation with religion in clearly defined areas.

## VI

Viewed historically, secularist ideology as defined in this essay proved to be a culturally sterile episode in Jewish labor history. Neither atheism nor irreligion has produced a single literary work of enduring significance despite the success it enjoyed from time to time during the early stages of the Jewish socialist movement. One cannot find an important Jewish poet or novelist who has ever been inspired by the irreligious notions entertained by the proponents of secularist ideology in this country. The great Yiddish literature, probably the most important achievement of the immigration from Eastern Europe, has from the beginning been secular in spirit, not secularistic. Insofar as secularism did not represent a complete break with Jewish religious tradition, it has created values that will forever enrich Jewish culture here in America, in the State of Israel, and in other lands.

# CULTURE

# The East
# Side:
# Matrix of the
# Jewish
# Labor
# Movement

ABRAHAM MENES

When the Jewish immigrants from Eastern Europe began settling in great numbers in New York's East Side in the early 1880's, they little dreamed that they were opening a new chapter in the history of Jewish life in America, let alone in the history of the Jewish people throughout the world. The East Side ghetto came into being without plan. Indeed, the seething and frenetic life that filled the narrow streets and crowded tenements of the East Side resembled chaos and planlessness. But despite this external impression, there was profound historic sense in this mass concentration of Jewish immigrants within the narrow confines of an old part of the City of New York. Here, under gruelling sweatshop conditions over a half-century ago, a pioneering generation of poverty-ridden tailors and cloakmakers set the path of Jewish history for our generation and for others still to come.

The importance of the rise of the immigrant Jewish community on the East Side becomes readily apparent when we recall some significant figures. Roughly a century ago there were about five million Jews in the entire world. Eighty-five percent of this number lived in Europe. Only slightly more than one percent lived in America, and the remaining thirteen percent were scattered throughout Asia and Africa. The number of Jews in Eretz Israel was insignificant at that time. Ninety years later, at the time of the outbreak of World War II, the number of Jews in the world exceeded sixteen million. In the course of not more than four generations the Jewish population in the world had more than tripled its numbers. The distribution of the Jewish population had radically shifted. America and Eretz Israel had become important centers. But the bulk of the Jewish people still remained in Europe, primarily in the eastern part of the continent.

World War II brought about the greatest catastrophe in Jewish history. A bare remnant has survived from the large European communities. Fully two-thirds of European Jewry cruelly perished at the hands of the Nazis. Today the bulk of the Jewish people is concentrated in Israel and America, the two countries that contained a mere two percent of the Jewish people one hundred years ago.

Tragic and painful beyond compare as the catastrophe in Europe has been for us, it would have been still more crushing to us as a people had it not been preceded by the miracle of the mass emigration from Europe which commenced in the 1880's. The pioneers of the East Side, and of Jewish sections in other large cities of America, played a leading role in bringing about this miracle.

Today there are about five million Jews in America. This is a significant number. It is generally assumed that the mass Jewish emigration from Europe was caused by external factors, and that the emigrants themselves performed only a passive role. It is undeniable that the economic pressure within the Jewish communities in Eastern Europe, and the wave of anti-Semitism and pogroms that swept Southern Russia in the early eighties, were potent factors. Nevertheless it would be a grievous error to overlook the fact that the Jewish emigrants themselves were the chief factor in the historically decisive exodus from Eastern Europe. It was not the weak elements, ready to resign themselves passively to fate, who began the trek. Even under the conditions of disenfranchisement which prevailed in Russia it required abundant courage to resolve to leave home and family and native town. Effort, determination, and pioneering initiative were required to embark on the long, and then unfamiliar, journey. Though many rumors were current regarding opportunities in America, it remained a remote and strange country. It must also be borne in mind that it was the poorest elements, who in most cases even lacked the fare to a port city, who were the ones to go. So far as paying the ocean passage was concerned, the majority did not even dream of possessing the requisite one hundred rubles ($50)—a sum that was considered a veritable fortune in the impoverished Jewish towns of Poland and Russia.

How, then, did they reach America? Some of the emigrant pioneers made the trip in stages. The first stage of the journey brought them across the Russian border. At the time of the pogroms in Russia in 1881-2, the commercial city of Brody on the Austrian side of the Russian border, was the first main stopover. In 1881 alone, about four thousand emigrants received assistance in Brody from the large Jewish philanthropic organizations which gradually provided them with the means to continue the journey to America. Others settled temporarily in Germany, France, or England. If luck was with them they obtained employment there and saved enough to resume their trip. The number of emigrants who left home with sufficient means to pay for the entire trip was infinitesimal.

But this trickle did not by itself account for the mass emigration of hundreds of thousands. The path of these pioneers was not an easy one even after they reached America, yet despite their hardships it was they who made possible the subsequent flood from Eastern Europe in the later eighties. The decisive factor stimulating the mass Jewish emigration to America from 1885 to 1890 was the assistance from relatives already in America who were themselves still strangers in the country.

"Everyone who came here," writes B. Weinstein, one of the pioneers of the Jewish Labor Movement in America, "constantly cherished one hope—to save enough money to bring other members of the family."

The remarkable growth of the East Side becomes comprehensible from Jewish writing in America five and six decades ago. Here we find a host of touching descriptions of how poor immigrant laborers, burdened with a sense of guilt, worked far beyond their strength, denied themselves necessities, and went into debt in order to provide passage for some member of the family still in the Old Country. Family loyalty was characteristic of all immigrant groups, but among the Jewish immigrants this became the very essence of life. The cause of this intense feeling was quite simple: emigrants from Germany, England or Italy left their friends and families among their own people, and the emigrant himself often dreamed of returning to his native land. The Jewish emigrants from Eastern Europe had no such feelings. Their emigration was a form of exodus from a land of slavery into a land of freedom. They were constantly troubled by the problem of enabling their dear ones to share this freedom with them.

They were therefore obsessed by one idea: to work as hard as possible and to spend as little as possible in order to save passage for the family. The accusation levelled against the Jewish immigrants of that time that they were themselves to blame for the intolerable working conditions in the sweatshops was not entirely unfounded. A theory was then propounded that it was in the "nature" of Jews to work endless hours and to drive themselves at their tasks, in disregard of the fact that Jews were the historical pioneers of the idea of definite periods of rest (Sabbath and holidays) and firmly defined hours for prayer and study during weekdays. That the sweatshop system had had a long tradition in America was also overlooked. It is undeniable, nevertheless, that the sweatshop system became especially acute in the needle trades at the time when Jews became prominent in this industry as workers and contractors. It is equally an established fact that the manufacturers and contractors met with but little resistance from their workers when they tried to extend the work day. The workers themselves wished to work longer hours and thus earn a little more, to hasten the day when they could bring their families to America. It was this intense devotion to family and friends in the old home that made possible the mass influx of Jewish immigrants in the later eighties.

The aid, in its diverse forms, that was extended by the new immigrants to their relatives still overseas, merits our attention as an example of the decisive role that can be played by purely moral factors in the life of a people. Had the concern of the Jewish arrivals in America at that time not been directed so intensely to their native towns, they would have sent less material assistance, and the number of immigrants would have been much smaller. Had a "normal" attitude prevailed, we would probably have no more than two million Jews in America at the most. The mere formulation of the question: "What would be the shape of world Jewry today, were the American Jewish community to number not more than two million?" makes an answer superfluous. It is impossible to estimate in full the debt we owe to the pioneers of the East Side.

The distinctive nature of the Jewish immigrant is readily confirmed by statistical analysis of the immigration trends, as a whole, to America at that time. Our attention is at once drawn to the fact that the Jewish immigrants came to America to stay. As a general rule about one-third of all immigrants left the United States; but Jewish re-emigration amounted to somewhat less than five percent. The immigration figures also show that the percentage of women and children was considerably higher among Jewish immigrants than among others. This fact imposed a greater burden of duties on the family heads and compelled them to work harder and longer hours. Like Joseph in the Bible, these later day immigrants could maintain that Providence had sent them to become the rescuers of their brothers.

The pressers and operators of the East Side provided their kin with more than mere passage money: they also secured for them opportunities to earn their livelihood. As long as Jewish immigration was limited in scope, the problem of employment was virtually non-existent. As late as the seventies of the last century, the majority of Jewish immigrants found their livelihood in peddling and trade. These callings were especially characteristic of the Jewish immigrants from Austria and Germany. It should be noted in passing that peddling was a gruelling occupation, and that the immigrant peddlar of the frontier performed a difficult and responsible task.

But such middlemen's occupations could absorb only a small number of immigrants, and many opportunities in commercial life were not available to the newcomers because of language difficulties. This hardship was not a major problem for the Jewish immigrants from Germany, because they came as part of a tidal wave of general German immigration which, during the five decades 1841-1890, comprised fully one-third of the total immigration to the United States and exceeded even the immigration from Ireland. Knowledge of the German language thus opened to many the doors of opportunity in commerce, and developments among German Jewish immigrants largely paralleled those of the general German immigrant community. German Jewish immigrants scattered far and wide throughout the country.

The mass immigration of Jews from Eastern Europe was confronted with an entirely different situation. Their arrival occurred at a time when the industrial revolution was in full swing. The frontier era was virtually ended, and the rapid growth of large cities and huge empires of capital overshadowed all else. Industry was the sole area of the economy which could, at this time, absorb the hundreds of thousands of immigrants who annually streamed into the country. Jewish immigration had to adapt itself to this economic fact.

Though rich in opportunities, however, industry did not everywhere welcome the immigrants. A number of trades excluded them altogether. The skilled and organized workers looked askance at the newcomers as competitors who served as instruments in the hands of capital to depress the wage scale. These suspicions were not unfounded. Religious factors added to the difficulty of economic integration. Most of the Jewish immigrants of that time tried to observe the Sabbath and *kashrut* laws as far as possible, and many avoided employment in factories and businesses where the majority of workers were non-Jewish. Not knowing the language, they felt themselves strangers in such shops and factories, and whenever need compelled them to take such employment, they did not give up their search for work in traditional Jewish vocations.

Since the characteristic Jewish trades were not yet in existence in America, they had to be created. The garment industry was still in its infancy in the eighteen nineties, as is demonstrated by the following table:

### Production of Women's Clothing

| YEAR | NUMBER OF ENTERPRISES | NUMBER OF WORKERS |
|------|------|------|
| 1879 | 562 | 25,192 |
| 1899 | 2701 | 83,739 |
| 1914 | 5564 | 168,907 |

Thus, the opportunities in this field, for workers as well as for manufacturers, were considerable, and it was not necessary to storm an already occupied economic position. The opportunities were still further enhanced by the fact that as far back as the seventies Jews, largely from Germany and Hungary, were already prominent in the garment industry both as workers and as employers. The dominant role of the Jews in the garment industries of Eastern Europe, whence most of the immigrants now came, was still another factor contributing to the ease with which they entered this field.

Concentration in specific trades was a distinctive feature of the Jewish communities in Eastern Europe. In America this concentration assumed extreme forms. More than half of all Jewish workers (wage workers and self-employed) were engaged in garment manufacturing. Of the wage workers, two-thirds were employed in the needle trades. Since the eighties the needle trades increasingly passed into Jewish hands.

The sweatshop system may have contributed to the predominance of Jews in the needle trades, but it was not the sole, or even the most important factor. There is no doubt that Jewish skill in these trades, as well as initiative, played the chief role in the development of the garment industry, which in turn contributed significantly to democratic processes in American life in general.

Thus it came about that the pioneering labors of the tailors and cloakmakers during the eighteen eighties and nineties paved the way for "the great migration" early in the twentieth century, when nearly one and one-half million Jews entered the United States in the course of fifteen years.

The great Jewish immigrant concentration in New York's East Side, as well as in a number of other ghettos in large cities, was not an accidental development. The miracle that is the Jewish community in America was forged with hard labor and the devotion of generations of pioneers.

As might have been expected, the growth of the East Side was also marked by negative aspects which at one time were quite prominent. The sweatshops may have performed a necessary function in the development of the garment industry which was then in the period of primitive exploitation characteristic of pioneering capitalism. But the methods it employed could not but retard the emergence of a sound and normal community.

The dangers of primitive capitalist exploitation were still further enhanced by the rootlessness of an immigrant community. The industrial revolution, the growth of cities and the influx of immigration upset the equilibrium even of the long settled population which for generations had lived serenely in their small communities:

"The influx of alien tides to whom our precious heirlooms are as nothing, the growth of cities and the inextricable perplexities of their government, the vast inequality of condition between man and man—what room is there for the little primary council of freemen, homogeneous in stock, holding the same faith, on the same level as to faith and station?" [1]

The Jewish immigrant coming to America from his small native town was even more profoundly shaken by this transition. For though there had been no social equality in the East European town, the Jewish community nonetheless felt united by family bonds:

"In my town everything was done in common. The town was like one large family . . . Jews clung together, like children abandoned in a desert . . . The Jew felt more secure when he was with others . . . Should anything happen to a small town Jew, the entire community would share his joy or his sorrow." [2]

Upon coming to America the immigrants clustered together and tried to recreate the *shtetl* (small East European town) in the guise of the *landsmanschaft*. The Jewish immigrants from Russia felt little sympathy for the czarist empire whose victims they were, but they cherished powerful nostalgias and boundless longings for their families and native towns.

The cultural and historical role of the *landsmanschaft* was beautifully described by Professor Morris Raphael Cohen in his autobiographical work, *A Dreamer's Journey*. Though Morris R. Cohen became integrated in American culture, he displayed a profound understanding for the generation of pioneers. He commences the story of his life with a letter to his grandchild:

"Dear Gene Maura:
Your father and mother knew my parents who were of that heroic generation that tore up their roots in their old homeland, and unaided and with no equipment other than their indomitable faith and courage, built new homes in this land and raised children who have made invaluable contributions to the life of this country in the fields of art, science, industry, education and philanthropic work."

[1] Samuel Adams, *The Man of the Town Meeting*, quot. by Edward N. Saveth, *American Historians and European Immigrants*, p. 24.
[2] M. Olgin, *Mein Shtetl in Ukraine*, p. 54.

Morris R. Cohen belonged to an intermediate generation. He did not break completely with the old home, though spiritually he had become an integral part of the culture of the new home. His *landsleit* (fellow townsmen) from the town of Neshvies remained close to him. On November 5, 1936, two days after his mother's death, he wrote:

"My last two years with her made me appreciate her qualities more than I did in the years when I saw little of her. If I had to make a speech, I would have spoken of the spiritual importance of the Neshvieser Verein—how it enabled the hardy pioneers to adjust themselves to the new land, to keep people in self-respect and to make a home for the new generation; how the tradition of learning was a light—not like the modern electric but like the ancient candle or torch—which enabled people to interpret the new life." (p. 283)

The *landsmanschaft*, however, could not take the place of the *shtetl*, because the immigrant now lived in the turmoil of gigantic New York where he frequently felt isolated and alien, with that peculiar sense of alienation of one uprooted from his old home who has not yet struck roots in his new domicile. Economic adaptation was the easiest aspect of the problem, and the process of Americanization proceeded rapidly in this direction, while cultural and social integration proceeded at a slow pace. Both trends were accented by the fact that during his first years in America the immigrant had no time for anything except material survival.

It is therefore not surprising that economic success became the center of the immigrant's ambitions, and that its attainment also paved the way to social recognition. Material success became the yardstick with which all values were measured, and this, in turn, engendered an attitude of contempt for spiritual values and for the cultural traditions of the old home. The successful *"allrightnick"* was not content with his place in economic life but asserted his claim also to the position of spiritual leader. This accounts for the defeatist moods that seized some of the intellectuals. America was lampooned in the pun *Ama Reka* (hollow people) which recurs in a large number of articles and critical essays both in the Yiddish and Hebrew press of the past century. The situation of the intellectuals was indeed difficult, and especially so in the case of the older ones. These could no longer hope to adapt themselves to a regimen of manual labor, and their intellectual attainments were not in demand. The great upheaval which the migration caused created many weird situations. Former *melamdim* who were sufficiently aggressive assumed posts as rabbis, whereas the modest and gentle scholars could not even attain positions as teachers. In desperation they turned to hard physical labor. The following is a touching description of this phenomenon:

"There are few more pathetic sights than an old man with a long beard, a little black cap on his head and a venerable face—a man who had been perhaps a Hebraic or Talmudic scholar in the old country, carrying or pressing piles of coats in the melancholy sweatshop; or standing for sixteen hours a day by his pushcart in one of the dozen crowded streets of the ghetto." [3]

Since material success seemed to make up for all shortcomings, there appeared to be no need to ascribe importance to moral principles. The danger of moral degeneration became still greater, because the success of the self-made man brought out in greater relief the want and loneliness of the immigrant mass. Concentration in the most neglected sections of the big cities, overcrowding, dirty streets and equally dirty tenements, combined to undermine the foundations of the moral discipline of the older generation, and to provide a poor backdrop for the moral education of the young. The insecurity of the immigrant went hand in hand with uncertainty regarding moral values. He lived in two cultural realms and was estranged from both. Hillel Rogoff, an authority on the East Side, gives the following description of the spiritual instability that prevailed at the turn of the century:

Physical exhaustion was aggravated by moral and spiritual anguish. The old-fashioned religious Jew saw his traditions dis-

[3] Hutchins Hapgood, *The Spirit of the Ghetto*, pp. 11-12.

carded and even ridiculed. He saw his children drift away from him to pick up strange new ways. The safe old moorings of Jewish family life loosened, the privacy of the home was invaded and its sanctity frequently profaned by boarders, the minds of the children were often poisoned against their parents by the ridicule of the gutter and by the ill-digested enlightenment of the school.[4]

Many immigrants held financial success to be synonymous with the ideal of Americanization. This fallacious conception was based on partial truth. The American philosophy of rugged individualism, which was in part a heritage of Puritan theology, was vulgarized. Furthermore, the dominant strata in American society had little understanding and still less respect for the culture of the later arrivals, even though they were themselves children or grandchildren of immigrants.

America was built by pioneers confident of their strength and luck. This gave rise to a tradition of stubborn individualism and unquenchable optimism that was justified by everyday experience. Faith in the individual no doubt contributed heavily to the fantastic growth of America. In a land of such unlimited opportunities, consistent effort nearly always paid off in the end. This was true at least as long as America was a land of independent farmers and medium-sized business enterprises.

Nearly everyone in America had started out with his bare hands. The cult of the self-made is therefore quite comprehensible. The unique development of spiritual life in this country extended its sanction to this cult, and thus helped the ideology of individualism to strike deep roots.

The sociologist, Max Weber, tried to demonstrate the immense influence of the Puritan ethic on economic developments in England and America in his epoch-making work, *The Protestant Ethic and the Spirit of Capitalism*. Weber's theory aroused widespread debate, and it appears certain that he had overextended himself on some points. Yet, the basic premises of his theory are well established.

For the purpose of this essay we are primarily concerned with the Puritan attitude toward economic activities in general, and

[4] *An East Side Epic*, p. 5.

toward the problem of individual success. The Calvinist Puritan ethic elevated man's economic activities to the level of a religious commandment. God can and should be served also through labor. It is therefore the duty of every man to guard his position in economic life and to respect his calling:

God doth call every man and woman . . . to serve in some peculiar employment in this world, both for their own and the common good . . . The great Governour of the world hath appointed every man his proper post and province, and let him be never so active out of his sphere, he will be at a great loss, if he does not keep his own vineyard and mind his own business.[5]

The dividing line between religion and economic life was thus obliterated. Work, trade, and even banking are part of God's plan, and it is our duty to endow our everyday labors with religious emotion. If it is a religious duty to conduct business sensibly, then it follows that the ambition to make profits and to expand business is likewise in agreement with God's plan:

If God show you a way in which you may lawfully get more than in another way (without wrong to your soul or to any other), if you refuse this, and choose the less gainful way, you cross one of the ends of your calling and you refuse to be God's steward.[6]

The Puritans endowed the establishing, organizing and conducting of business with endless devotion. Economic initiative became the highroad to success on earth and bliss in the hereafter. The merchant, the manufacturer, even the banker lending money on interest, rose to the highest rungs of the social ladder; and capitalist drive for profits acquired supreme moral sanction.

Equally important in the theology of the Puritans were the principles of predestination and election. Though all men were created equal, not all had the good fortune to enjoy divine favor in equal measure. Calvinist Puritan theology teaches that there exists a class of the elect upon whom the Creator bestows His favor both here and in the hereafter, while He withholds it from

---

[5] Richard Steele, *The Tradesman's Calling*, quot. by R. H. Tawney. *Religion and the Rise of Capitalism*. Mentor ed. p. 200.

[6] Baxter, *Christian Democracy*, quot. by R. H. Tawney, *Religion and the Rise of Capitalism*. Mentor ed., p. 202.

others who, incidentally, constitute the vast majority. Why this
is so, we do not know, for the ways of God are inscrutable. According to Puritan theology, material success is therefore the best
indication of God's blessing, and it is only natural that those who
are successful should feel secure and satisfied with themselves.
Ralph Barton Perry pointed this out:

According to this philosophy, if a man is rich, he has himself
to thank; if he is destitute, he has himself to blame. The rich man
is an object of commendation, and not merely of envy; to be a
pauper is not a misfortune, but a disgrace.[7]

From this it follows, as a matter of principle, that radical social
reform is intolerable. Since God chose to create the poor, we
must not interfere with His plan. The poor, by the way, are to
blame for their misfortune:

Poverty being a sign of spiritual weakness, the Puritan cure
would be found in reprobation. Poverty is to be condemned
rather than pitied or relieved.[8]

The theory of election seemed to be made to order for the
pioneers of capitalism. It spared them many sleepless nights and
relieved their conscience of the nagging doubt: Why do I deserve
so much fortune, and what sin has my brother committed that
he should be destined to live in need and an outcast? The philosophy of success left no room for the problem of a Job.

A small group of liberal intellectuals in America realized as
far back as the eighties and the nineties of the past century that
the profound changes engendered by the industrial revolution
in America necessitated also a new approach to the problem of
poverty. This group included such Social Settlement workers as
Jane Addams, Lillian Wald, Florence Kelley and others. The
workers of the East Side encountered these idealistic representatives of American humanism during the early days of the Jewish
Socialist movement. There was a measure of rapport between
these two elements, though, as a general rule, the Jewish Labor

[7] *Puritanism and Democracy*, p. 302.
[8] Ibid. p. 304.

movement followed a different path—one that had been determined by the specific historical experiences of the Jewish people.

The Jewish immigrants from Eastern Europe brought an entirely different approach to the questions of happiness and misery in life. Jews found it hard to become reconciled to the idea
that material success is an outstanding indication of God's favor,
The Puritan theology was well suited for the courageous pioneers who blazed new trails, and achieved their goals by means
of stubborn diligence. But Jewish historical experience was of a
different kind, and scholarly thought was preoccupied with those
who failed despite all efforts. The Jewish way of thinking propounded the theory of the election of the injured and the suffering. Job's tragedy consisted not so much in his physical suffering
as in his painful recognition that not even his friends believed
in his innocence. "You have sinned," they repeatedly said to
him, "and God has punished you for it." Job protested with all
his strength against being abandoned by God, and deprived of
consolation and encouragement even from his closest friends.

The problem of Job and the Jewish problem were basically
alike, and to the question posed by the existence of suffering in
the world, the Jews counterposed the old answer of faith in the
coming of a new world at the end of time. This old, yet ever-new,
Jewish solution to the problem of suffering was now propounded
by the tailors and cloakmakers of the East Side.

It is impossible to account for the unique response of the East
Side to socialist propaganda without taking into consideration
the Messianic tradition. To the Jewish masses, socialism was in-
comparably more than simply the program of a political party.
It was more than merely a dream of a beautiful future. For the
workers of the East Side socialism was a new faith which helped
them endure the great hardship and disappointments of everyday
life. Still more important, socialism bolstered their faith in
themselves: it saved them from despair and from the loss of respect for both themselves and their fellows in need.

The problem of human dignity was not less important than
that of material want. In the *shtetl* even the poorest Jew was a
personality in his own right. "In my *shtetl* every Jew was a se-

cret prince; every pauper concealed within himself the spark of secret aristocracy," wrote M. Olgin. The individual was not easily lost in a small town, and everyone had his recognized status, even though this was on the lower rungs of the social ladder. In the capitalist metropolis, on the other hand, it was much easier to lose one's individuality. Of what account is an individual among millions of his fellows? True, there were some among the immigrants to America who had left the old home with the express desire to "disappear," to shed their past and to become "new" people. But only seldom was it possible genuinely to become a new person with a distinct individuality.

Work in the sweatshops could not provide moral satisfaction. The attitude of the bosses and subcontractors, themselves mostly former workers, was most galling. It was an everyday occurrence for workers to be abused and fired without cause, and there were even instances of bosses beating their workers. Some of the early strikes were called because of such mistreatment of workers. The workers also lacked permanent homes. The bachelors lived as boarders, three or four to a room which was merely a place to spend the night. Even the married workers with families seldom had homes to themselves. The sense of forlornness was great even when there was employment; when the worker lost his job, his situation became intolerable. Of what worth was an immigrant without home, family, friends or even a job?

There has been a tendency to overlook the moral factors influencing the social and political conflicts of our time. It is very easy to see the material needs of the masses. Yet the unrest which agitates so many is often the product of the mounting depersonalization characteristic of modern society. This unrest is the protest of the *mass man* who refuses to become reconciled to his fate. He resents having to remain a *mass man* all his life. He wants recognition as an individual. The class conflict between rich and poor is becoming overshadowed by another social conflict—the struggle between those who have status in social life, the class of *somebodys*, and the great and nameless mass lost in the turmoil of modern life, the class of the *nobodys*. The East Side fought with especial vigor against this trend toward depersonalization.

The entire labor movement in the country fought the same battle, but there was one distinction between the general and the Jewish labor movements. Until the time of the New Deal, the American labor movement, as represented by the American Federation of Labor, had been most strongly influenced by the Puritan philosophy. This was apparent in the structure of the union movement. The principle of industrial unionism would, without a doubt, have been more practical in many instances, yet the unions stubbornly clung to the principle of craft unionism. The Puritan philosophy of "calling" was effective here, in my estimation. The skilled and better paid workers proudly guarded their superior status, and their privileged position as skilled labor. They did not care to mingle with the unskilled and thus lose their separateness.

The Jewish workers lacked this attitude toward a "calling" that was so characteristic of the Anglo-American tradition. For one thing, the conditions of work were so different here than they were in the old home. The skilled workman, in particular, was frequently depressed because his craftsmanship was superfluous here. Furthermore, most of the workers were what was then known as "Columbus' tailors," people who had learned the work after they came to America. As a result of the division of labor, few truly skilled workers were needed. This was one reason why the needle trades largely escaped the conflict between craft and industrial unionism. The ideology of "unionism pure and simple," as it was classically formulated by Samuel Gompers, likewise found little response here. Even trade unionism, as such, appealed but little to the workers of the East Side.

The East Side needed a re-evaluation of values. It needed a philosophy that would give the worker comfort and status. In the course of generations of trials, the Jew found consolation for himself and for his people in his faith in his chosenness. This faith was now shattered, and the spiritual crisis of modern times generally undermined the authority of religion. Moreover, the old-fashioned religious leaders were themselves at a loss in America; they did not comprehend the new reality and had no answers to the problems it posed. The philosophy of Reform Judaism,

"Yahudim," was altogether alien to the workers of the East Side.

The socialists introduced a new scale of values. Today we can scarcely grasp what the teachings of the socialist propagandists, who stressed the unimportance of individual success and the insignificance of money as a yardstick for social values, meant for the poor workers of the East Side. If the poor were indeed the righteous ones, and if the workers were the true creators of wealth for society, the poor laborers need not be ashamed of their social status. Socialism restored to them their human worth and aroused their sense of individual pride. Not only could they respect themselves as the true creators of wealth, but the future, too, was to be theirs.

Socialism gave added prestige to spiritual values. As was pointed out above, a segment of the Jewish intellectual class found it especially hard to adapt itself to the new conditions, and felt superfluous. This was not the case within the socialist camp. The socialist intellectuals enjoyed the advantage of a sense of historic mission, as well as enthusiastic audiences, and since they were in the forefront of the struggle against the cult of success, they found it easy to stress the importance of spiritual values. Enlightenment and social justice were the two main themes of socialist propaganda. Young workers, boys and girls, enthusiastically undertook their self-education. They read, studied, discussed problems after their hard labor in the shops. The ancient Jewish tradition of individual and group study was revived in a new form. How important these intellectual pursuits were, can be judged from the fact that the majority of Jewish immigrants came to this country with but scanty education—many were, in fact, almost illiterate. Intensive educational work was therefore required in order to prepare a reading public for the socialist newspapers, books, and Jewish literature in general. Much devoted labor was invested in this task, and the goal was attained.

Socialist educational work on the East Side was integrated into the broad framework of the social and political problems of the world. These were extensively reflected in the Yiddish socialist press as far back as the nineties. Morris R. Cohen wrote:

As I look back on the Yiddish and English press in the last decade of the nineteenth century I cannot help feeling that the former did more for the education of its readers than the latter. Having no army of reporters to dig up sensational news, the Yiddish press necessarily paid more attention to things of permanent interest. It tried to give its readers something of enduring and substantial value . . . The Yiddish press has prepared millions of Jewish people to take a worthy part in American civilization while also promoting the natural self-respect to which Jews are entitled because of their character and history.[9]

The pioneers of the Jewish labor movement gave the Jewish worker a sense of his own dignity; they also contributed to the respect with which the East Side came to be regarded in the non-Jewish world. First they won for the Jewish worker the respect of the general labor movement. The working conditions prevailing in the sweatshops of the East Side were not of a kind to win the sympathy of organized labor. But this attitude changed almost overnight when a series of bitter strikes in the garment industry aroused public opinion, and the world became aware that the Jewish workers knew how to defend their rights and interests.

The Jewish labor leaders were keenly aware of the importance of winning public opinion in times of conflict, perhaps because Jewish labor was still weak and urgently needed the moral support of the native American workers. The Jewish workers gained a reputation as good strikers but poor union people. This reputation was not unfounded, though their shortcomings as union people were not the result of a lack of understanding of the importance of organization.

How account for the fact that Jewish workers so frequently resorted to strikes when their unions were so weak? There were even instances when they struck before formulating their demands.

The workers of the East Side often went on strike for reasons other than formulated economic demands. For them the strike

[9] *A Dreamer's Journey*, p. 220.

was frequently a way of expressing their protest against a form of society that tried to transform the laborer into a robot. In such instances the strike was an instrument to win recognition for the role of the worker in economic and social life.

In an article published in *Forward* (July 27, 1910) concerning the historic cloakmakers' strike, the poet A. Leyssin characterized the mood of the workers as follows: "The seventy thousand zeros now became seventy thousand fighters." The worker refused to maintain his passive role in the shop or in social life, and struck for his rights as citizen and man.

The great cloakmakers' strike in 1910 marked a turning point in the history of the Jewish labor movement. It may even justly be maintained that it was a turning point in the history of the American Jewish community. The strike ended in a remarkable fashion. The embittered fight of the workers aroused the entire Jewish community. Prominent personages like Jacob Schiff, Louis Marshall, Louis D. Brandeis, and others became involved as intermediaries. Agreement was reached after long negotiations, and both parties signed a Protocol of Peace which became a milestone in the history of industrial relations in America.

The authors of the Protocol of Peace did not regard it as a temporary agreement, but as a kind of constitution for labor that should make possible peaceful resolution of conflicts between employers and workers. For this purpose a Board of Arbitration was set up, consisting of three members: "One nominee of the manufacturers, one nominee of the unions, and one representative of the public." In this manner the right of labor to bargain about working conditions even when no strike was in progress, and the right of the public to intervene in industrial disputes, were officially sanctioned.

The pacific philosophy underlying the Protocol sharply clashed with the ideology of a number of socialist union leaders. In time, however, it became obvious that the system of impartial arbitration had many advantages and helped strengthen the position of the unions in the shops. The system of arbitration was familiar to the Jewish workers from the old country. It also appealed to a number of employers and to the liberal elements in the Jewish community at large. The harsh working conditions in the needle trades lowered the prestige of the Jewish community, and leaders like Marshall, Brandeis and Schiff understood that the workers were also fighting for the good name of the Jewish people. Even some of the employers understood this. "I do not want my children to feel ashamed," one employer said, "when they say that their father is a clothing manufacturer."

As the unions gained strength and influence, they could increasingly protect the interests of the workers without resorting to strikes. In recent decades it has been the pride of the needle trades unions that they have solved most conflicts through negotiation, and we are confronted with the remarkable phenomenon that the unions which had been influenced most by socialist ideology became the pioneers of cooperation between employers and workers. It should also be observed that this cooperation between unions and manufacturers extends far beyond the mere settlement of conflicts. The sense of security which the worker now enjoys, and the fact that his status in the shop and in society is now recognized, has virtually eliminated the strike as a form of social protest.

From the start the Jewish labor movement was distinguished by the fact that it did not confine itself to a narrow sphere of activities. Parallel with the unions there arose a variety of organizations and institutions,—political groups, the *Forward,* Workmen's Circle, Jewish National Workers' Alliance, and others. Some feared that this variegation might diffuse the strength of the labor movement. These fears proved unfounded. In times of trial these organizations aided one another loyally. The entire movement became as one family, and the struggles of one organization always evoked warm sympathy from the others.

The Jewish labor organizations often had to devote much time and energy to a variety of relief activities at home as well as on behalf of numerous Jewish and non-Jewish labor organizations overseas. In this area, too, the Jewish labor movement distinguished itself. At the time of the great cloakmakers' strike in 1910, the *Forward* collected the sum of $70,000—a substantial amount for that time. Some years later the cloakmakers contributed tens of thousands of dollars to the strike funds of the furriers and men's clothing workers. During the great steel strike in 1919, the Jewish needle trades contributed $175,000—a sum equal to one half of that contributed by all the other unions in the country. Moreover, this was accomplished at a time when Jewish workers were engaged in a great relief campaign for the Jews in Europe. Today the needle trades and other Jewish labor organizations contribute annually between seven and eight million dollars for relief and educational purposes.

The Jewish labor movement is also proud of its record in the struggle against discrimination. Today the overwhelming majority of workers in the needle trades are non-Jews. The influence of the Jewish leaders of the unions has not diminished nonetheless, and they enjoy the full confidence of the rank and file. Jewish workers have learned from their experience, and have succeeded in establishing an atmosphere of mutual understanding and cooperation among the various ethnic groups that are now employed in the needle trades. Selig Perlman, an authority on the American Labor Movement, points out that,

"As members of the ethnic group with the longest record of persecution and adverse discrimination, they cannot but feel pride in their own clear record on the minorities issue as when judged by the test of deed. It is doubtful that there is another union milieu where a Negro feels as much at home." [10]

The general labor movement in America has not succeeded in attracting or utilizing the intellectuals for its purposes. In part this was an intentional estrangement. Samuel Gompers had no confidence in the socialist intellectuals. His distrust was well founded. The ideological conflicts between the various political trends in the eighties and nineties caused no little harm to the labor movement. The political wrangling and the bitter polemics that engaged the various party groups were also not without effect on the East Side. But here labor and the intellectuals never parted ways. The dividing line between workers and intellectuals

[10] "Jewish Unionism and American Labor," *Publications of the American Jewish Historical Society*, Vol. XLI, p. 337.

was not sharply drawn on the East Side. Nearly all Jewish immigrant intellectuals began by working in shops. On the other hand, numerous workers came to America possessed of a considerable education. Moreover, the two elements needed each other too urgently. The intellectuals needed the workers of the East Side as an audience. In turn, the labor movement was a powerful influence in Jewish cultural life and Jewish literature. Gradually the spheres of influence were marked out. The unions and the Workmen's Circle were dominated by workers—more correctly, by a group of leaders who came from the shops. The Jewish labor movement created a mighty press where the intellectuals dominated and exerted their influence on the entire movement. It should be noted that the Jewish workers were the only labor group in America who created a press of their own possessing high standards and a mass circulation that exceeded by far the circulation of the non-labor papers in Yiddish. The purely political organizations, on the other hand, lost much influence and prestige. The "non-partisan" socialists, who fully supported the socialist parties in America and in Europe, assumed the spiritual leadership.

The Workmen's Circle effectively fulfilled the role of a socialist party on the practical level, though it did not conduct political campaigns. In this respect, too, the East Side blazed a new path, and students of modern social movements can learn much from the experience of Jewish labor organizations in America.

Until 1903, cosmopolitanism was the dominant trend in the Jewish labor movement. The pogrom in Kishineff in the spring of 1903, which aroused Jews everywhere, did not fail to leave its impress on Jewish labor. The remarkable growth of Yiddish literature raised the prestige of Yiddish as a cultural language (and contributed its share to the new sense of national self-consciousness). Jewish workers were increasingly drawn into the sphere of Jewish interests and problems, at the same time that they were becoming more integrated into the life of America, and establishing closer relations with the general labor movement in the country. Americanization and Jewish self-consciousness went hand in hand. Its very prominence made the

Jewish labor movement feel keenly responsible for the fate of the Jewish community as a whole.

The foregoing traces the general contours of the development of the Jewish labor movement in America up to the twenties of this century. The radical changes introduced in the immigration laws after World War I, gave rise to an entirely new situation in the "Jewish trades" and brought about far-reaching modifications in the social and economic structure of the entire Jewish community in America. The Jewish labor organizations are now confronted with new problems. But this is another theme.

The East Side has contributed its share to the totality of the cultural assets of America. It helped create the necessary climate for the understanding of want, poverty, and the fate of the unsuccessful. The East Side demonstrated that there can be dignity in poverty. This was a surprising discovery for the idealistic pioneers of social reform who went to live in the slums in order to help the people.

Thus, the social worker, Mary K. Simkovich, writes as follows about life in the East Side tenements at the turn of the century:

I spent 1898 at the College Settlement, visiting these tenements and getting acquainted with the life of the East Side. What a deep chasm exists between publicity and facts! The word 'slums' is used indiscriminately for poverty, disease and crime. These generalizations are not only inaccurate but misleading. For life in the tenement can and often does exhibit the loftiest character and the finest human relationships. But it is against great odds . . .[11]

Much light came from the East Side. The historians must note it and record it. Coming generations ought to remember it.

[11] *Here is God's Plenty*, p. 30.

# American

# Jewish

# Scholarship

## SOLOMON B. FREEHOF

When Plato dreamed that philosophers would be the guide of the ideal republic, he did not envisage a cultured community. The young men who participated in the symposia were scions of the Athenian aristocracy. The ideal republic was to have an aristocracy of learning. Chinese culture was more democratic. It resembled Jewish culture insofar as all were invited to the reverent study of ancient texts. Yet actually it was restricted to government circles and to its limited number of recruits. It was a mandarin culture, a tool for those selected to govern the land. In the Christian Middle Ages, it was presumed that anybody could join a monastery and if so inclined attain some scholarship. Universities flourished and thousands of disciples followed the great medieval Christian philosophers during the heyday of Scholasticism. Nevertheless, illiteracy was the rule. Any man in England who could recite the one verse in the Vulgate (Psalm 51:1) could claim to be a cleric and thus free from civil law, and could demand "benefit of clergy."

Any sound opinion on Jewish scholarship must be based upon

the realization that the traditional Jewish learning was basically different from any other in the world. Its uniqueness inhered in its social penetration. There never was a culture before modern times that was so far-reaching in the lives of the people that carried it. There was, of course, some Jewish illiteracy. The fact that the simple morning blessings which were originally intended to be recited at home were, in Spain, transferred to the synagogue so that the cantor could say them for the illiterate, is evidence enough. (*See Seder Rav Amram* at the end of the first paragraph of the responsum.) Also, the more difficult *piyutim* (poetry) with their complex language and obscure midrashic references were intended, primarily, for the *Chakhamin* (The Wise) and *Novonim* (The Intelligent). Nevertheless, a people whose worship was through regular daily prayers from a prayerbook must, of necessity, have become almost entirely literate; and the tremendous spread of Talmudic studies in almost every land indicates that Jewry was drenched with the waters of the Torah. There can be no doubt that there never was another culture that reached so far and penetrated so deeply into the life of its people. It was this all-pervasive learning which produced the practitioners of modern Jewish scientific scholarship.

Old-fashioned Jewish learning of this unique pervasiveness can never be re-established in America. There is, first of all, no such adoration of it as had existed in every Jewry in the past. It would have been impossible to have developed great Talmudic centers in the various lands, a phenomenon which occurred time and time again, if there had not been a basic adoration of Jewish learning as a religious duty and a pathway towards the presence of God. Today, Jewish learning does not evoke enough religious devotion for it ever to become again a pervasive phenomenon. Moreover, general culture has advanced and has become available to everyone. It is the indispensable instrument for a career. A life-long devotion to the old Jewish learning is a hindrance to the modern learning which is necessary to life. It is always possible, of course, to establish a number of *Yeshivoth* (Talmud Schools). It may even be possible to isolate a certain small per-

centage of the Jewish population and devote it to the study of
the Talmud, but it will never amount to more than what the old
*Yeshivoth* are in Israel or in the United States, or the two lone
ones in Switzerland, namely, a reminiscence and a survival. The
great Jewish learning of the past, omnipresent, ever self-
renewing, deeply penetrative, is never likely, unless the world
changes radically, to conquer the Jewish people again.

This has a vital bearing upon modern Jewish scholarship. It is,
of course, possible to conceive of modern scholarship without an
individual background of the old learning. Such profound
knowledge as the old-fashioned Jewish scholars had is not entirely indispensable. After all, if a modern professor of Chinese
knew half as much of the *Analects* of Confucius as the average
yeshiva graduate knew of the Talmud, he would be one of the
great savants in the field of Chinese literature. Certainly very
few of the historians of ancient law are as thoroughly at home
in the Codes of Justinian as the average able Orthodox Rabbi
in Europe was in the Code of Maimonides and the *Shulchan
Arukh* (The Set Table—A Legal Code) and all its commentaries.
Modern scholarship is so different in method from ancient learning that perhaps the older method of broad and almost complete
knowledge (*Bekiyut*) is an irrelevance to it.

This hope of scholarship without mass learning is denied by
the facts of history. Every great development of modern Jewish
scholarship came from the first generation offspring of the older
Jewish learning. There was only one step from the *Beth Hamidrash* (The Talmud School) to the Seminary. When a community
completely steeped in the old Jewish learning came into immediate contact with modern culture, it was then that Jewish scholarship developed. German-Jewish scholarship, the pioneering
*Juedische Wissenschaft,* arose when the generation of the
*Yeshivoth* still existed and the old rabbinic education was still
widespread. As a matter of fact, the famous Yeshivah at Fuerth
was still conducted by Wolf Hamburger as late as 1850. Young
men left the Yeshivah to enter the universities. The great Posen,
Galician and Hungarian centers of scholarship were all devel-

oped by people who were steeped in the old-fashioned studies. In sum, there was no Jewish scholarship without a nearby background of the old Jewish learning.

Of course, only a certain percentage of the students in the Yeshivoth embarked upon an academic career. Of these, only a small percentage rejected the possibilities of medicine or physics or mathematics and decided to bring modern scientific methods to bear upon the Jewish learning which they already possessed. Accordingly, in the great countries of creative Jewish scholarship, there had to be tens of thousands of competent Talmudic students in order to produce ten creative scholars in modern Jewish scholarship. But with the Jewish learning presently restricted in the western world to a small proportion of the ultra-pious families, there are not enough private soldiers from whom generals and marshals can be developed. American Jewish scholarship and English Jewish scholarship and, for that matter, Israeli Jewish scholarship just do not have the broad human background of the Jewishly learned upon which to build and upon which the pioneer generations of scientific Jewish scholarship built their foundation. How, then, can there be much development of modern Jewish scholarship in the western world when the basic Jewish learning is so limited?

There is an additional difficulty which goes beyond the confines of our specific Jewish experience. The whole mood of our western civilization is turning, for the present at least, from pure science and tends to encourage chiefly practical training. In the earlier days of modern science, a century ago, the ideal of study and learning swept over the western world. In England alone in the fifth decade of the nineteenth century there were hundreds of Mechanics' Institutes founded by workingmen for the purpose of hearing lectures and studying scientific matters. Vast numbers of books were published popularizing scientific knowledge. There was an intense desire to study, a hunger for learning. This mood has vanished from the modern world, partly because science through its recent atomic discoveries has for the first time brought danger into the world; and perhaps in a more general way because men of science and scholarship have been

brought under control of governments, especially in the auto-
cratic lands, and science, which two generations ago was adored
as a leader, is now looked upon perhaps unjustly as a slave.
Learning as an ideal has lost its exalted status in the eyes of average folk. We seem to be entering upon an anti-intellectual era.
We therefore lack two advantages which the founders of Jewish
scholarship possessed. As their point of departure they had the
widespread Jewish learning which had formed their mind, and
as their goal they had the hunger for scientific truth which
evoked their intellectual idealism.

All of which would indicate that Jewish scholarship in the
western world is not likely to be a general characteristic of the
era ahead but rather the professional occupation of specialists.
We are not likely to develop gifted amateurs in Jewish scientific
scholarship, businessmen who will devote themselves to scientific
study of Jewish matters, a *Baal Ha-Bayith* (householder or business man) like Solomon Buber who devoted his life to the publishing of exact texts of Midrashic classics. This is, alas, impossible nowadays. There will be only as many practitioners as the
faculties of the rabbinical colleges, of Dropsie College and of the
few universities with Hebrew departments can absorb. There will
also be a small number of rabbis who will be able to steal some
time each week from the busy public life of the modern rabbinate
to devote to Jewish scholarship. There will not be more than a
small number of such rabbis, for the rabbinate, too, has changed
its nature. The earliest of modern rabbis still inherited congregations who were raised in the tradition that the main function of
the rabbi was expertness in Jewish law and that he would honor
the community through his learning and the fame he acquired by
his constant study. The modern rabbinate is an entirely different
profession. "The needs of Thy people Israel are many." The
rabbi is constantly engaged in organization work, in charity work,
and in preaching. How a modern rabbi with a hunger for scholarship must sigh when he reads Isaac Hirsch Weiss' description
in his *Reminiscences* of the rabbis of Hungary whose rabbinical
obligations were so few that they had time not only to study constantly but to maintain a Yeshivah attracting students from sur-

rounding districts. There are only a handful of rabbis who manage to fight off the demands of daily duties to devote some hours to study and perhaps even to creative scholarship.

Yet, in spite of the distractions of American life, a great amount of scholarly work has been produced. Of course, as is to be expected, it is mostly the achievement of those who were fortunate enough "to come here with their learning already in their possession" (Pesachim 50a). The special historic situation of European Jewry, with its vast democratic pervasive Jewish learning flowering into modern university education and research techniques, had produced so many practitioners of modern Jewish scholarship that for a number of generations we were blessed with the overflow from Europe. There was hardly any technically competent scientific Jewish scholarship in America before two generations ago. Jewish scholarship in Europe had itself not yet expanded sufficiently to have a superabundance of scholars and those who did come here in the earlier days were too busy teaching and preaching to engage in private research.

Generally speaking, the upsurge of Jewish scholarship in America coincides with the launching of the Jewish Encyclopedia at the beginning of the twentieth century. The rearing of this monument of Jewish information stimulated older scholars and served to develop young scholars recently arrived in America. Before the beginning of the Encyclopedia, Jewish scholarly talents were chiefly centered on theological controversy, sermonic literature, editing of prayerbooks, and the like. The wide learning, for example, of Samuel Hirsch and David Einhorn expressed itself in philosophic discussion and sermonic controversy; but Samuel Hirsch's son, Emil G. Hirsch, and David Einhorn's son-in-law, Kaufmann Kohler, began to write modern scholarly articles for the Encyclopedia. Solomon Schechter's chief work in the Genizah material was done overseas. In America his *Studies in Judaism,* however, pioneered in popular Jewish scholarship, a genre in which many must follow his footsteps if some day we are to have an appreciative readership for technical Jewish studies. Of world stature in Jewish scholarship were the Genizah studies in *Geonica* by Louis Ginzberg and by Jacob

Mann. Jacob Z. Lauterbach's researches in Talmudic origins,
Midrash and Mishnah, the Pharisees, exerted wide influence.
Solomon Zeitlin's many articles in the *Jewish Quarterly Review*
are illuminating the period of the second commonwealth. A
host of younger men are now working in the various fields producing articles and books in Jewish history, biography, legal
and Biblical literature. As the Jewish Encyclopedia constituted
a landmark for correlated Jewish learning, so a number of efforts of a similar cooperative nature have stimulated Jewish
studies in America. The *Jewish Quarterly Review,* which had
ceased in England, was brought over to America and published
by Dropsie College. This new series, now in its forty-sixth volume, is a monument of Jewish scholarship. The Hebrew Union
College Annual has reached its twenty-fifth volume. As a background for future scientific work great libraries, rich in books
and manuscripts, and constantly growing, have been established.

Thus, in spite of the basic difficulties due to the lack of a
broad basis of popular Jewish learning and the tension of the
rabbinical life in America, a creditable shelf of scholarly works
has already been produced. As for the future, it is clear that,
although Jewish scholarship in America struggles under disad-
vantages, it has certain clear sources of strength.

Thus, it shares with the "founding fathers" of Jewish scholarship the spur of a strong social motivation. The founders of
Jewish studies had a motivation beyond the attraction which
modern culture had for the graduate of the old Yeshivoth and
beyond the personal desire to attain inner harmony by merging
the traditional loyalties with modern cultural aspirations. They
had also a powerful social drive, a great sense of obligation to
the Jewish people. These men felt that they were leading Jewry
out of darkness into light. As far as the non-Jewish world was
concerned, the new and more scientific descriptions of what Jewish history and Jewish literature really were like and what high
levels they had attained in the past, constituted the foundation for
demands for the complete emancipation of the Jews. The first
great classic of Jewish science, Zunz's pioneering work on the
Jewish sermon, has an introduction that reads like a political

manifesto. It sounds the battle-cry for Jewish rights, for Jewish dignity and calls upon the non-Jewish world to attain decency and enlightenment.

This is not the motive spurring modern Jewish scholarship. In certain lands Jewish rights are hopelessly lost. In other lands the battle is won. Nevertheless, the motive that inheres in modern Jewish scholarship is as compelling as the older battle for Jewish rights. It is directed not outward but inward. Jewish life in America is confronted with urgent problems and these knock at the door of the scholar's study.

Jewish life in America is different from that of the older communities, or rather Jewish life in America may be at that early formative stage, no longer clearly discernible in the history of the older communities, but whose existence is self-evident. It is an unfused group of subcommunities of separate origins and different points of view and different degrees of religious observance. Are there precedents in the Jewish past for such a predominantly non-orthodox community? How did such communities in the past gradually move to a greater consistency, a greater religiosity? Modern scholars of strong orthodox loyalty cannot brush aside the great American Jewish community as non-religious and build merely a little enclave of righteousness in a wicked world. In order to justify orthodox effort in America, there will undoubtedly be consistent historical investigation of the early stages of other great communities. Perhaps many of them began this way. Did not the Turkish community, which later became so great, reveal a startling neglect of all the laws of *mikvah* (ritual bath) (Isaiah Trani the Elder, JQR, O.S., 1892, IV, p. 99, article by Schechter)? Was not the great French community careless about such observance as the putting on of *tefillin* (phylacteries) (*Tosafoth*, Sabbath, 49a, s.v. *K'elisha*); to say nothing of the wearing of hats? Clearly there is a strong impulse in America for orthodox scholars who are scientific in their methods to begin paying attention to what was never adequately studied hitherto; namely, the early formative stages of the great Jewish communities, the battles between the various disparate elements as the Italian, the Spanish and the Greek elements in Turkey, the widespread non-observances and then the growth of study and the deepening of Jewish life. History may well serve to give courage and promise to the hopes of a renewed orthodoxy in the United States.

To the non-orthodox scholar, this American neglect of ritual observances will likewise provide an impulse to a closer study of the Jewish past. While the strictly orthodox may look upon the Jewish community in America as a sinful one since it is sketchy in its observance of old Jewish custom and law, the non-orthodox may well think of the American Jewry as experimental and perhaps creative of new modes of expressing the eternal truths and attitudes of Judaism. Therefore the interest of more liberal scholarship may well turn to the original and the creative periods in Jewish history, the time when new *minhagim* (customs) arose in large numbers. American Jewish scholars may begin studying the thousands of instances where Moses Isserles comments on the *Shulchan Arukh saying,* "The custom in these lands is thus and thus." These numerous customs will be traced back to their sources until perhaps we discover some century in northern France of the Rhineland where the Jewish people, just the people anonymously, suddenly became creative and achieved customs and habits which became the norm in later Judaism for centuries. A creative Jewry in America has a strong motive to search out and study the original and the creative Jewry of the past.

Besides these religious needs of American Jewry which will send the scholar searching in history, there is also a large and more general social need. Our American Jewry as a nationwide phenomenon presents a rather confused picture for which the past does not give us adequate parallel. Our American Jewish communities are virtually without precedent. So many diverse interests exist side by side and no one group has any official standing above that of another. To what extent is this a community? To what extent can it become a community? In the old world where there was a close church and state relationship, the church or the synagogue was the leading communal organization since it had official status and all the rest were incidental. But in

America, no one group has special status. Who then shall lead
in the integration of the community? We need guidance in building. Therefore to us the history of the Jewish community becomes a vital matter. How did the various communities in the
past become organized? How did they achieve their purpose, and
with how much control? These questions have already been studied with considerable profit by a number of Jewish scholars and
will continue to be studied and investigated. The rise and growth
of the Jewish community everywhere will always be a central
interest in this land of new communities.

On the national level our communities are only vaguely bound
together. Certain groups within our communities are in national
relationships with similar groups in other communities but any
attempt to unite our local communities as totals with other
communities has never succeeded and is not likely to succeed for
a long time. This is, perhaps, due to the general American
situation. Since there is a separation of church and state, there
is no temptation to organize any religious group or semi-religious
group into a strong, integrated, governing organization in order
to stand on equal terms with the secular state. The tendency in
America, therefore, is towards congregationalism. There are
Christian churches which are nationally organized and some of
them strongly so, but even these strong, nationwide churches or
communities would be much more tightly organized if they had
to stand in some official relationship to the state. For the fore-
seeable future, therefore, American Jewry will be at best a loosely
federated entity as far as intercommunity relationships are concerned. Can we maintain proper cooperation without too strict
a control? How strict was the control of the Council of the Four
Lands? How successful were nationwide organizations of the Jews
in the past? There is considerable social need impelling students
to study the nationwide organization of older Jewries.

Beyond the problems of American communities and of American Jewry, there is a need today to reconsider the interrelations
of world Jewry. It is a long time since we had to search out a
new basis for world Jewish unity. Up to the modern era all Jews
were united by the fact of their common faith. Now, aside from

the fact that many modern Jews no longer adhere to a religious faith, we have to face for the first time in two thousand years the question of what bonds there can be between one Jewry which is now an independent state and all the rest of the Jewries which are parts of other states as they have been for two thousand years. This search for a new relationship will spur Jewish scholarship. Undoubtedly there will be a new study of the one historical parallel to our present situation, namely, world Jewry during the Second Commonwealth when there was a Jewish state and also a large diaspora. Much has to be rediscovered and reevaluated of that past relationship. Among modern scholars in Palestine, the problem of interrelation has already produced new studies, but in the field of medieval and post-medieval history. They are gathering and editing the scattered literature of Jewish travellers to the Holy Land and also the records of Jewish emissaries from the Holy Land to all the scattered Jewries. Many Jewish scholars in Israel and elsewhere will be devoting much time and energy toward the discovery of whatever light history can shed as a guide to the building of suitable relationships in this new situation among the Jewries of the world.

This new impulse to scholarship, spurred by the integrational needs of the Jewish community, as the earlier Jewish scholars were spurred by the citizenship needs of their communities, will, of course, make use of the techniques of text study, the comparison and the dating of documents, and all the other methodologies used by the older scholars. The older science of Judaism had, quite properly, borrowed techniques which were developed in general historical and textual studies. The methods used in determining the text of Homer, the documentary study of Latin classics were carried over into the Jewish field. These techniques are still ours, but in addition to them we have the advantage of new sciences and new developments of older sciences. There are new points of view which lead to new methods and new insights into the material presented to us by the Jewish past. There is, first of all, the science of archeology. That which was a century ago mostly an amusement for well-to-do travellers or a desire to fill up museums with antiquarian oddities has become virtually an exact science with precise datings and exact methods of comparison, aided by radiophotography which enables us to judge by chemical means the exact age of many an ancient bit of material. The archeology of the Near East has already had a tremendous impact on the study of the Bible, as is well known, and further discoveries and greater precision will give us deeper insight into the earliest levels of recorded and non-recorded Jewish life.

The mood of historians has changed. The life of average folk has become a central interest. How people once earned a living, the details of common craftsmanship, even their folklore and superstitions have become subjects for the study of historians. A modern historian is likely to spend a good deal of time describing the modes of dress, the structure of the houses and of the streets, the songs people sang, their fads and their fancies. Economics has become part of history. Scholars are interested now in what possessions people had, where they came from, the silk culture, the travel routes over Asia to Europe. There were two recent discussions, for example, on the Merino sheep, whether they came from North Africa into Spain and how in the Napoleonic era they were brought to America and raised in Vermont and from there were sent to Argentina and Australia and changed the economics of the world. History has become human and intimate. Also, the great developments in individual psychology lead to an entirely new concept of biography combined with social psychology.

These new approaches are already affecting Jewish scholarship and are beginning to express themselves in new types of studies. The epochal lecture which the unforgettable Louis Ginzberg gave at the University of Jerusalem in 1931 is an outstanding example of the new mode in Jewish scholarship. The debates between the school of Hillel and the school of Shammai had been discussed for centuries and now in the modern spirit Dr. Ginzberg explains the difference between them upon an entirely new basis, namely, that each group had in mind a different social level of society, the school of Shammai suiting its emphasis in the law to the more comfortable classes, and Beth Hillel to the poorer classes, a type of explanation which would have been impossible or which would not even have occurred to a scholar a century ago. There is room for an entire social reworking of Jewish history and, in fact, Dr. Baron has already achieved pioneer work in this field with his *Social and Religious History of the Jews.*

There is today a sizable group of Jewish scientific scholars in the various institutions of American Jewish life and the universities, even though the recruiting of successors may not be easy. These scholars will find an abundance of living problems (as Zunz did) to spur them to fruitful investigation. New scientific disciplines will give them new instruments of research. There remains, however, the uneasy question of whether all such scholarship will be appealing enough to the American Jewish community to evoke their approval and their support. The lack of a Jewish population steeped in Jewish learning such as had existed in the past becomes here a serious weakness. It is a much more urgent problem than the fact that there will be fewer potential scholars. What if nobody cares to support Jewish scholarship?

The Jewish community of America is heavily burdened with urgent needs which simply cannot be set aside and which lay a heavy and continual tax on available financial resources. These demands are not only urgent, they are practical and thus can easily be made to appeal to a businessman. The community of the United States, largely a business community, has been successfully appealed to for charitable and Israeli causes. But Jewish scholarship, while it will surely eventuate in practical benefit and social guidance, is on the face of it highly theoretical. What chance has Jewish scholarship to win for itself a portion of the money given for the urgent needs of world Jewry? American Jewry is American, which means that it is practical. The same tendencies that lead to anti-intellectualism among all Americans, tend to anti-intellectualism among Jews. A theoretical study of ancient documents would seem to be useless, or if not useless, at least not urgent. It is, therefore, a crucial question of whether our present American Jewry can really be expected to support Jewish scholarship. Of course, the general American public does support investigations into old texts and Oriental archeology;

but the truth is that these studies are supported almost inad-
vertently. What American donors are concerned with are physics
and chemistry, plastics, training for business managership. If
pure humanistic studies are also supported, it is only by accident.
The universities support them; but the universities themselves
are supported chiefly for their so-called practical usefulness.

In the same way, Jewish scholarship will be supported in
America. The people want rabbis for their congregations, and for
that they will support rabbinical seminaries. If it happens that
the professors at the seminary do some Jewish research, that
fact is almost unknown to the supporters of the school, and is
just carried along by the support of the school. But Jewish scholarship requires more than rabbinical colleges and their faculties.
Chairs, too, need to be established for Jewish studies at general
universities. Dropsie College needs support. It is clearly necessary
to re-establish some sort of widespread interest among American
Jews for pure "impractical" studies, in learning for its own sake.
It is here that we are hurt most by the disappearance of the mass
Jewish study which existed in the past. That scholars and students should properly be supported for their theoretical studies,
*Torah Lishmah* (study for its own sake), was taken for granted
in a Jewish world in which almost every Jew did some Jewish
studying of his own even if he belonged only to a *Chevrah
Tillim* (Psalm study association). To a community aspiring to
knowledge, great scholars represented the height of social development; but to a Jewish community, in whose individual life
personal Jewish studies no longer exist, the greatest scholars
in the Jewish field are at worst a curiosity or at best an anachronism. There will, therefore, never be any real support for Jewish scholarship until we re-establish a widespread general Jewish
learning. This aim should be a major undertaking and must
engage the attention of our best scholars.

The intellectual of the past was not scornful of this task. One
of the earliest efforts made by the broken fragments of the great
Spanish Jewry arriving in the Balkans was the re-establishment
of widespread popular Jewish study. It was for that reason that
Jacob Ibn Chabib was not above excerpting from the Talmud

all the easy, narrative passages in order to provide some sort of learning within the reach of the masses. This book *Ain Yaakov* (the Well of Jacob) has been studied since by millions of Jews and become their main contact with Talmudic literature. Joseph Caro simplified the *Tur* (the Rows—A Legal Code) and his own great *Beth Yoseph* (a Commentary on the *Tur*) into an elementary code (without citing authorities) for the benefit, as he said, of the small disciples; and this folk-book became perhaps the best read and most studied book in Jewish life for centuries. Is it too much to expect that American Jewish scholars should begin to write books for the American Jewish people? We have more fields to draw upon than did our predecessors. There is much more now than Jewish law and the Talmudic literature. There is Jewish history and Jewish philosophy. There is a story of Jewish institutions. There are Jewish prayers and new and appealing commentaries on the Bible. We do not presume to say that any modern scholar can duplicate Rashi's great popular achievement in his Biblical commentaries; but the sort of thing he did should be our aim; namely, to produce a Bible commentary that thousands of Jews will read and re-read every week of their lives.

American Jewry has already felt the need of creating a new type of widespread Jewish learning. The pioneer work of the Jewish Publication Society is evidence of that. But we must have more than *reading* books for our people. Jewish learning was always more than reading, or, it was deep reading rather than wide reading. We must work towards a few books that will have the grand destiny of being studied again and again all through life, as once among the Christians, Foxe's *Book of Martyrs,* Bunyan's *Pilgrim's Progress,* and once amongst us, Rashi's *Commentaries* and *Ain Yaakov* were studied again and again. A plan for adult Jewish studies, the production of books to be studied all through life, merits the full devotion of all who are interested in the future of Jewish scholarship. We can find the scholars. We have the themes. We have the methods. We need to reconstruct the background of a reading and studying Jewish people.

# Hebrew Culture and Creativity in America

## JACOB KABAKOFF

That the Bible and the Hebrew language have deep roots in the soil of America and that they are among the forces which helped shape the thoughts and actions of the founders of this nation are by now well-recognized facts. It is thus no accident that the first book printed in the American colonies (1640) was the *Bay Psalm Book,* a translation of the Psalms containing Hebrew type and a preface by Richard Mather on Hebrew poetry and the Hebrew language. The large number of Hebrew grammars and lexicons published in this country over a long period attests to the popularity of biblical and Hebraic learning among non-Jews.

While a number of studies have been published on the history of Hebrew language instruction in America, there is still no full account of this fascinating aspect of early American higher education. Hebrew has played an honorable role in the history of our republic. Charles Seymour, former president of Yale University, one of the institutions which made Hebrew a required subject, put it well when he wrote: "The influence of Hebrew culture went far beyond the bounds of technical scholarship and professional training for theologians . . . it has pervaded and colored the thought and feeling of this nation ever since its beginnings." [1]

Although we may justifiably take pride in the fact that, through the Bible, Hebraic culture has made a deep impress on American civilization, this does not alter the fact that Hebraic endeavor on the part of American Jews is of comparatively recent origin. It was not until the large East European immigration that we witnessed the development of an American Hebrew press and literature. Moreover, it was not until the period of World War I that Hebrew literature and expression threw off its provincialism and began to become an integral part of the spiritual life of the American Jewish community.

The knowledge of Hebrew among American Jews in the early period of Jewish settlement was meager, particularly prior to the Revolutionary War. In 1735 there appeared the first Hebrew grammar to be published in America. This grammar was the work of a Jewish convert to Christianity, Judah Monis, who prepared the text for the use of his students at Harvard College, where he served as instructor of Hebrew. Monis had to obtain special Hebrew type from England for the printing of his grammar, which took a number of years.

It is only at the beginning of the 19th century that we begin to find several people who brought with them Hebrew knowledge. It comes as a pleasant surprise, therefore, to read of the career of the American-born *hazzan* Gershom Mendes Seixas (1745-1816), who achieved some degree of proficiency in Hebrew. For the most part the early spiritual leaders of American Jewry had to be imported because educational opportunities were rare here.

It is one of these spiritual leaders, Rabbi Isaac Aboab, who is credited with the distinction of having composed the first Hebrew book in the New World. Aboab, who emigrated from Holland to Recife, Brazil, in 1642 together with a group of Spanish and Portuguese Jews, was the author of a collection of poems

[1] *Hadoar*, vol. XXXI, no. 12, Jan. 17, 1941, p. 189.

and hymns entitled *Zekher Rav* (Great Memorial), written to commemorate the struggle between the Portuguese and Dutch in Brazil. While the collection remained in manuscript in Amsterdam, where it was taken by Aboab when he returned in 1646, it still has the honor of being the first Hebrew work composed in the Western Hemisphere. Moreover, this work is the product of events which occurred on this continent and bear their imprint.

In explaining the purpose of his work, Aboab wrote: "I have just put up a memorial of the wonders of God and of the great Kindness which He in His compassion and His great mercy showed to the house of Israel in Brazil, when there came over them the hosts of Portugal to destroy and to exterminate all that is called Israel, children and women in one day." The author composed a poem in which he described the sufferings of the Jews during the Portuguese-Dutch struggle in 1646 and their miraculous salvation when two Dutch ships arrived in the port on the 9th of Tammuz of that year. He also included prayers of supplication and penitence which were used by the Jewish community of Recife at that time.[2]

From the few Hebrew documents of the early period which have come down to us, the lack of acquaintance of the Sephardic Jews with Hebrew is more than apparent. The use of Hebrew was confined mostly to religious purposes, such as the writing of marriage contracts, divorce bills, Shechitah certificates and tombstone inscriptions, and forms of services which contained Hebrew prayers.

During the first half of the 18th century, however, we find that a Hebrew diary was kept by Benjamin Sheftall who settled in Savannah, Georgia, in July 1733. Sheftall, who came with a group of Portuguese Jews, was English, originally from Bavaria. His diary of events contains important data on the history of Jews in the southern colonies. That he translated his diary into English at the request of his son is sufficient indication that his

[2] For the text of Aboab's writings, see Kayserling, M., "Isaac Aboab, the First Jewish Author in America," *PAJHS* (*Publications of the American Jewish Historical Society*), vol. V, Appendix, pp. 133-136.

family did not continue the chain of Hebrew knowledge. Extracts in English from this diary were first published in the *Occident* by Mordecai Sheftall, his son.

The records of Congregation Shearith Israel, which virtually span the history of Jewish settlement in America, are a treasure-trove of information regarding the cultural level of American Jews as far as Hebrew knowledge is concerned. An interesting example of the use of original Hebrew prayers in worship was the *Form of Prayer* composed by Joseph Jessurun Pinto, leader of the congregation from 1759-66, for recitation on the "General Thanksgiving for the Reducing of Canada to His Majesty's Dominions," on October 23, 1760. The English translation of this service, which appeared in the same year, contains the note: "N.B. The foregoing prayer may be seen in Hebrew, at the Composer's Lodgings," indicating, as George A. Kohut has pointed out, that "apparently Hebrew scholarship was a curiosity in New York City in 1760." [3]

By the middle of the 18th century the need became evident for an English translation of the Siddur, for Portuguese and Spanish was beginning to be unknown to American Jews. In 1761 there appeared an English version of the Sephardic ritual for the evening services of the High Holy Days, which is said to have been translated by Isaac Pinto. Five years later Pinto issued a complementary volume containing a translation of the morning and afternoon services for Sabbath, Rosh Hashanah and Yom Kippur. While professing a high regard for the Hebrew language in the preface to his translation, Pinto expressed the hope that his work would "tend to the Improvement of many of my Brethren in their Devotion." He explained his motives as follows:

"A Veneration for the Language sacred by being that in which it pleased Almighty God to reveal himself to our Ancestors, and a desire to preserve it, in firm Persuasion that it will again be re-established in Israel, are probably leading Reasons for our performing divine Service in Hebrew: But that, being imperfectly

[3] In his article "Early Jewish Literature in America," *PAJHS*, vol. III, p. 122.

understood by many, by some, not at all; it has been necessary to translate our Prayers, in the Language of the Country wherein it hath pleased the divine Providence to appoint our Lot."

Apparently, the large majority of worshippers at this time were dependent on the English language for religious purposes. Men with Hebrew knowledge, like Isaac Pinto, were certainly the exception. Thus, when Haym Salomon addressed a Hebrew letter to Rabbi David Tevele Schiff in London in 1784 concerning the matter of a certain inheritance, he asked Joseph, the son of Wolf Karpeles of Prague, to write it for him.[4]

An outstanding example of an original Hebrew prayer composed for synagogue use in 1784, is the one published by Raphael Mahler from the Shearith Israel documents of the Lyons Collection of the American Jewish Historical Society.[5] The author of this prayer, which was composed following the American Revolution and the reconstitution of the Jewish community in New York, was Rabbi Hendel Johanan Van Oettingen, a Dutch Jew of German extraction. In addition to expressing thanksgiving for peace, the prayer singles out Governor Clinton and General Washington for special approbation and vouchsafes unto them the blessings of the kings and heroes of Israel. The prayer concludes with a hope for Jewish redemption and the restoration of Zion. Both from the point of view of content and style, this prayer is an admirable production, marred only by a few slight errors.

An extremely interesting example of the use of Hebrew for secular purposes at the turn of the 19th century was Sampson Simson's Hebrew oration. This was one of a series of addresses delivered in the classical languages by graduates of Columbia College at the commencement exercises on June 21, 1800. The Hebrew text of the oration, entitled "Historical Traits of the Jews, from Their First Settlement in North America," was ap-

[4] For the text of the letter, see Grinstein, Hyman B., "A Haym Salomon Letter in Hebrew to Rabbi Schiff," *PAJHS*, vol. XXXIV, pp. 107-111.

[5] "American Jewry and the Idea of the Return to Zion in the Period of the American Revolution" (Hebrew), *Zion, vol.* XV, 1950, pp. 122-124.

parently written by Gershom Mendes Seixas.[6] The introductory
note by Seixas to the address in the original manuscript states:
"One of the professors of Columbia College has requested me to
write something for Master Sampson to speak in public in the
holy tongue on Commencement day . . ." While the address is
not free from errors in Hebrew, it is nevertheless a notable
document.

It must be remembered that Seixas' Hebrew training was not a
formal one. According to David de Sola Pool he acquired his
knowledge from Joseph Jessurun Pinto, the *hazzan* of Shearith
Israel, and from his home environment.[7] When he prepared the
Hebrew address, Seixas was a trustee of Columbia College. Sampson Simson, the first Jewish graduate of Columbia, who delivered
the address, became an attorney and took an active part in Jewish communal life.

Sampson Simson's Hebrew oration, however, is but an isolated
instance of the use of Hebrew for secular purposes. That Jewish
leaders were concerned with the role of Hebrew in the preservation of synagogue and Jewish community life during the 19th
century is clear from Mordecai Manuel Noah's admonition in
his discourse delivered at the consecration of the Mill Street
building of the Shearith Israel Synagogue in New York, in 1818,
that "with the loss of the Hebrew language may be added the
downfall of the house of Israel." Again and again we meet com-
plaints by Jewish leaders on the decline of Hebraic knowledge.
If the results of Jewish educational efforts were unsatisfactory
during this period, they must be viewed against the background
of the struggle of a small Jewish community to strike roots in
a new land.

American Jewish historical records reveal a number of instances in which Hebrew served as a link between Jews in this
country and throughout the world, particularly Palestine. George
A. Kohut adduces as the "first vestige of Jewish literature in
America" an inquiry sent in 1636 by the Jews of Brazil to the

---

[6] For the Hebrew text of the oration, see Meyer, Isidore S., "Sampson Simson's Hebrew Oration, 1800," *PAJHS*, vol. XXXVII, pp. 430-431.
[7] *Portraits Etched in Stone*, 1952, p. 348.

Salonika Rabbi, Hayim Shabbatai, asking whether the prayer
for rain was to be recited during the Brazilian winter.[8] Hebrew
continued to be used for such purposes down to the modern era.

We know also of a Hebrew correspondence with the forgotten
Jews of Cochin, India. In 1787, Solomon Simson, the father of
Sampson Simson, received a Hebrew letter from the Jewish community of Cochin and was in communication with them. Some
years later, in 1794, the same Solomon Simson endeavored to
contact the Jews of Honan Province, China, and addressed to
them a Hebrew letter, which he sent along with a certain Captain
Howell. However, we are informed that the letter was never delivered.

It was only natural that Hebrew should serve as a bond between the American Jewish community and Palestine. As Abraham Yaari has shown in his comprehensive volume *Shluchey
Eretz Yisrael* (Emissaries from the Land of Israel, 1951) a constant stream of emissaries from Palestine came to these shores,
where they were usually well received. Dr. Ezra Stiles, the famous president of Yale University and the Hebrew scholar, tells in
his diary of his meetings with a number of rabbis from Palestine
and elsewhere with whom he conversed regarding Hebraic
learning. The most important among these was Rabbi Chayim
Isaac Carigal of Hebron. Stiles records, in June 1773, that during
one of his meetings with Rabbi Carigal the latter showed him a
Hebrew letter received from Isaac Pinto, the translator of the
prayerbook referred to above, requesting an explanation of some
Arabic words in Abraham Ibn-Ezra's commentary to the Bible.
He also observes that Rabbi Carigal showed him an edition of
the *Zohar* and gave him considerable information about the Holy
Land. After Carigal left Newport he continued to correspond in
Hebrew with Stiles. On one occasion, when a Hebrew letter from
Hebron was received in 1771 by Isaac Hart, in Newport, it was
Ezra Stiles who furnished him with a translation of it.

With the gradual increase in Jewish immigration and the arrival of greater numbers of German Jews we find more frequent
examples of the use of Hebrew. When in 1826 the trustees of

[8] *Supra, PAJHS*, vol. III, p. 104.

the newly organized Congregation B'nai Jeshurun in New York decided to purchase a synagogue building, they sent a Hebrew circular letter requesting financial aid from the various existing congregations.[9] One of the trustees of the congregation was Israel B. Kursheedt, a German Jew and the son-in-law of Gershom Mendes Seixas. Kursheedt is said to have been the most learned Jew in rabbinics in America at the beginning of the 19th century.

In 1834 Rabbi Bernard Pique, also of German origin, composed an original Hebrew hymn for the dedication of the new synagogue building of Shearith Israel in Crosby Street, New York City.[10] Rabbi Pique was in charge of the Polonies Talmud Torah, maintained by the Congregation and was first appointed to his position in 1818.

During the 1840's and 50's the field gradually opened up for Jewish religious functionaries and rabbis, who came for the most part from Germany. They brought with them Hebrew knowledge which they tried to foster under difficult conditions. At the same time there continued to arrive a trickle of Polish Jews who retained their loyalty to Hebrew. There are even a number of cases on record where Hebrew was the cause of sharp differences of opinion between German and Polish Jews. Thus, one of the reasons for a split in the membership of a San Francisco synagogue in 1855 was the failure to keep the minutes in Hebrew. The following year the same issue occasioned a sharp division of opinion in a B'nai B'rith lodge in Boston.[11]

In the 1840's and 50's there were organized a number of congregational all-day schools, in which Hebrew as well as general subjects were taught. The rise of the public school system and the increased enrollment of Jewish pupils in the non-Jewish private schools, however, gradually emptied the all-day schools of their pupils. To meet the demand for Hebrew, instruction in this

[9] For the text of the letter, see Grinstein, Hyman B., *The Rise of the Jewish Community of New York*, 1945, Appendix XIII, p. 520.

[10] For the text of the hymn, see Drachman, Bernard, "Neo-Hebraic Literature in America," in *Proceedings of the Seventh Biennial Convention of the Jewish Theological Seminary Association*, 1900, pp. 94-95.

[11] Steinberg, B., "A Contribution to the History of Jews in America" (Yiddish), *Yahrbuch fun Amopteil*, vol. II, 1939, p. 148.

subject was offered in some of the non-Jewish private schools. In New York, a number of Jews petitioned the Community Council in 1850 for the introduction of Hebrew as a language in the public schools. The following year a similar petition was made by Philadelphia Jews to give Hebrew equal status with other languages in the public schools of their city. No favorable action was taken regarding these petitions. The afternoon school, conducted chiefly by the congregations, became the primary agency of Hebrew instruction.[12]

It was due to the efforts of the pioneer spiritual leaders of American Jewry beginning with the 1840's that the vineyard of Hebrew was not left entirely unattended. The efforts of such rabbis as Isaac Leeser, who came here as a young man in 1824 and began his widespread activities in the 40's; Abraham Rice, who came in 1840; Bernard Illowey, in 1850; Sabato Morais, in 1851; Benjamin Szold, in 1859; and from the Reform group— Max Lilienthal, in 1844; Isaac Mayer Wise, in 1846; Isidor Kalisch, in 1850; Bernhard Felsenthal, in 1854; Henry Vidaver in 1862; Adolph Huebsch, in 1866 and others—embraced in varying measure Hebrew literary activity and a concern for the perpetuation of Hebrew learning. The number of intellectuals in America saw an increase in the 1860's when additional rabbis, teachers and *maskilim* ("enlightened" Hebrew Scholars) arrived, some of them with "literary reputations." The East European Jews, who began to develop their own social groups in the 50's and 60's, felt the need for spiritual leadership and in 1852 Rabbi Abraham Joseph Asch, the first rabbi of Russian-Polish origin, arrived to take a post in New York. Six years later came Rabbi Joshua Falk Ha-Kohen, the author of *Avney Yehoshua*, the first Hebrew book to be printed in this country.

Isaac Leeser, who helped fill the void in American Jewish literature by providing educational texts and catechisms and by translating the Bible into English and who agitated for higher Jewish study, is notable also for his positive attitude to Hebrew.

[12] Grinstein, Hyman B., "Studies in the History of Jewish Education in New York City (1728-1860)," *Jewish Review*, vol. II, nos. 1, 2-3, April and July-Oct., 1944.

For more than twenty years he edited the journal, *Occident*, which he founded in 1844, and he made it a forum for positive Judaism. The pages of the *Occident* contain not only translations from Hebrew literature and researches but also original contributions in the form of Hebrew essays on religious questions and even Hebrew poetry.

Among the contributors of Hebrew material to the pages of the *Occident* was Rabbi Abraham Rice of Baltimore, who is said to have been the first Rabbi in the United States to be called to a congregation. In volume V of the periodical, we find him engaged in a controversy with Menahem Goldsmith of New York concerning the use of citrons from the West Indies as *etrogim;* Rice permitted their use. In volume XI he published a review strongly critical of Isaac Mayer Wise's *History of the Jews.* Rabbi Illowey also made Dr. Wise's book the target of an attack, which elicited a Hebrew rejoinder from Wise. Illoway was the author of a number of other Hebrew articles in which he was critical of Reform; he also wrote Hebrew verse. Among the Hebrew verses published in the pages of the *Occident* there should be mentioned those by Sabato Morais, who was an ardent supporter and lover of Hebrew. That Leeser fostered Hebrew writing on rabbinic matters in the traditional style and encouraged even modern poetic efforts speaks well for his love of the language and his understanding of its role in Jewish life. That Hebrew found adherents from among the ranks of traditionalist and liberal rabbis alike attests to its unifying value.

For lack of Hebrew forums of expression the Hebrew intellectuals beginning with the 60's sent their literary efforts to Hebrew journals overseas. The pages of such Hebrew periodicals as *Ha-Karmel, Ha-Maggid, Ha-Meliz, Ha-Shachar* and *Ha-Zefirah* published in the European Jewish centers and of *Ha-Lebanon* and *Chavazelet* published in Palestine are dotted with the correspondence and poetic efforts of *maskilim* not only from New York City but even from as far west as San Francisco. This material is of considerable historical importance and offers a vital source of information regarding the development of American Jewish life. From time to time we also come across Hebrew material in English-Jewish periodicals, such as the *Jewish Messenger*, the *Hebrew Leader* and later the *American Hebrew*. Thus, Isaac Goldstein was the author of an "Acrostic on Abraham Lincoln," published in the *Jewish Messenger* of May 26, 1865 after the president's assassination.[13] The development of the Yiddish press in the 70's saw the introduction of Hebrew material by their contributors who were very often at home in both Yiddish and Hebrew. Virtually all the early Yiddish newspapers printed Hebrew contributions as a regular feature.

Reference has already been made to the first Hebrew book printed in America, *Avney Yehoshua* by Rabbi Joshua Falk, which was published in 1860. Of Polish origin, Falk first served as rabbi in Newburgh and Poughkeepsie and then became an itinerant preacher. For some time he was the *maggid* (preacher) of the first synagogue of the Russian-Polish Jews in New York, of which Rabbi Asch was the spiritual leader. In the introduction to his book, which is a commentary on the Ethics of the Fathers, Falk relates his difficulties in getting it published. He says that he received the support of Rev. M. J. Raphael of B'nai Jeshurun Synagogue, and appeals to his readers to purchase copies. He tells his readers that one of the benefits of this support will be the fact that it "will be to your glory that in America, too, there are to be found people who labor to write in the holy tongue." Isaac Rivkind has correctly commented on this work that it "leads to the sad reflection that it took fully two hundred years from the arrival of the Jews in North America before the pangs of Hebraic culture produced a Hebrew book in the full sense of the term." [14] It is noteworthy that a considerable number of the Hebrew titles published in America down to this day can be classified as rabbinic literature, thus following the pattern first set by Rabbi Falk.

During the 1870's the trickle of East European immigration, which before long was to become a mighty stream, was accelerated. Among the *maskilim* to arrive was Zvi Hirsch Bernstein (1870), who was a pioneer of both the Yiddish and Hebrew

---

[13] Reprinted in Goodman, Philip, ed., *Lincoln's Birthday Program Material for Jewish Groups*, 1953, p. 53.

[14] "Early American Hebrew Documents," *PAJHS*, vol. XXXIV, p. 53.

press. After publishing the first Yiddish newspaper *Die Post* in 1870 and engaging the following year in a short-lived journalistic venture, the *Hebrew News*, which he issued in four languages—Hebrew, Yiddish, English and German—he turned to the publishing of the first Hebrew newspaper *Ha-Zofeh ba-Arez ha-Chadashah*, which lasted for a period of some five years (1871-1876). Bernstein apparently had two motives in mind in undertaking his venture: to provide the new immigrants with a link with the Old World and to give them an organ which would help integrate them into their new life. To further these aims Bernstein solicited literary contributions from Hebrew writers in Europe and encouraged the publication of material on American history.[15] Associated with Bernstein in his task were such men as Leon Horowitz, who agitated for the emigration of the persecuted Rumanian Jews to America, and Mordecai Jahlomstein, who was later to issue in Hebrew translation a book on early American history. At this time the activity of Henry Gersoni began. He had a checkered career as a journalist in Hebrew, Yiddish and English, and his translation of Longfellow's poem "Excelsior" marked the first effort to give Hebrew garb to an American literary work.

Except for the publication in Chicago of a Hebrew supplement to the Yiddish newspaper *Die Israelitische Presse,* which served as a forum for the local *maskilim,* no other journalistic effort was made until the 80's. In 1877, however, there appeared a small volume of verse which has the distinction of being the first printed work of American Hebrew poetry. Moreover, since its author, Jacob Zvi Sobel, rendered three of his four poems into Yiddish, it is also the first printed book of American Yiddish poetry. The volume, entitled *Shir Zahav Likhvod Yisrael ha-Zaken* (A Golden Song in Honor of Israel of Old), contains, in addition to haskalah motifs and laudatory verses in praise of the Hebrew language, a poem about a "Polish Talmid Chacham in America." The poem, obviously a reflection of the author's strug-

---

[15] For a study of this periodical as a source of American Jewish history, see Davis, Moshe, "Ha-Zofeh ba-Arez ha-Chadashah," in the Hebrew section of the *Alexander Marx Jubilee Volume,* 1950.

gles, reveals what happened to a learned Jewish immigrant who had to bear the peddler's pack in America. Here we have expressed what became a recurring motif in American Hebrew writing throughout the immigrant period.

A concomitant of the increased immigration of the 80's was an increase in the still circumscribed Hebrew literary creativity. In 1880, there was founded in New York the *Shochare Sfat Ever* (Friends of Hebrew), which has the distinction of being the first organized Hebrew society in the world. The aims of the society were to provide a public forum for Hebrew, to maintain a library and to foster the study of the language among the youth. The society also included in its plans the publication of a quarterly magazine, of which only the first number appeared in 1881 under the title *Ha-Meassef ba-Arez ha-Chadashah* (The Compiler in a New Land). The officers of the new society included Kasriel Zvi Sarasohn, pioneer publisher of the Yiddish press, Zvi Hirsch Bernstein, Moses Aaron Schreiber, who was one of the early Hebrew versifiers and the author of a patriotic poem on the centennial of American independence (1876), and Judah David Eisenstein, who was to become known as the editor of various Hebrew encyclopedias, and others. While it lasted only about one year, this society was the prototype of scores of others which arose throughout the country in later years and which constituted the pioneer expression of an organized Hebrew movement. Thus, in 1889, we find a similar society organized in Chicago, which continued to be active for some thirty years. This society sponsored the literary organ *Keren Or* (Ray of Light), the first Hebrew monthly in America. In addition to contributions by the editor, Leon Zolotkoff, the two issues which appeared contained articles by Peter Wiernik, Rabbi Bernhard Felsenthal and others. Many of the early Chovevei Zion societies in America during the 90's not only bore Hebrew names, such as *Shavei Zion, L'Maan Zion,* etc., but also engaged in Hebrew activities and gave support to existing Hebrew journals and literary efforts.

In Baltimore, the efforts of the local Hebrew society were supported by Rabbi Benjamin Szold, whose scholarly Hebrew commentary on the book of Job was published in 1886. A notable Hebrew literary society which was active during the nineties was the *Ohale Shem* (Tents of Shem), organized in 1895 and encompassing the leading Hebrew writers and intellectuals in New York.

There is hardly need to document the bitter lot of the Hebrew intellectual during the 80's and 90's. The repeated advice of those who had already immigrated to America to their colleagues and friends in Europe was to stay home. Moshe Weinberger, author of the book *Ha-Yehudim v'ha-Yahadut b'New York* (Jews and Judaism in New York), published in 1887, states explicitly that his caustic criticism of Jewish spiritual life in America was meant to discourage his Hebrew readers in Russia, Poland and Hungary from coming here. He paints a sorry picture of the small band of American Hebrew writers who were unable to devote themselves to literature but had to engage in peddling, business and the like in order to eke out a meager living. While there were a good number of Hebrew readers, "they gave preference to the dollar over literature."

In the face of all this, we must marvel all the more at the persistence of the Hebrew writers who came here and labored to keep the spark of Hebrew alive. In 1889, three attempts were made in New York to establish Hebrew weeklies. The initiators of these efforts were: Ephraim Deinard, who founded *Ha-Leumi* (The Nationalist) and who was later to become known as a collector of Hebraica for American libraries; Michael L. Rodkinson, who issued *Ha-Kol* (The Voice) and was later to publish an English translation of the Talmud; and Wolf Schur, who edited *Ha-Pisgah* (The Summit). All of these efforts were short-lived. However Schur, whose journalistic attempt had preceded those of Deinard and Rodkinson, was not a man to be discouraged by a single defeat. The full story of his pioneering efforts in behalf of Hebrew journalism and the Jewish rebirth cannot be told here, yet a few highlights of his work will serve as indication of the courage and perseverance required by Hebrew writers in the 90's.

Determined to establish a Hebrew organ for American Jewry,

Schur renewed *Ha-Pisgah* in 1890. He stated editorially: "If the
select few will not arise to act for spreading a knowledge of
the language among our brothers so that the new generation
should at least understand what is written in our Bible, then our
people and Judaism must indeed fall." In addition to his aim
of advancing the "ancient Hebrew language among the American Israelites," Schur desired to make his weekly a forum for
the interests of Russian-Polish Jewry, as well as for the cause
of Zion. With various interruptions, Schur continued his publishing efforts for over a decade in New York, Baltimore, Boston and Chicago successively, finally issuing his weekly under
the name of *Ha-Techiyah* (The Rebirth). His was a significant
contribution in agitating for Zionist activity in the pre-Herzlian
period. After the appearance of Herzl, Schur succeeded in
making his weekly a "semi-official Zionist organ." In addition,
he produced one of the more important books of the 90's—
*Nezach Yisrael* (Israel Eternal), which appeared in 1897. He
wrote it to combat the anti-religious views of Jewish Socialists and Anarchists and the extremism of Reform, on the one
hand, and to demonstrate the validity of Judaism against the
claims of other religions, particularly Christianity, on the other.

Schur is but one of the many unsung heroes of Hebrew literary
effort in America. The nineties bore tragic witness to the efforts
of such men as Gerson Rosenzweig, Isaac Rabinowitz, Menahem
Mendel Dolitzky and Naphtali Herz Imber to continue to nur-
ture their Hebrew muse. Their literary hopes were dampened by
economic struggles and setbacks. Rosenzweig, who during the
nineties edited *Ha-Ivri* and afterwards issued other Hebrew journals as well, turned to satire. Some of his well-turned epigrams
hit at various evils in American Jewish life. Rabinowitz, who in
Europe had been a part of a circle of Hebrew haskalah writers,
lost his splendor here and made his poems a vehicle for his
disappointment and despair. Dolitzky, while still sustained somewhat by the romantic dream of Zion, also succumbed to a spirit
of sadness and futility and turned to hackwriting in Yiddish,
among a variety of other occupations, in order to support himself. Imber even engaged in English writing, yet the vagabond

and tortured existence which he led here is indicative of the hopelessness that characterized the life of the author of *Hatikvah*.

There were also lesser literary lights like Goetzel Selikowitch, Moshe Ha-Kohen Reicherson, Abraham B. Dobsewitch, Joseph L. Sossnitz and others who were unable to find themselves in the new land. Hutchins Hapgood, whose interviews with many of the Hebrew intellectuals are recorded in his *The Spirit of the Ghetto* (1902), aptly termed these intellectuals "Submerged Scholars."

During the nineties, also, a number of journalistic ventures were made, most important among which was the Hebrew literary review *Ner ha-Maaravi* (The Western Light), issued by the Society for the Advancement of Hebrew Literature in America. In addition to K. Z. Sarasohn and J. D. Eisenstein, who served as president and treasurer of the Society respectively, we find Israel Davidson listed as secretary. That the publication of the journal entailed a bitter financial struggle may well be gauged from the fact that its last editor, S. B. Schwarzberg, was led to pen a vehement tract entitled *Tikatev Zot l'Dor Acharon* (Let This Be Recorded for Future Generations), in which he bitterly denounced the Hebrew-reading public for its lack of support of culture.

Among the important works which appeared during this last decade of the 19th century were the concluding volume of Alexander Kohut's *Ha-Arukh ha-Shalem* (Arukh Completum), the first two parts of A. H. Rosenberg's *Ozar ha-Shemot* (Cyclopedia of Biblical Names) and Arnold B. Ehrlich's *Mikra ki-Fshuto* (The Bible According to Its Plain Meaning). Nevertheless, the general picture of Hebrew cultural and literary creativity in America at the close of the century was a bleak one indeed. Even as ardent a Hebraist as Mordecai Z. Raisin, who was already active in Hebraic activity and Hebrew letters at that time, expressed serious doubts about the future unless the ranks of the stalwarts of Hebrew were to receive additional reinforcement from overseas.[16]

---

[16] "Hebrew in America," *Dappim mi-Pinkaso Shel Rabbi*, pp. 386-387. This Hebrew article appeared originally in *Ha-Shiloach*, vol. VIII, 1901-02.

It was with the arrival of the new type of Hebraists imbued with the ideals of the Hebrew rebirth that the modern period began in American Hebrew literature and activity. Daniel Persky, the veteran American Hebrew journalist, has on more than one occasion described how the representatives of modern Hebraism gradually conquered the positions held by the *maskilim* of the old school. They joined the *Mefize Sfat Ever* (Disseminators of the Hebrew Language), a society which had been founded in 1902, and they propagated the ideals of Hebraism which they brought with them from Eastern Europe. In 1906 they started the publishing venture *Ivriah*, which issued modern Hebrew writings by Joseph Chayim Brenner and Joseph Klausner. They endeavored to bring Hebraic activity in America into line with that of Eastern Europe and to have it share in its growth. When Ben-Avigdor, the European Hebrew publisher, arrived here in 1908, he stressed in a public lecture the need for founding a periodical which would become a medium for modern Hebrew literary expression. Such an attempt was made the following year with the issuing of *Shibbolim* (Ears of Corn), under the editorship of M. Ben-Eliezer. Some of the writers who later achieved distinction first tried their literary wings in this magazine.

The old-time Hebraists did not give up without a struggle. They continued to issue journals and to fight for their ideas. After editing the weekly *Ha-Leom* (The Nation), Moses Goldman launched in 1909 and again in 1913 the daily newspaper *Ha-Yom* (The Day), which in both instances appeared for but a short interval. By that time, however, a sufficient number of young Hebrew writers had arrived to turn the tide. They established the *Achiever* (Hebrew Brotherhood), which eventually became a federation of twelve Hebrew societies and which can be viewed as the precursor of the present-day organized Hebrew movement. In addition to conducting various Hebraic activities, *Achiever* initiated in 1913 the publication of *Ha-Toren* (The Mast), which continued to appear under various auspices down to 1925. At first the periodical was edited by a group which included Abraham Goldberg, Simon Ginsburg, S. M. Melamed,

S. B. Maximon, B. N. Silkiner and Daniel Persky, but it was later to benefit also from the editorship of such leading writers as Isaac Dov Berkowitz and Reuben Brainin. Through their efforts *Ha-Toren* came to play a leading role in the fostering of creative Hebrew writing in this country. Another Hebrew publication of high caliber, edited for the Mizrachi by Rabbi Meyer Berlin, was *Ha-Ivri,* which appeared from 1916 to 1921 and transcended narrow party interests.

In the meantime, the movement for the teaching of Hebrew as a living language by the use of the *Ivrit b'Ivrit* method had gained momentum. This movement did much to create enthusiasm for Hebrew and to modernize Hebrew schools in community after community. By 1909 the Teachers Institute of the Jewish Theological Seminary, under the direction of Dr. Mordecai M. Kaplan, was organized. The Mizrachi Teachers Institute was opened in 1917 by the Mizrachi Association, under the direction of Dr. Meyer Waxman. This school was later to become the Teachers Institute of the Rabbi Isaac Elchanan Theological Seminary. Similar teachers' institutes in New York and elsewhere were to be established during the 20's and 30's.

Few could have foreseen the development of a virtually new center for Hebrew literature in America. Yet this occurred as the result of the appearance on the American scene of a few good editors and a member of talented poets and writers who gradually turned to new themes and modes of expression. In 1910 *Achiever* published a slim volume, entitled symbolically enough *S'nunit* (Swallow) and containing the poetic offerings of a group of young Hebrew poets. Among the poets represented here who made their mark in American Hebrew poetry were Benjamin N. Silkiner, Ephraim E. Lisitzky and A. S. Schwartz. Gradually a whole group of poets developed here. In addition to the above, there were Simon Ginsburg, Israel Efros, A. H. Friedland, Hillel Bavli, Simon Halkin, Moses Feinstein and later Eisig Silberschlag and Abraham Regelson.

A number of factors have combined to give relevance and significance to the work of these men. Unlike the Hebrew writers who preceded them here in the 90's, they did not have to go through the adjustment of a difficult immigrant period. Most of them came in early youth and received their general schooling here. Moreover, they quickly mastered English and became intoxicated with the American spirit and the beauties of English literature. No wonder then that a number of them (Silkiner, Lisitzky, Efros, Bavli, Halkin) undertook to translate Shakespeare's plays into Hebrew.

The strongest voice in American Hebrew poetry prior to World War I was that of B. N. Silkiner. He early sounded a lyrical, individualistic note which characterizes much of the new American Hebrew poetry. He was led to deal with American themes which became a concern of most of our American Hebrew poets. In 1910 he published an epic poem on Indian life during the Spanish rule of America entitled *Mul Ohel Timurah* (Facing Timura's Tent). The American Indians later served as material for two other poets who devoted epic poems to them. Lisitzky dealt with this theme in his *Medurot Doakhot* (Dying Campfires), while Israel Efros devoted to it his *Wigwamim Shotkim* (Silent Wigwams). All three epics are permeated with a sense of deep sympathy for the tragedy of the American Indians. Indian motifs are to be found also in the poetry of Abraham Regelson.

Not only the Indian but also the Negro provided American Hebrew poets with thematic material. Lisitzky is the author of the volume *B'Ohale Kush* (In Negro Tents), dealing entirely with the folklore and suffering of the American Negro, while Eisig Silberschlag and Hillel Bavli also turned their attention to Negro motifs.

There are other aspects of American and American Jewish life which have received treatment by our poets. Efros is the author of an epic poem on the California gold rush entitled *Zahav* (Gold). S. Ginsburg devoted poems to the city of New York and the Hudson River. H. Bavli has written idylls full of perception about *Mrs. Woods*, an aged New England woman, as well as the Mormons. S. Halkin has dealt with Cafe Royal types in New York and has written fine descriptive nature poetry. He is also the translator of Whitman's *Leaves of Grass*. Reuben

Grossman (Avinoam), the American-born Hebrew poet now residing in Israel, recently issued a *Hebrew Anthology of American Verse,* containing translations from the best in American poetry. Both in style and in theme, Gabriel Preil is an American poet writing in Hebrew. The realistic poems of Abraham Z. Halevi reflect various phases of city life, while American motifs and cadences are easily discernible in the poems of E. D. Friedland and of such younger writers as David Kramer and T. Carmi. In addition to translating from English and American literature, some of our American Hebrew poets have also written essays and criticism in this field.

The claim has sometimes been made that in writing about Indians and Negroes our American Hebrew poets have been guilty of escapism. However Lisitzky, in a statement on "American Hebrew Poetry," has endeavored to explain the motivation for this preoccupation with themes out of the American past.[17] He perceives a close relationship between the struggle of the American Indian who was being displaced from the soil, the American Negro who was being oppressed by the white man, and the American Jew who was fighting for spiritual survival on the American scene.

Another factor which led the poets to deal with specific American themes was their desire to strike root here. Unlike the immigrant generation of poets which preceded them, they felt at home in the natural beauties of America and in its literature. And they wished to transmit their appreciation of the American spirit as their contribution to modern Hebrew letters. In so doing, they helped free American Hebrew writing from the dominance of the Russian Jewish center and to give it character of its own.

The theme of Americanism is by no means the only facet of the Hebrew poetry produced here. An intense national feeling and love of Zion characterizes the work of all of our American Hebrew poets. If Americanism is their bond with this country, then the ideal of Zion is their link with the people of Israel and its age-old aspirations. In poems of yearning and in hymns to the builders of Israel, our poets have closely identified themselves

[17] *Hadoar,* vol. XXIX, no. 7, Dec. 17, 1948.

with the Jewish homeland. As a matter of fact, a number of poets who were active on the Hebrew literary scene here chose to settle in Israel and continue their literary work there. Reuben Grossman, Baruch Katznelson and more recently Simon Halkin and Abraham Regelson have continued their literary work in the Jewish homeland. American Hebrew poetry runs the gamut of lyrical themes as well, and prominent among its interests are poems on biblical subjects and characters (Silkiner, Lisitzky, Ginsburg, Bavli, Efros and others) and poems of an introspective, contemplative nature (especially Halkin, Regelson).

American Hebrew prose represents a much later development. It is neither as varied nor as extensive as the poetry, having come on the scene rather late. Little of value was written until our own century and the process of adjustment to the American scene on the part of some of our prose writers has been difficult. It is only in comparatively recent times that we have a number of thoughtful and mature novels of American Jewish life.

Isaac Dov Berkowitz, who was an active influence in American Hebrew letters during World War I and the twenties, was far too much a son of the Russian Hebrew center to become fully integrated into American life. The excellent monthly journal *Miklat* (Refuge) that he edited during 1920-21 for the American branch of the Stybel publishing house, which he headed, was more a forum for European than American writers. Even in his short stories which have America as their locale, Berkowitz remained attached to his spiritual homeland overseas. The characters in these stories are forlorn and alienated people.

Abraham Soyer also remained sentimentally attached to the Old World and the East European town and his two-volume collection of short stories *Dor Holekh* (A Generation Passes) is rooted in that milieu. L. A. Arieli, some of whose American short stories were recently published in Israel in his posthumous volume *L'Or ha-Venus* (By the Light of Venus), was caustic and bitter and took a dim view of Jewish life here. S. L. Blank, who recently published a volume of short stories of American life *B'Maarbolet ha-Chayim* (In the Stream of Life) and has a number of other American stories to his credit, has nevertheless made his mark chiefly as the interpreter in novel and short story of Jewish life in Bessarabia.

The first among our American Hebrew prose writers to throw off the "yoke" of the Old World and describe realistically characters on the American scene was Abraham H. Friedland. In his *Sippurim* (Stories) he recorded with psychological insight incidents from various areas of Jewish life, including religious and communal activity. B. Isaacs has also been able to shift his interest to the American Jewish scene and in his latest collection of short stories *Amos Mokher Tapuzim* (Amos the Orange Vendor) he interprets the mind of both integrated and ambivalent American Jews.

But by far the most significant contribution in this area has been made by Simon Halkin and Reuben Wallenrod. Halkin is the author of a trilogy of American Jewish life. Its first part, *Ad Mashber* (Towards a Crisis), describes Jewish life in New York in the late twenties. Underlying the thread of the loose narrative is the author's attempt to evaluate the varied pattern of Jewish life here and to probe its spiritual and cultural trends. Wallenrod has given us many short stories describing Jewish life in New York, as well as two novels dealing with other segments of the American Jewish experience. *Ki Fanah Yom* (The Day Wanes) is set in the Catskills and depicts the disillusionment of Jewish farmers who have turned to hotel-keeping, while *B'Ein Dor* (Lost Generation) treats of the adjustment of postwar Russian-Jewish immigrant youth to America.

Prominent among the other American Hebrew prose writers are Harry Sackler and Yochanan Twersky, both of whom have dealt with historical themes—Sackler in the short story and Twersky in the novel. Sackler, who is also a dramatist, has written a play on the life of Mordecai Manuel Noah, while Twersky, since settling in Israel, has published extracts from a novel on Noah. A younger writer, Chayim Abramowitz, who was educated in America, is the author of *Al ha-Lechem Levado* (By Bread Alone), a novel of Jewish life in Brownsville. Other short story writers who have described various aspects of American Jewish life are S. Kushtai, S. Damesek and J. Tarkow-Naamani.

This survey of American Hebrew creativity would not be complete without taking account of the writers who have enriched Hebrew scholarship. There is scarcely a field of research in which significant works have not been produced by American scholars. The writings of Israel Davidson, David Neumark, Louis Ginzberg, Henry Malter, Ben Zion Halper, Chaim Tchernowitz, Michael Higger and Samuel J. Feigin, to mention but some of the scholars who are no longer with us, are enough to indicate the contribution which has been made to Hebrew learning.

It is encouraging also that a good number of our present-day Jewish scholars are continuing to publish their researches in Hebrew. In the field of rabbinics Saul Lieberman published an edition of Maimonides' *Hilkhoth ha-Yerushalmi* (Laws of the Palestinian Talmud) from an unknown manuscript and Abraham Weiss has written on the redaction of the Talmud. Of our American-born Jewish scholars, Louis Finkelstein has published Halakhic researches and texts in Hebrew, Robert Gordis has written on Wisdom literature and other biblical subjects and Moshe Davis has devoted two volumes to American Jewish history.

In the essay, too, we can point to a group whose efforts cover a variety of fields, from literary criticism to various scholarly subjects. Menachem Ribalow not only edited an *Anthology of American Hebrew Verse* but was also the author of five volumes of sensitive criticism. His most recent work *MeOlam l'Olam* (From World to World) was issued on the occasion of the first anniversary of his passing. J. J. Wohl interpreted both European and Hebrew literature in his collection of essays entitled *Bishtey Reshuyot* (In Two Realms), while Abraham Epstein gave us sympathetic evaluations of many of our modern Hebrew authors. Of particular interest is his two-volume collection of studies *Sofrim Ivrim d'America* (Hebrew Writers in America), published in Israel shortly before his death. Other leading essayists among the departed were Zevi Diesendruck, who wrote on philosophical subjects; Nissan Touroff, who issued authoritative works on psychology and education; Chaim Tchernowitz, who set down his memoirs; and S. B. Maximon, Abraham Goldberg and Moshe

Halevi, whose collected essays touch upon various phases of Hebrew culture and literature.

A considerable number of writers and scholars contribute regularly to our American Hebrew periodical press, but we can consider here only those authors whose writings have appeared in book form. Among those who have given us scholarly monographs is Meyer Waxman, whose latest work is entitled *Galut u'Geulah b'Sifrut Yisrael* (Exile and Redemption in Jewish Literature). Simon Bernstein and Shalom Spiegel have been active particularly in the field of medieval Hebrew poetry, while Simon Federbush and Samuel K. Mirsky have given us studies in rabbinic literature. Pinkhos Churgin contributed a volume of researches on the Second Commonwealth. In the field of philosophy, M. H. Amishai (Moshe Meisels) has dealt competently with both Jewish and general thought in his two-volume *Mahashavah VeEmet* (Thought and Truth). Zvi Scharfstein has written extensively on the history of modern Jewish education and pedagogy, while I. Z. Frishberg has published a collection of essays on educational and publicist themes.

The veteran Hebrew writer M. Z. Raisin has given us two volumes of delightful essays on various phases of American Jewish life, particularly the Reform movement. Daniel Persky has collected his feuilletons on the holidays and has issued also his *Ivri Anokhi* (I Am a Hebrew) on various aspects of the Hebrew language and culture. Isaac Rivkind and E. R. Malachi have put us in their debt with their useful bibliographical and literary studies. Joshua Ovsay has written on the world of Torah in Eastern Europe and on various literary themes, while Isaiah Rabinowitz has expounded a humanistic approach to modern Hebrew literature.

Among the scholars and authors from overseas, who have continued their literary activity in America, is Simon Rawidowicz. He has contributed additional stimulating essays on the relationship between the State of Israel and the Diaspora and has edited the seventh volume of *Metsudah* (Fortress). Nahum N. Glatzer and Abraham J. Heschel have also published Hebrew studies, while Aaron Zeitlin has written impressive poetry in addition to essays. Mention has already been made of the fact that most of our American Hebrew poets have produced essays and criticism.

The gains of American Hebrew letters in the modern period are largely a result of the efforts of the *Histadruth Ivrith* (National Organization for Hebrew Culture), which was founded in 1916. World War I saw the concentration in America of a number of important Zionist and Hebraic leaders who gave impetus to the launching of a revitalized Hebrew movement. There were Shmarya Levin, Isaac Ben-Zvi, David Ben-Gurion, Eliezer Ben-Yehudah and others. Reuben Brainin, who had been in America since 1910, was elected to the presidency of the Histadruth Ivrith and edited for it a series of popularly priced classics as well as a volume in honor of the 60th birthday of Ben-Yehudah. Various popular pamphlets on the Hebrew revival by I. Ben-Zvi, Brainin, Ben-Yehudah and others were issued.

The launching of *Hadoar* (The Post) in November 1921, initiated a new era in American Hebrew journalism. That it was begun as a daily newspaper, under the editorship of M. Lipson, indicates the high hopes which American Hebraists had for the Hebrew revival in the postwar years. It soon became a weekly, however, and the position of editor was occupied by Menahem Ribalow. An indefatigable worker, Ribalow nurtured *Hadoar* until it became the central organ of American Hebrew writers and soon launched additional literary projects. He made the supplements *Hadoar Lanoar* and *Musaf Lakore Hatzair*, containing suitable reading material for children and young people, regular features of his magazine. Ribalow was the guiding spirit and editor of the *Sefer ha-Shanah Lihude Amerika* (The American Hebrew Year Book), of which nine volumes have appeared, and of the *Ogen* (Anchor) publishing house, which has issued the works of American Hebrew writers. During 1953, the last year of his life, he started the publication of a new literary quarterly *Mabua* (Fountain), to which both American and Israeli writers contributed. His passing came as a severe blow to the Hebrew movement and to Hebrew literary effort in America.

A number of other literary endeavors of high caliber must be considered as part of the total picture of American Hebrew creativity: the monthly *Bitzaron,* the scholarly quarterly *Talpioth, Shevile ha-Chinnukh,* an educational journal, and *Megillot,* a review of Jewish education and culture.

The organized Hebrew movement in America, represented by the Histadruth Ivrith, has sponsored over the years a variety of activities in order to focus attention on the centrality of Hebrew in American Jewish life. In addition to its literary endeavors, the Hebrew movement has been responsible for initiating a number of educational ventures, such as the Massad Camps. Since the establishment of the first Camp Massad in 1941, the Hebrew camping movement has advanced considerably. The Ramah camps, conducted by the United Synagogue of America, and Camps Yavneh and Sharon, maintained by the Chicago College of Jewish Studies and the Boston Hebrew Teachers College respectively, are examples of the gains made by this idea.

In Eastern Europe the Hebrew movement and Hebrew literature were able to draw their supporters from the ranks of those who had been educated in the schools. The ability to read and speak Hebrew were the accepted goals of a large segment of the school system. This, however, is no longer the case here. Whether our own educational system will be able to provide a sufficient number of Hebrew intelligentsia is, therefore, still a moot question. Against the decline in the Talmud Torah, as a result of the steady shift in the Jewish population and the growth of the Congregational school, some educators have pointed to the development of Hebrew nursery and foundation schools and to the remarkable increase in the day schools as hopeful signs. From a total of 17 day schools with an enrollment of 4,600 children in 1935 the number, as of the end of 1954, jumped to 176 day schools with an enrollment of over 30,000. This figure includes elementary, junior high and senior high schools. Then, too, there is the unprecedented phenomenon of the teaching of Hebrew as a foreign language in the public high schools and junior high schools in New York City, as well as in 12 out-of-town communities, with an annual enrollment of over 5,000. To this number must be added close to 2,000 students engaged in the study of Hebrew in the colleges of metropolitan New York. Still another

factor in favor of Hebrew is the variety of available Israeli tours
and study opportunities for youth and adults. Educators look to
these sources, as well as to our schools of higher Hebrew learning, to help supply the readers for American Hebrew literature
and the human material for an Hebraic-oriented program of cultural activity.

The establishment of the Jewish State has given new impetus
and relevance to Hebrew in America. Aside from the survival
value of Hebrew as a bond with the past and as a medium of
religious expression, it now looms as a potent factor in the
achieving of world Jewish unity. We do well to recall the historian William Lecky's statement, "Hebraic mortar cemented
the foundations of American democracy." This same mortar can
and must be made to serve as a cohesive force in strengthening
the mosaic of American Jewish life.

# Jewish Literature in English

## CHARLES ANGOFF

Contemporary Jewish-American creative writers in English find themselves in the strange position of having to justify themselves to some of the more aggressive writers in Yiddish and Hebrew. The dogmatic Hebraists incline to look down upon any writing by Jews in any language other than Hebrew, though one must add that it is a question whether they object more to those who write in English than to those who write in Yiddish. The dogmatic Yiddishists insist that nobody writing in any language other than Yiddish can possibly pretend to write truly about Jewish life and the Jewish people, at least in America and Eastern Europe. The two groups have organizations of long standing and considerable vigor, and through them they propogandize their points of view. Jewish writers in English have no such organizations.

The irony of the situation is that, though Yiddish as a vital language appears to be declining in the United States, as is evidenced by the sad state of the Yiddish press, the Yiddishists are probably the more vociferous of the two. The *Jewish Daily Forward*, whose editors are well versed in world literature and

should know better, recently gave considerable space to one of
its staff writers to argue his chauvinistic Yiddishist philosophy.
Apparently it has not occurred to him that if his basic philosophy
is valid, then the writings of James Joyce about Ireland are worthless, since they are not written in Gaelic, and the writings of Sean
O'Casey about the Irish are also worthless, for they, too, are written in a "foreign" tongue. According to the same philosophy, *The
Rise of David Levinsky,* by none other than Abraham Cahan, late
editor of the *Forward,* must also be considered of small value,
since it is written in English—and was not translated into Yiddish,
in the very same *Forward,* till nearly four decades after its first
appearance in English.

It is no wonder, then, that books on American-Jewish life in
English generally get such piddling notice in the Yiddish press,
and that dozens of them are not noticed at all. In the Hebrew
press they are almost entirely ignored.

There is another obstacle put in the way of Jewish-American
writers. They must submit to a sort of religious caste system if they
wish to be taken seriously or published by some of the Anglo-
Jewish periodicals. One such periodical refuses to print any
stories that do not extol the Orthodox Jewish virtues, while the
editor of another has told one short story writer that his magazine
"is interested only in those characters and situations that would
be familiar to men and women of the Reform persuasion." The
periodicals sponsored or edited by men and women who incline
toward the Conservative wing of Judaism appear to be more tolerant, and yet, the editor of one of them has criticized two prominent Jewish-American writers because their works do not concern
themselves chiefly with religious issues, though he admitted that
both authors are fully aware of such issues and do give them due
and sympathetic consideration in the context of their works.

A third obstacle that the Jewish-American writer must hurdle
is the general indifference of the whole Anglo-Jewish press, especially the weekly press. The editors of the latter would rather
devote columns of space to social events than to the publication
of short fiction or the critical discussion of Jewish-American literature. One of the oldest and most affluent weeklies in America re-

fuses to print any short fiction whatever, and it is only of late that it has decided to devote any space to intelligent reviews of Jewish books. Most of the more pretentious monthlies and quarterlies —with few notable exceptions—are little better. They do print short stories, but only on occasion. The editors of some of them insist that while they are not at all ashamed of being basically Jewish publications, they nevertheless prefer to print articles, and they frankly like to have many of their articles deal not so much with Jewish problems as with minority problems in general, as if Jewish problems were pretty much solved and therefore Jewish publications should earn some extra *mitzvahs* (merits) by discussing the problems of the American Armenians, American Czechs, American Indians, Puerto Ricans, and so on. Many Jewish-American short story writers must therefore turn to the general periodical press for publication. Fortunately, there are several general literary periodicals that are glad to publish good Jewish stories.

Finally, American-Jewish writers still have to contend with the obstinate conviction among the editors of important American book review organs that novels and short story collections dealing with Jewish-American life are "special"—on a level with books on stamp collecting, Iranian grammar, fox hunting, and the cultivation of silk worms in Japan. It has done little good to point out to these editors that if books on Irish-American life by James T. Farrell or Armenian-American life by William Saroyan belong to the category of "general books," of interest to every intelligent American and to be reviewed at length, then certainly books on Jewish-American life by equally gifted Jewish-American writers also deserve to be reviewed at length and to be considered "general books." Perhaps in time, the book review editors will reform, but meanwhile, Jewish-American writers must be satisfied with such brief and unintelligent notice as most of them get in the general reviews.

If it is hard to be a Jew, it is possibly even more difficult to be a Jewish writer, but the aforementioned obstacles will disappear with time. In any event, there is an abundance of compensations, and all of them glorious to the genuine writer. The material is of almost incredible richness. Jewish-American life is, in some respects, unlike the life of any other hyphenated group. It bears the accumulated tears and joys and sorrows and exhilarations of some two thousand years of exile. It is thus freighted with a range and intensity of human experience perhaps never before recorded of any other people. The whole gamut of human emotion forms an integral element of it. American Judaism is a mosaic of world Jewry but it is also an amalgam, and will probably become more so with time, as the melting pot among American Jews continues to boil and churn.

While American Jewry bears within it the burden of its unparalleled history, common to Jewry in all other lands, it has the additional advantage of having soaked up, for three hundred years, the spirit of the American tradition, which has probably been more congenial to it than the tradition of any other country. Early America was steeped almost as much in the Old Testament as in the New Testament; the "Christian" names of large numbers of the early settlers came out of the Old Testament, and so did many of their mores and political sentiments. Their insistence upon the primacy of learning and education paralleled that of the Jews. The early Americans sensed this deep kinship with the Jews, so that while the Jews in Colonial times were not entirely free from discrimination and even persecution, they suffered less from both than did some of the Christian sects. Jews were thus pretty much at home in this land from the beginning, and they have been at home, by and large, in this country ever since.

This should have given to the American Jew a dimension of pride. Actually it took decades for this pride to become a part of the consciousness of American Jews. For a long time their dominant attitude toward the new country was one of thankfulness and understandably so. A people does not soon forget an experience like the expulsion from Spain, nor does it soon forget the persecutions that took place in Russia, Poland and Rumania three and a half centuries later. It is true that German Jews, French Jews and English Jews did not suffer from the periodic pogroms visited on Eastern Jews, but a people's misery is not divisible, any more than the pain inflicted upon one part of the human body can be ignored by the rest of the same body.

The pervading feeling of thankfulness, as has been said, was thus perfectly natural, and while it restrained the Jews, for a long time, from feeling properly proud of themselves as a people in a country founded upon so many of its own principles of living, it propelled the Jews to an experience of Americanization that was perhaps deeper, and to an active participation in American communal life that was probably more extensive, than that of any other immigrant group. The history of the *Galuth* seems to show that the Jews are an intensely patriotic people, attaching themselves to whatever land gives them harbor. They loved Russia and Poland and Rumania, even though these countries persecuted them. It was, to be sure, partly love for the land of their parents and grandparents, but it was more than that: it seems to reveal, within the Jewish people, a deep desire to give of themselves freely to almost any land that takes them in. In any case, what was true of Eastern Jews was also true of German, French and English Jews, though to a somewhat lesser extent. That so many Jews for so long after they came here spoke of the countries they fled from as "home" is very significant.

But while in some of the older countries, especially in Eastern Europe, Jewish expression of patriotism was limited to sentiment, in America they could express themselves openly, for here they stood on the same political plane as Christians. They became judges, they became Governors, they became mayors and Congressmen and United States Senators, and State Senators and legislators, and they became members of School Committees and State Planning Boards and Child Welfare Councils and Park Commissions and Federal and State Crime Commissions. They became thoroughly American, and they brought their Judaism to bear upon almost every aspect of American life—upon law and music and drama and dancing and business and architecture and sculpture and literature. Their influence was not always a direct one. It was often indirect, and in a singularly American way. Jewish musicians steeped themselves in the spirit of the land, the compound of this immersion, so to speak, then reacted with a fresh vigor and a novel attitude, and the result of this vigor and attitude comprised an alloy of Judaism and Americanism. George Gershwin's music is thus thoroughly Jewish-American, for it represents an Americanized Jew's musical version of America.

II

With the coming of the First World War something historic happened to American Judaism. It came of age— just about the same time that Louis D. Brandeis, at the age of more than fifty, became, spiritually, *bar-mitzvah*. Almost suddenly, it seems, it became fully conscious of its maturity, of its two-thousand-year-old maturity. It became conscious of its peoplehood, and the old tunes and the old folk tales and the old pieties and the old mores and the old communal habits returned with greater meaning and urgency. It became fashionable again to discuss Jewish problems openly, and Zionism ceased being the complete madness that so many Jews had imagined it to be. Yet there remained a hard and very large core of American Jewry that soon after the Balfour Declaration—when the first, fine frenzy of the Declaration had cooled, and it became plain that it would be a long time before Palestine would become the Jewish homeland again—reverted to type and were again Jews by occasional observance only. It was not till another generation had passed, and Hitler had done his evil work, and Israel became a full-fledged state that virtually all of American Jewry had, so to speak, returned to the fold—and at long last, after three hundred years, has become fully mature. When that has happened to a people one can safely say that it is at the beginning of a cultural era of true and enduring worth.

In the literary realm the potentialities of this culture are incalculable. Alas, one must still speak, in the main, of potentialities when one speaks of Jewish-American writing in English. Up to about the time of the First World War nearly all worthy Jewish-American literary culture was in Yiddish. It was and it continues to be of high quality, and has yet to be properly evaluated. Even today, with but two Yiddish dailies remaining in America, a fine body of short fiction and poetry and essays and general commentary appears in Yiddish. This literature, one must, however, point out, has been written almost entirely by men and women who had emigrated from Europe. The writers wrote mostly about life in Russia or Rumania or Poland, for they knew it best and felt more drawn to it emotionally than to their new life here. Such writing as they did about Jewish life in the United States—with a very few exceptions—was cerebral rather than emotional and hence of inferior artistic worth.

In this one respect, Jewish literature in English has had one virtue that most Yiddish writing did not have: it has had the quality of real intimacy. Unfortunately, for some two centuries, it had little more than this. The few short stories and novels of post-Revolutionary and Civil War times that can still be obtained in libraries are generally overly romanticized portraits of Jewish-American types—especially older folk—that remind one of contemporary Sunday supplement "human interest" features. Barely any attempt was made to reveal character or to present a Jewish-American situation fully.

There was a marked improvement in the quality of this literature—in the creative and other realms—around the time of the First World War, especially in the East. In Boston and New York, there were several Anglo-Jewish periodicals that, for a while at least, made an honest and heroic attempt to give expression to good writing: short stories and essays in particular. Indeed, one of the Anglo-Jewish periodicals of those days, the *Boston Jewish Advocate*, rivalled some of the best contemporary American periodicals. Alas, the periodicals under discussion have virtually disappeared as organs of much value.

The years 1913 and 1917 mark two very important events in the history of Jewish-American literature. The first saw the publication of Mary Antin's *The Promised Land*—and the end of an era in Jewish-American life—and the second saw the publication of Abraham Cahan's *The Rise of David Levinsky*—and the beginning of an era in Jewish-American life. Mary Antin's autobiogra-

phy was the most complete and perhaps the best statement of
Jewish gratitude to the American ideal. It was the last such statement on a major scale, though it was probably the first general
Jewish book in America to achieve a wide reading public and
considerable critical attention. It actually marked the conclusion
of a 250-year period in the evolution of Jewish-American life.
It was American Jewry's farewell gesture of thankfulness toward
the land that gave it shelter from the persecutions of the Old
World and that offered a way of life—politically, economically,
and spiritually—that had so much in common with basic Judaism.
*The Promised Land,* despite its excitable prose, is still worth
reading. But even as it was being hailed all over the nation, something new was already a-borning in American Jewry. American
Jewry was finding its own soul, straightening its shoulders, and
realizing that it had an identity of its own.

The book that heralded this change was Abraham Cahan's *The
Rise of David Levinsky.* It is in some ways a sad book, for it
portrays an American-Jewish Babbitt—five years before Sinclair
Lewis portrayed George F. Babbitt—in the clutches of his own
business success, which brings him only loneliness. It also presents
East Side New York in all its tawdriness, and the garment industry in all its gaudy shabbiness. But there is also something
fundamentally positive about it: a realization that Jews could not
only take from but also give to America, that they could outdo
Americans in several respects (in dress designing and merchan-
dising, for example). And David Levinsky's heartache over his
lost Judaism—his pining for the soft and deeply satisfying atmosphere of the yeshivah, his admission that the woman of his heart
had been right in abandoning him for a *luftmensch* (impractical
dreamer)—implied that Judaism had a set of values of its own
that the Jew can reject only at the peril of his own soul. And what
David Levinsky realized so poignantly reflected what all American Jewry had come to realize—that it must become more Jewish in answer to its own deepest spiritual needs, and uncon-
sciously it also realized that it must become more Jewish if it was
to become fully American in the best sense of the term.

In the history of Jewish-American literature in English, *The*

*Rise of David Levinsky* has an additional importance. It is perhaps the first truly good novel produced in that literature—and
one of the few very good ones in American literature in the first
two decades of the twentieth century. It can stand on the same
level with anything Sinclair Lewis has written and with some of
the works of Theodore Dreiser.


III

Abraham Cahan encouraged other Jewish fiction
writers in English. But very few of his followers have even approached him in skill, in sympathy, in understanding. In the late
twenties and the thirties, Jewish-American fiction came under the
same evil influence as did general literature: the proletarian "literature" hammered together by innocent and talentless young men
and women who were taken in by the spreading Communist
philosophy in the United States. The hoopla engendered by this
philosophy was truly fantastic, so much so, indeed, that critics
and editors who were otherwise very astute were soon praising
stories and novels and semi-autobiographies that were shoddy
from every conceivable literary point of view. Thus even H. L.
Mencken was taken in by Michael Gold's *Jews Without Money,*
chapters of which he first published in *The American Mercury.*
To Gold, America was the land of despair . . . the land where
the rich got richer and richer and found special pleasure in piling
misery upon misery upon the poor, who were, of course, getting
poorer and poorer.

To Gold, the East Side Jews had very few special problems of
their own; they were only part of the vast silent majority of proletarians in this country, which, according to him, was far below
Soviet Russia. To Gold, the Jews he wrote about possessed no
Jewish soul, no special cast of spirit, no singular yearning. They
were chiefly Jews without money. To the misfortune of American
Jewry this book was hailed as a fine portrait of Jewish America.

The miasma of proletarian literature for a while darkened the
horizon of the resurgent pride among American Jews. But then

something happened in the world that in one fell swoop brushed aside the vulgarity of proletarian literature and its even more vulgar philosophy—the materialistic interpretation of the human heart—and the American-Jews realized, as did Jews all over the world, that they were a truly heroic people. Subconsciously, they began to think that perhaps there is something chosen about them if after 2,000 years of exile a nation with a culture as advanced as that of Germany could stake its bid for world power upon the theory that the Jews were the cause, not only of Germany's misery, but of the misery of the whole world. This theory posited an almost mystical power in a little group of 15,000,000 in the midst of a world population of more than 2,500,000,000. In America, it wiped out, almost over night, nearly every last vestige of anti-Zionism, for American Jews saw clearly that the Jews of the world could not always depend upon the kindness of Christian countries, even those allegedly most civilized. They must have a haven of refuge of their own.

This upsurge of national or perhaps one should say peoplehood feeling had, and continues to have, tremendous effects in every aspect of Jewish-American life. The cultural benefits from it will probably not become fully apparent for another century. Meanwhile, in the realm of literature, one thing is already clear. More short stories and novels and essays on general Jewish subjects and Jewish-American subjects have appeared in print since the dark days of Hitler than, perhaps, in all our previous history in this country.

## IV

But it seems that many of our inept writers were the first to get into print with their Jewish books, and such was the climate of the times that many of them sold well, and the American people were treated to some very shoddy portraits of Judaism and Jewish men and women. For a while, there was a rash of novels dealing with intermarriage. One of the most successful of them from a commercial and critical standpoint, presented a Jewish father and mother who were the paragons of stupidity and cruelty, at a total loss as to what to do with their son who had strayed from the fold by falling in love with a Gentile. The picture of the life led by these parents was such that the girl began to wonder whether this was the kind of family she wanted to marry into. The novel did have drama, but only as a grade B movie has drama, and it won the author a reputation, among Gentiles and some Jews, too, as an authority on Jewish life.

Still another novel, which reached a sale of many hundreds of thousands, and which was made into a highly profitable motion picture, was a superficial plea for tolerance but so lacking in understanding of Jewish life that it was almost a caricature. It had no value as literary anthropology or as literature. It revolved around a gimmick—a Gentile masquerading as a Jew and thereby "getting into the Jewish heart," a trick that only a poster writer with the soul of an advertising hack could think of—and it was oblivious of the open and covert psychological burdens of the Jew, not only in small Connecticut and Long Island communities where anti-Semitism is generally more subtle, but also in the big cities where it is sometimes so much an accepted part of certain businesses and professions that even genuinely tolerant and perceptive Gentiles become hardened to it.

But sad as was this sort of pulp about Jewish life, there was one development that perhaps was even more depressing. Some avant-garde Jewish writers began to make copy out of the Jew, with the result that the advanced intellectuals of the Gentile world—and newly self-discovered non-literary American Jews, too—got the idea that most Jews were neurotic and had ulcers and went from one psychiatrist to another and found special delight in an occasional non-Jewess on the side. And they got the further idea that there were not many Jews in America who didn't connive at getting virtually everything wholesale.

Then there was, and alas still is, a strange group of Jewish-American writers, many of them former Communists and fellow-travelers, who had sneered at the whole concept of Jewish peoplehood and exulted in being interested only in "people, no matter what they believe." One segment of this group makes a specialty of looking down upon Jews, particularly those who reside in the more modest sections of big American cities. If you should read a story or an article by one of them about, say, the Jewish sections of Brooklyn or the Bronx, you would get the impression that all the Jews there found pleasure only in eating and haggling with one another, that their sons, by and large, went into accounting and dentistry solely because they offered the prospects of easy living, that their daughters were mostly money-mad when it came to looking for a husband, that they spoke dreadful English, that their mothers urged them on in their money-madness, and their fathers were almost incredibly henpecked—in short, that Jewish life was drab and cheap and offensive to cultured men and women. No hint about the vast learning going on in the colleges and yeshivoth in their midst, or about the large number of young men and young women who had devoted themselves to the fine arts, or about the parents who save and scrimp to send their children to some college or musical conservatory or dancing school. No hint that these are the People of the Book, the people with visions in their eyes, the people who from time immemorial have insisted upon learning and more learning, upon refinement of the spirit and humaneness. (*Lernen, edelkeit, menshlichkeit.*)

## v

And yet despite these unpleasant aspects of the contemporary scene in Jewish literature in English, aspects which will probably continue for some time, one can find ground for optimism. First, there is the fact already alluded to, that of the vast output of writing, which generally augurs well. If these writings have done nothing else, they have aroused a greater awareness of Jewish values and of the sheer romance of the Jewish story, and this awareness is bound to have a heightening effect upon the latent creativity in Jewish-American men and women. Many of the new novels and stories are sound and solid works, as good as and often better than current American best sellers.

Any critical listing of the more memorable works in this area would include the following works:[1] Abraham Cahan's *The Rise of David Levinsky* is the first major, and still the best, over-all novel about Jewish immigrant life in America. It is centered in New York City and teems with memorable characters and insights. Hyman and Lester Cohen's *Aaron Traum* likewise takes the East Side of New York as its locale. Its special emphasis is on the progress of Americanization, in both its integrative and disintegrative aspects. *The Old Bunch* by Meyer Levin is a massive and superb novel on Jewish life in the depression thirties. It is a chronicle of a group of young Chicago Jews, vibrant with both genuine Jewish characters and the harrowing realities of the period. The book seems to have all the earmarks of endurance and probably will be read for many decades to come. In many respects, it excels *The Rise of David Levinsky*.

Perhaps the most memorable novel on the theme of the Jew who seeks to escape his Jewishness is Ludwig Lewisohn's *The Island Within*. Charles Reznikoff's *By the Waters of Manhattan*, the story of a group of Russian Jewish immigrants in America, is notable for its aura of tenderness. *Blessed is the Man* by Louis Zara is the story of a Chicago *all-rightnick* (*nouveau riche*), done with emphasis and gentleness, and yet deeply incisive.

The harvest of the Jewish short story, while more meager than that of the novel, includes a number of significant contributions. *Hungry Hearts* by Anzia Yezierska, while published in 1920, still holds up remarkably well. Miss Yezierska has an extraordinary ear for immigrant speech and for certain types of immigrant characters. A more recent collection of short stories about contemporary American Jewish life is James Jaffe's *Poor Cousin Evelyn*. Most of the tales reveal a richness of insight. The two best anthologies in this genre are the volumes, *This Land, These People* and *These, Your Children*, both edited by Harold U. Ribalow.

Especially noteworthy is the larger number of first novels by

---

[1] An excellent guide for further reading in the realm of American Jewish fiction is Harold U. Ribalow's pamphlet, *American Jewish Life*, Jewish Education Committee, New York, N. Y. 1953.

young Jews. Many of them—perhaps most—are of inferior literary
worth, written too hastily, too green spiritually, not sufficiently
suffused with the essence of Jewishness. But they do reveal a
growing concern with Jewish life in this country from the fictional
standpoint, a vague realization that here is great wealth for the
creative artist in the realm of prose. Most of these novels concern
themselves chiefly with Jewish self-hate (as practiced by the parents of the authors), anti-Semitism in the fashionable suburbs,
intermarriage, of course, and the barriers set up against Jews in
business firms. These problems are dealt with in first novels because they inflict so much pain upon the sensitive soul of the
young writer. He writes about them dramatically, for he is
shocked and wounded. He doesn't realize that in order to write
about them with enduring artistic effect he must experience all
their myriad subtle implications—and such experience demands
time.

Perhaps even more important for the future of Jewish-American literature is the new spirit of acceptance and pride that is
obvious all over the land. More and more American Jews are less
and less furtive about their Judaism, and they are beginning to
take pride in it—and there is reason to believe that they will
experience still more pride as time goes on. If the Hitler massa-
cres and later the Communist canards tended to bring together
the Jewish community the world over and especially in America,
the establishment of Israel tended to bring out into the open the
deep-rooted attachment that American Jews had always had for
things Jewish. Their hearts lifted with the unprecedented historical event that took place in Israel, for never before in all human
history has a nation been revived 2,000 years after its apparent
destruction by a foreign power.

What promises to take place in the Jewish-American community culturally will perhaps be almost as historic as what has already taken place in Israel on another level. America now contains nearly five and a half million Jews, or about half the Jewish
population in the world. This fact alone places American Jewry
at the forefront of world Jewry. That America is not Israel has
less significance than is generally imagined. The Diaspora is not

at all an abnormal concomitant of Jewish life. It has been normal through the major part of Jewish history, including most of the period of the Kings and Prophets. At the time of the destruction of Jerusalem in 70 C.E., about half of the Jewish population of the world, in so far as available records reveal, lived outside the Jewish state, and free choice was undoubtedly an important factor in the mass migration of Jews.

Wherever Jews lived in Western, Central or Eastern Europe, their environments impinged significantly upon their life and thought and found expression in their contributions to world Jewish culture. From a literary angle, this is a point of vast importance, for it means that Jewish literature is inevitably a literature of astounding variety and great riches, for in every country it bears both its own Jewish stamp and the stamp of the country. Jewish literature in the Diaspora—which is to say Jewish literature among the greater number of the Jews of the world—is thus more than an amalgam, it is an alloy, with the Jewish strain dominant.

American Jewry seems to be ripe for a literature of its own such as it has never had before. It has been here 300 years and in that time it has soaked up the fullness of the spirit of Americanism—and it has also affected the American community. If there is validity to the theory of some cultural historians that it takes about 300 years for a culture to reach its full maturity, then this glorious time has begun for American Jewry—as it probably has begun for the American nation as a whole.

The field for the creative Jewish writer in America is virtually untouched. There are numberless situations and characters, dramas and dreams and secret yearnings and regrets and sheer color. It is presumed, of course, that the creative Jewish writer will naturally seek to exploit this material to which, as a Jew, he brings a native understanding. There is the hinterland Jew, who is often a Jew chiefly by memory and who struggles to maintain his Jewishness largely by contributing to the various appeals and by reading his lodge paper. There is the small town Jew who is rapidly being Westchesterized or Long Islandized. There are the sisterhoods and the brotherhoods, most of them very sincere and worthwhile organizations, all of them relatively new in American life and of great value to the creative writer—for in these sisterhoods and brotherhoods boil and seethe and flourish all the magnificent age-old Jewish characteristics.

There are the new types of rabbis that are coming out of the seminaries. Some are vastly learned, true *Geonim,* and with profound spiritual influence. There are also rabbis who are, unfortunately, little more than masters of ceremonies. Finally, there are rabbis who, to put it politely, should have entered some other profession. They all merit the most careful fictional treatment— as types, as individuals, as sources of influence—to be portrayed kindly and with understanding. There is the itinerant peddler, who roamed the countryside, bringing Jewishness to the hinterland Gentiles, and glimpses of hinterland America to the big town Jews. The Yiddish press has attempted to present him, but he deserves fuller and more effective treatment. There is the old time *melamed* (elementary Hebrew school teacher) who knew little of the science of pedagogy and, alas, not too much about Jewish history either, but he did know his *chumash* (pentateuch) and he did much good—and there is enough material in him for several dozen novels and numberless short stories. There is the more modern teacher in Temple Sunday schools and in the Jewish parochial schools, who probably has fewer problems of discipline than the *melamed* did, but who has special problems of his own.

And there is the real estate operator, who has changed the outline of our major American cities, but who also is intensely interested in the upbuilding of Israel. There are those who have returned to the fold, the former radicals who have become mystics or so orthodox as to make some *Hasidim* look with surprise upon them; the former plain free-thinkers who now have taken to *Hasidism;* the new style cantors who are like the old *Chazonim,* yet different—better versed in Jewish liturgy, but a bit more, shall we say, "businesslike"; the new type of American Gentiles in our midst, some of them Christian ministers, who are even more zealous about the welfare of Israel than some American Jews, and who are fertile with suggestions for the enrichment of Jewish-

American life; and dozens and dozens of other characters and situations.

They are all begging to be portrayed in short and long fiction— and also in poetry and drama, two departments wherein American Jewry has not yet produced anything truly noteworthy. One hazards the guess that they will be portrayed, and in the not too distant future. American Jews are now more ready than ever before to read about their own life, for they now better appreciate what it means to be American Jews. The American audience in general is likewise more receptive to novels and stories of the life led by the five million odd Jews in its midst, as is revealed by the larger number of Jewish stories that are appearing in general and even in so-called sophisticated general magazines. Then, Jewish-American writers are beginning to feel that they need no more look upon themselves as martyrs, that they are being more widely accepted by their fellow Jews and by Americans as a whole, not as much as they should be, true enough, but still far more than they were twenty-five years ago or even ten years ago. These developments indicate a future resplendent with literary culture. All literary history appears to offer ground for belief in such a future. And it may well be that the next hundred years will see the flowering of a Jewish-American literature in English that will add lustre to the annals of world Jewry.

# Yiddish

# Literature in

# America

## NOCHUM B. MINKOFF

The Yiddish speaking group is the only American
cultural minority that has produced and is now at
the zenith of producing a vast, pulsating, many-
faceted literature of high enduring quality. Its study reveals a
set of values that constitutes an important mirror of the Jewish
experience in America. But description of this variegated phenomenon, in its every aspect, is a complicated task. Not the
least of the difficulties for the literary historian inheres in the fact
that the literary physiognomy of many Yiddish writers was
formed abroad, though their major contributions were made on
American soil.

Bearing the impress of European culture and already spiritually mature at the time of their arrival, they showed little initiative or interest in the newer literary forms current in this country.
Despite their American residence, they remained relatively im-
mune to the spirit of their environment. The new atmosphere
could not substantially alter their perspective or their methods.
Their literary visages were already cast and not subject to altera-
tion.

214

Despite this, their contribution to American Yiddish literature is of ranking importance. In this category of writers, whose literary maturity preceded their arrival in America, one counts such significant figures as Dovid Einhorn, I. Bashevis, Aaron Zeitlin, I. I. Trunk, Shlomo Bickel, Rokhl Korn, Chayim Grade, Mordecai Shtrigler, Yehuda Elberg, and Z. Diamant.

This observation applies to Yiddish literature since its very dawn in America. It is as true of the early folk poet, Eliyokum Tzunzer as it is of such latter day figures as Sholem Asch, Abraham Reisen, Peretz Hirshbein and I. J. Singer.

The transplantation of Yiddish literature to America and the problems it poses to the literary historian is not the only complicating factor in the history of the development of American Yiddish literature. In all, it is an intricate web of literary movements, groups, forms, and of individual figures. A summary essay must necessarily limit itself to the most characteristic aspects of these varying trends.

## II

There is evidence that the first Jew to reach American shores, Jacob Barsimson, was an Ashkenazi Jew, which means a Yiddish-speaking Jew. Barsimson landed in New Amsterdam a few weeks prior to the arrival of the twenty-three Jewish refugees from Brazil in 1654. Among the latter, Asher Levy, whose full name was Asher Levy Van Swellen, was a Yiddish-speaking Ashkenazi. Within a year, there is a historical reference to two groups of Jews, Sephardi (Spanish-Portuguese) and Ashkenazi. It is estimated that about the beginning of the eighteenth century, fifty percent of the Jewish population in America consisted of Ashkenazi Jews—that is, Jews from Central and Eastern Europe, whose vernacular was Yiddish.

Although spoken Yiddish was used from the very beginning of the Jewish settlement in America, Yiddish literature in the United States began its career with the establishment of the Yiddish press in 1870. The first sixteen years, 1870-1886, may be called the pre-historic years. The Yiddish poetry of the period came from the pens of persons as diverse as Meir Rabinovitch, by profession a *shochet* (ritual slaughterer), *Chazzan* and scribe; Yankev Zevi Sobel, a former Rabbi and student at the University of Odessa; Arnold B. Ehrlich, an eminent Biblical scholar. For the record, the first Yiddish poem written by Rabinovitch appeared in 1871 and took the form of a satire on the convention of Reform Rabbis held at that time in Cincinnati. Shortly thereafter, there appeared from his pen a satiric fable whose background was the national elections of the year 1872. A prolific writer, his verses, which appeared in many Yiddish publications of the period, took their themes from the then current scene in America and in American Jewish life.

Sobel's first poem in this country appeared in the *Yiddishe Gazetten* in 1876. Its title is significant. It really bore two titles, one in Hebrew, *The Golden Song of Old Israel,* and one in Yiddish, *Old Israel.* The most important poem in the booklet was entitled *Der Polnisher Talmid Chochem in America* (The Polish Scholar in America). Sobel describes a European Talmudic scholar and his experiences in the new country during his first days here. The scholar becomes a peddler and thus improves his financial status. But he bewails the lack of spiritual ideals among the immigrants of the seventies.

The last versifier of this formative period was Professor Arnold B. Ehrlich, a noted Hebrew scholar, who wrote scholarly studies in Hebrew and German, and poetry and novels in Yiddish.

III

This early, formative period of Yiddish literature in America came to an end with the great impact of the new mass immigration. The Russian pogroms in 1881 set in motion great waves of Jewish immigration bound for America. This sudden, continuing influx of newcomers changed the entire picture of Jewish life in the United States. Victims of oppression, the immigrants were imbued with deeply-rooted Jewish values and lofty ideals, ethical, cultural and social. In time, these immigrants were to become the source for the highly articulated Jewish life that was to develop in America in the forms of religious institutions, philanthropy, social welfare, education, labor movements, Yiddish press, theatre and Yiddish literature.

With this new impetus, Jewish religious life enjoyed a period of efflorescence and was strengthened through the medium of the Orthodox daily Yiddish press, which included the *Yiddishe Gazetten, Dos Yiddishe Tageblatt, Der Morgan Jhournal* and others that were short-lived. Oral Yiddish found lodgement in the old style Yeshiva, where it is still to be found today.

In the second decade of the present century there emerged the Yiddish school. Today, such schools are conducted under the auspices of the Jewish National Workers Alliance (*Farband*), Workmen's Circle (*Arbeiter Ring*), and Sholem Aleichem Institutes, many of which maintain high schools in addition to elementary divisions. The schools are staffed in large measure by graduates of the Jewish Teachers Seminary. Within recent years, courses in Yiddish linguistics and literature have been introduced in such institutions of higher learning as Columbia University, City College of New York, the New School for Social Research and Brooklyn College. This development must be credited both to the earlier establishment of Yiddish courses and to the extraordinary growth in Yiddish literature. Yiddish scholarship in the fields of linguistics, philology, folk-lore and history has found encouragement and expression in the Yiddish Scientific Institute (Yivo) and its scholarly publications.

While the organization of the Jewish labor movement was primarily motivated by the desire to improve the economic lot of the Jewish worker, it soon developed important cultural implications. The Jewish worker became the devoted reader of the Yiddish press and through it made acquaintance with the vital and vigorous literature that was published in installments in the Yiddish newspaper. Much of this literature was directed towards the worker and his social and cultural situation. In popularized form, the Yiddish press served, and still serves, as a potent medium for adult education. From its very inception, reportage played a relatively small role in the Yiddish newspaper. Most of its columns were given over to commentary and opinion-forming articles on the actualities of the day, from a variety of points of view. At least one page, and occasionally even more, was devoted to various novels (or short stories) in installment form.

Yiddish cultural and literary criticism in America found its first expression in the Yiddish press. Theatre criticism by Getzil Zelikowitz began to appear in the *New Yorker Yiddishe Folks-Zeiting* in 1887. David Edelstadt, a poet, was the first literary critic (1890) whose work appeared in the *Freie Arbeiter Shtime*. Since that date, literary criticism has formed a regular feature of the Yiddish press. Its outstanding practitioners have been Joel Entin, Samuel Niger, Dr. Abraham Mukdoni and Dr. Solomon Bickel. The publicistic and philosophic essays was also represented in the daily press. It was through his daily newspaper that the Yiddish reader first made the acquaintance of the first-rate Yiddish thinkers, such as the late Hayim Greenberg, Chayim Zhitlovsky, Nachman Syrkin and Abraham Koralnick.

The Yiddish theatre, too, played a significant role in stimulating and providing an outlet for a number of first rate Yiddish dramatists.

## IV

By 1886, two currents in American Yiddish literature were already discernible, currents that were to gather increasing momentum in the years to come. The first found its expression in a literary movement that derived its basic impulse from a growing social conscience. The second sought to give literary form to the traditional Jewish consciousness and a revived set of Jewish national aspirations.

The point of departure for the first was the central preoccupation and emotional experience of immigration life: how to eke out a livelihood in the new environment. The avenues of economic endeavor open to the newcomers were as few as they were

competitive. Around the strange world of the sweat shop there
was no horizon of hope of improvement. The peddler knew only
a day-to-day security, and the small retail shop keeper saw no re-
lease from his endless hours, which brought him a meager return.

The facts of life for the immigrant—a sense of alienation, grind-
ing poverty, long hours—hard as they were did not extinguish
the dream of a better future for his children, nor his commitment
to the ethical values of his tradition. Out of these social and economic conditions there emerged a powerful stream of social
awareness. The situation and the aspirations found literary expression through the pens of writers who constituted the folk
intelligentsia. For the most part, they had themselves experienced the oppressiveness of the sweat shop. From their own experience and observation the writers of this school—former Yeshiva
students, or Russianized, Polonized Jews—created a genre that
found immediate appeal. One distinguishes in their writings a
number of recurrent moods and themes. Morris Rosenfeld's poetry ("I Am a Millionaire of Tears"), particularly his famous
poem, "My Little Boy," are perhaps the best examples of the
self-pity and the tears and the social sentimentality that suffused
much of this writing. Morris Winchevsky's poetry ("Three Sisters") expressed the same mood. Again and again, in the literature of this school, one hears the cry of struggle and the yearning
for improvement of the workers' lot ("You can kill only our body,
our flesh, but not our Holy Spirit"). The mounting resentment
and bitterness found expression in satire, directed against the
"bosses" and all who were allied with the capitalist class. Out of
the personal misfortunes and frustrations, traceable to adverse
economic conditions, there grew the motif of social lyricism. As
persistent as any of these, and growing in intensity with the advancing years, one meets the motif of revolutionary romanticism;
the demand for universal justice and the dream of a brighter
future, when the claims of justice will have been met. To the
names of Rosenfeld and Winchevsky, the outstanding poets of
this period of social awareness, one must add those of Bovshover
and Edelstadt. A complete list of some of the lesser lights would

add up to some two score. Among the pre-eminent prose writers of this school, one includes Z. Libbin, Leon Kobrin, S. Levine, B. Gorin and the dramatist, Jacob Gordon.

The second main current in Yiddish literature, at the end of the last century, consisted of two main streams. One drew its themes from the traditional Jewish motifs of moral ideals and religious aspirations. The other turned to the hope of national pride and revival. The poet Yehoash (Solomon Bloomgarden) was perhaps the most gifted and creative of the poets who drew their material from the national aspects of Jewish life. His poetry employs traditional Jewish images against a background of universal romanticism. Leyssin, on the other hand, turned Jewish national motifs into symbols of both revolution and martyrdom.

By the turn of the century, acclimatization to the American scene was rapidly taking place and newer, younger voices in Yiddish literature emerged. The new writers were inclined toward personal lyricism. Yiddish poetry now took an individualistic turn. The former motifs, based on social and national consciousness, began to recede and served merely as backgrounds for individual self-expression. The writers displaying this tendency might be considered the forerunners of the later impressionists. Prominent among the former, one recalls J. Adler, H. Rosenblatt, the earlier Rolnick, and Joel Slonin among the poets; and Schmuelson and Haimovitch among the novelists. These writers were harbingers of the new impressionist movement and gave it its first impetus. The movement gained its real momentum, however, with the coming of the great stream of immigration that arose after the failure of the First Russian Revolution in 1905.

Impressionism was not merely a caprice of a group of literary aesthetes. It was a new approach to reality, a new feeling, a new mentality. For the impressionists, reality was not exhausted by the outward appearance of the world. An object was more than its outer form. In every object there was an intangible element. It is this intangible element, in its impression upon us, that creates reality. Hence, reality is no longer a stable, static substance. The great impressionist movement, from Edouard Manet to pointillists like Georges Seurat, welded a decisive influence on the

impressionist school in Yiddish literature in America. The latter
appeared in 1907.

The basic aesthetic principles of European impressionism went
into the formation of its Yiddish literary counterpart. If anything,
Yiddish impressionism is more conspicuously individualistic,
more intensely personal, a-social, a-national, and the whole suffused with an aura of despair. This specific intensity is traceable
to the conditions of Jewish immigration life, essentially to its incompatibility with its surroundings and all the psychological com-
plexities arising from this incompatibility. The economic and cultural poverty of the time, the tragedy of being uprooted and
transplanted, these played an important role. Many of these writers, discouraged revolutionists, found their new circumstances too
brutal to accept, and they sought a form of escape. There was a
sense of being lost, alone and superfluous, in the great metropolis
of New York. Their feeling of apprehension strengthened them
in their defeatism and resignation and caused them to exaggerate
their rejected individualism and to recoil into a world of private
illusions. All of their works are replete with a misty, diffused
atmospheric indefiniteness. Such, at least, is the first impression
gained upon reading their poetry. Closer analysis, however, reveals two modes of Yiddish impressionism. Both are marked by
intense subjectivism. True, each poet of this group (*Die Yunge*)
displays a specific individual temperament. There is Moishe Laib
Halpern's or Opatoshu's quick temper and bluster; Joseph Rolnick's and Raboy's works are marked by an excessive calm; Leivick's by an impetuous will; Mani Laib's by a weary etherealness;
Zisho Landau's by a romantic preciosity; Rubin Ireland's by static
images of weary resignation.

One group leaned toward individualism, the expression of personal sadness or resignation, or momentary and fleeting joys.
These writers escaped into a private world of their own; their interests lay in art for art's sake. A second group of impressionists
found their themes in social, national and traditional problems and
hence were closer to reality. The main figures in this latter group
were H. Leivick, Joseph Opatoshu, I. J. Schwartz, Moishe Laib
Halpern, and the later David Ignatoff.

As an outgrowth of impressionism, there emerged a group of poets who stood somewhat apart from the impressionists. They occupied a position midway between the impressionists and the expressionists, who arrived a bit later on the Yiddish literary scene. The most suitable name for this heterogeneous school of writers might be the synthesizers. In their writing, they merged individualistic motifs with social or national themes. Many of them leaned toward impressionism and individualism, but not exclusively so; others among them accentuated social and national problems in their individualistic and sensuous verse. This group includes such poets as Ephraim Auerbach, Bialostotzky, Naftoli Gross, Nissenson, Nochum Yud, I. J. Segal, and A. Lutzky; the prose writers include Borukh Glazman and Shin Miller.

Although this school of poets never formally represented itself as such, it brought to the fore a manner and method which bridged the gap between the impressionists and the expressionists. Each of these poets differed in poetic orientation, in temperament, and in background. But their concepts of art were somewhat similar. They discarded that which was exclusively fanciful, the "swooning romanticism," the "grey monotony" and the "mysticism" of the impressionists. Nevertheless, they clung to an important tendency in Yiddish poetry: their work was suffused with an aura of other-worldliness. As these poets moved away from impressionism, the more weighty and concrete did their art become, the less did they stress "sweet singing," and the nearer did they approach realism, social motives, "themes" and problems.

During the war of 1914-1918, the entire world appeared to have become deformed. Before the chill blast of a general disillusionment, all ideals toppled. The crash was echoed in the subconscious of the creative personality. Deformity became almost synonymous with expressionism. The First World War and the Russian Revolution changed the entire outlook of Yiddish literature. The stability of the "old home," its staid and steady ties now became a thing of the past. They were replaced by a new psychological approach, a new attitude toward oneself and the world. A stranded and thwarted generation now seemed to be endeav-

oring to find its bearings, to re-establish its identity upon a new
foundation, amidst chaos and deformation. The ebb of past romantic experiences and the rise of a new art stimulus, occasioned
by a world now lying in ruins, were evidenced almost at the very
same time in the three centers where Yiddish literature perse-
vered.

Here in the United States, expressionism sailed under a Yiddish
name, *Insichism,* after the anthology and magazine which was
called *In Sich,* published in 1920. Two causes brought forth
*Insichism,* which really means expressionism. These were the
rapid permeation of the literati by Freudianism and the impact
and upheaval of the First World War. Years before the *Insichists*
appeared in our literature, Sigmund Freud had discovered an unfathomable and an abysmal world: our subconscious; its labyrinth
of layers representing the depths within our beings; the baffling
and complicated mechanism of remembering and of forgetting
emotional experiences through associations. *Insichism,* expressionism in general, is based upon this great discovery. This Freud-
ian revelation changed our entire vision, even our understanding
of the outer world. The expressionist thus sees his entire universe,
and all the events encompassing it, only as these are reflected in
his subconscious. In this connection, the fact must be stressed that
expressionism was not an escape into a private world and into
egocentricity *per se.* Expressionism, or its Yiddish equivalent,
*Insichism,* was on the alert to reflect the entire world and every
possible happening. Everything became suitable material for the
*Insichist* poet: the moon, as well as a strike; life on the "great
white way," as well as loneliness; national dreams, religious aspirations, as well as individualistic experiences.

But all of this was not taken from this outer world in a de-
tached, dry and objective manner. Having delved into the inner
depths of his subconscious being, the expressionist found a reflection or a refraction of his outer world. Hence, *Insichism,* a form of
expressionism, denoted a *poetic description of inner visions,* a
chain of associated *mental images.* This depicted a kind of psychological realism, such as we experience in the world of dreams,
or in daytime fantasies, when our eyes, though wide open, yet

peer within and their gaze is averted from the world without. Complex visions, complicated dreams, very often even incomprehensible symbols, these are all to be deciphered before the integral being can truly perceive.

The psychiatrist attempts to reveal the connections between inner symbols, dreams and their references to reality for the practical purpose of remedial treatment of his patient. The expressionist-artist, on the other hand, seeks to register and, very often, to depict the universal meaning of the inner and unknown entities, which reveal themselves in the guise of symbols. Poets of this school are extremely given to suggestiveness and a lavish use of allusions, the latter in the form of association of remote and apparently unrelated symbols. The style clearly indicates the influence of Freud and his psychoanalysis, as well as the dynamics of psychotherapy.

The great catastrophe of 1914 deepened all of these expressionistic tendencies in the direction of complexity. In the flames of the First World War, the world-order was destroyed beyond recognition. Havoc had taken over and the old secret diplomacy, so long relied upon, stood exposed as devastatingly inadequate. To this younger generation it seemed a mockery. Woodrow Wilson's slogan and philosophy—"to save the world for democracy"—was shattered to bits, as the Nazi-fascist regimes which followed somewhat later were to demonstrate. "I am a broken machine" were Woodrow Wilson's last great words.

In our subconsciousness, the totality of these events was registered as the expression of a deformed, bizarre, grotesque world. And when the artist endeavored to describe this appalling condition, he expressed it through a kaleidoscope outlook. He traversed a course from chaos to a state of variegation, from the one phase to many facets, from monotonous verse-form to free verse. To this group belong Leyeless, Glatshtein, Alquit, with a host of others on the periphery. To this sphere, too, belong L. Feinberg, Aleph Katz and Eliezer Greenberg.

By 1925, some sort of stability had been attained, a stability that effected a consolidation of social and, especially, of cultural forces. The world-spectacle having assumed more definite and

more distinguishable contours, the chaos and the disruption sub-
sided. Yiddish poets now achieved greater profundity and maturity in their work. The literature began, as it were, to retrace its
steps, to rediscover conservatism. Thus, traditionalism began to
be expressed in the work of those who were newly arrived upon
the literary scene, as well as in the evolution of the writers of the
previous decades. Traditionalism must not be construed as a return to petrified, dogmatically-accepted concepts, but rather as a
quest leading back to the groundwork, to the stability and order-
liness that existed long ago before the First World War. No doubt
it was not altogether possible to restore that stability, for the new
experiences had brought about too grave a transformation and
had left their all-too-significant impress. Nevertheless, the will to
be sound, moderate and concrete, was palpably evident in every
achievement, in every literary success or failure. This conservatism was true of almost every writer, no matter to what literary
school he adhered. Each in his own manner, in accordance with
his own experiences or temperament, sought to revalue a definite
tradition of the past and to continue its traditional pattern. The
return toward traditionalism brought forth: modern classicism,
neo-realism, and neo-romanticism.

Modern classicism was apparent in the works of almost all expressionists. A return to romanticism was evidenced in the works
of A. Tabachnick, Abba Shtolzenberg, Meir Shtiker, I. Teller,
and many others. Neo-realism came to the fore in the works of the
proletarian writers. Lyric realism is discernible in the short stories
of Chaim Pett, Metzker and Fershleisser.

The yearning for tradition was further deepened by the great
tragedy of the Nazi holocaust. Its meaning assumed an even
greater degree of depth with the establishment of the State of
Israel, for here was concrete verification that we had roots, that
there was continuity from the past to the present.

Thus, in our own day, we note the following important tendencies prevalent in Yiddish poetry. Contemporary verse is
preoccupied with a groping for religious values, for national consciousness and historic mythology, which simply denotes that figures out of the Jewish historic past are recreated by the artist into

universal symbols. But the basic motivation and the basic system of concepts in Yiddish literature in the United States, as in Yiddish literature in general, remains the same: it is firmly rooted in the earthly realities of Jewish life, while it strives to attain loftier reaches and more deeply conceived spiritual values.

# Jewish
# Education in the
# United States

## WILLIAM B. FURIE

Education involves the imparting of knowledge as well as the cultivation of aptitudes and attitudes in the minds of its educands. It concerns itself both with the nature of knowledge and with the good of man in society. Jewish education, Talmud Torah, representing the transmission of the body of teachings of Judaism as the guide and direction of Jewish life in its entirety, has, indeed, been the foundation of vital Jewish living wherever the Jew has gone during the millennia of his history.

Jewish life and consequently Jewish education have been characterized by a homogeneity born out of centuries of self-containment, isolation and detachment from the outside currents. For brief moments, at various points in history some of the barriers were partially let down only to be raised even higher following the relatively fleeting interchange of ideas, mores and experiences. It followed, therefore, that nearly every land harboring settlements of Jews practiced a program of Jewish life and education similar in objectives, content and methods. Almost universally similar conditions brought about a basically unified and identical process of traditional Jewish education.

227

This traditional teaching was not limited to children, as many narrowly construe it today. Jewish learning was regarded as the vocation of childhood and youth, and the avocation of every adult Jew throughout his entire mature life. The pursuit of Jewish knowledge has always been practical in its ends and synonymous with *living* a complete Jewish life. Indeed, our sages succinctly epitomized this point of view when they said that the study of Torah is equivalent in value to the performance of all of the commandments of Judaism.

II

Three centuries ago, the Jew migrated to the shores of the western world. Here the ghetto walls literally and figuratively were eliminated with telling consequences to Jewish living and to Jewish education. In this essay, we shall briefly survey the pattern of this process, evaluate its aims and goals, examine its present status and point up its trends and directions for tomorrow.

The absence of secular schools in the early years of Jewish settlement in the United States invested Jewish schooling with special significance; it literally spared Jews from illiteracy. Regardless of their countries of origin, most newcomers to these shores were still impelled by the common notion of instructing their children to live in accordance with the guiding principles of the Torah as a basis for making their way in this life and in the hereafter.

At maturity, this training aided them in the conduct of daily affairs and gave them status in their social group. It gave further worth to their life in this world by transmitting to them what they needed for the attainment of life eternal. The Jewish community reinforced this personal motivation by establishing the equivalent of a system of compulsory education long before the adoption of this principle by the general environment.

In spite of generally accepted and satisfying educational objectives, records indicate that knowledge of Hebrew and Torah was

noticeably lacking among children of early Jewish American settlers. Except for the few, pupils originally trained on these shores
were often grossly ignorant even of proper Hebrew pronuncia-
tion. This paucity of knowledge stemmed primarily from lack of
implementation of the goals of Jewish education in America. For
the most part, all that was achieved was the ability to read the
prayerbook by rote and a little translation of Pentateuchal passages.

Why was this so? Due to the exigencies and rigors of settlement
conditions, years would frequently elapse between Jewish settlement in a given locality and the organization of a synagogue
and/or an educational set-up. The home, during these intervening years, would then for the most part be the primary Jewish
educational influence, except for the fortuitous availability of
qualified private tutors. And then, where private instruction was
available, it could generally be taken advantage of only by those
with adequate economic means. As a matter of fact, it was the
community's concern for the offspring of the poor that frequently
hastened the establishment of a synagogue or similar organization
in order that these children might enjoy educational opportunities comparable with the opportunities of those able to defray
the cost of instruction.

Another deterrent to a more rapid development of Jewish
schooling in the United States was to be found in the nature of
the early immigrant. The majority of the earliest settlers were not
of learned stock. They were, by and large, average people who
had in Europe acquired only a minimum of Jewish education and
who, under economic pressures, were satisfied with less than
that minimum for their children. The few scholars who had haz-
arded the ocean passage to brave the conditions in the new land
made little progress against this wall of ignorance. Most efforts at
elevating the educational level during the first phase of settlement were frustrated by the cultural inertia of the masses who
wanted and received little.

It is to be noted, however, that the first generation of Sephardic
settlers displayed an interest in non-Jewish studies along with
their exposure to traditional sources and texts—a trend that was

not followed by the succeeding wave of early German immigrants, who concentrated what little educational efforts they made almost exclusively in the Jewish field. In the early Sephardic schools, Hebrew training no longer remained the main concern of instruction. The pupils' time was taken up primarily with English, reading, writing, arithmetic, grammar and spelling; and specifically Jewish studies were relegated to a position of secondary importance. Genuine educational progress became generally unattainable because of constant interruptions of schooling, abandonment of schools and frequent curricular changes, and the lack of qualified personnel. Each group of new arrivals of the Sephardic and early Ashkenazic migrations soon abandoned its cultural aspirations and reconciled itself to inferior educational standards.

In the mid-nineteenth century, later German immigrants arrived who, although not successful in immediately improving the situation, became very articulate in expressing their dissatisfaction with the status of Jewish instruction. The acutely inadequate situation led to the organization of the one-day-a-week classes in some communities and the congregational supplementary school in others. The pioneers in these new approaches themselves viewed their experiments as stop-gap measures rather than as sound and permanent educational devices. By-products of these efforts were the preparation of texts and curricula and the instruction of many children who otherwise would have been exposed to no Jewish education.

Since these were the years prior to the organization and introduction of the public school system, many congregations accepted the obligation of setting up Jewish School programs in combination with secular subjects, as their answer to the drastically challenging needs of the time. These early all-day schools served many a community well until some years following the introduction of the secular school system.

The firm establishment of the public schools coupled with the growth of the Reform notion of minimizing the importance of Hebrew, soon weakened the all-day schools and all but completely eliminated them. One and two-day schools meeting on weekends, in which religious history and other Jewish-content courses in

English predominated, became more popular and were for a time considered to be the ideal educational pattern for the majority of the Jewish community. Enthusiasm gave way to disappointment, however, when it became apparent that the educational harvest was indeed proportionately as poor as the pupils' meager investment in time and energy.

The second half of the nineteenth century witnessed a state of flux and instability in Jewish education. Teachers shifted from position to position without tenure and security, catering to the fancies of whimsical school committees, often holding additional jobs to eke out a meager livelihood. Though lacking scientifically constructed curricula and objectives, the basic aims and goals of Jewish study were clear and unchanging at all times. All strove to rear the new American generation to live lives of morality in accordance with Jewish practices, to fulfill the commandments of God and to worship Him meaningfully. The ideal was religious piety consisting of a knowledge of Torah and a strict observance thereof in practice.

Jewish education in the United States in the nineteenth century was almost exclusively limited to the elementary level, although several attempts were made to establish secondary schools. These efforts were motivated primarily by the need to train rabbis, Hebrew teachers and cantors. For a generation, beginning with 1840, a number of institutions of higher learning were opened in several communities with varying degrees of success, until finally the Hebrew Union College was successfully organized in Cincinnati in 1875. As this College's pattern crystallized and was aimed at serving the needs of the Reform elements, the Conservatives found it necessary a decade later to establish a similar institution, The Jewish Theological Seminary Association in Philadelphia, to disseminate the beliefs and tenets of modern traditional Judaism. The Seminary Association, after floundering for five years following the death of its founder, was reorganized in New York in 1902 as the Jewish Theological Seminary of America, designed to serve the needs of Conservative Judaism. After the founding of more intensive all-day schools, which will be described below, two of the emerging yeshivoth merged in

1915 and developed into the Isaac Elchanan Theological Seminary in New York. This institution served as a reservoir for Orthodox spiritual leadership. Since then, additional rabbinic training schools have been organized in other parts of the country.

Just as the basis of a permanent Jewish community was being established, a flood of immigration from East Europe set in, increasing the American Jewish population eightfold in one generation. The overwhelming majority of the new arrivals consisted of middle-class people, migrating from lands where life was completely steeped in Torah and its ideals. Social and economic pressure, however, denied parents the time and opportunity to supervise properly the educational activities of their offspring. This situation led to the invasion of the Jewish teaching profession by incompetent and often unscrupulous private itinerant tutors, *melamdim*, who, as they took root, opened the private afternoon and evening school which they named after its European prototype, the *heder*. The educative process sank to an all-time low.

Among this group of *melamdim*, there were fortunately a few capable and sincere teachers in many communities, who provided islands of qualified instruction in the wilderness of failure. These dreamers and workers, tilling the vineyard of the Lord, spread Torah intensively among thousands of American Jews. They laid the groundwork for what has blossomed forth as intensive education in the twentieth century.

As before, the children of the poor became the concern of the community. The new leaders of philanthropy, stemming from East Europe and imbued with the sanctity of Torah tradition, began to open adequate schools for the children of the poor, and naturally identified the institution established for this purpose with its old-country equivalent, the Talmud Torah. These institutions explored newer methods, attempted where possible to organize classes on the basis of graded groupings and classification, attracted more qualified personnel and were relatively stable. Ironically, many children were deprived of this improved type of schooling because parents considered their own offspring above the stratum of the "poor" children for whom community provision was made. Gradually, however, these Talmud Torahs overcame the handicaps of limited finances, poor housing and the identification with charity. To the extent that the supplementary afternoon schedule permitted, these schools followed the age-old traditional curriculum which had been in force in the European elementary school, consisting of mechanical Hebrew reading, Siddur prayers, *Chumosh* (Pentateuch) with Yiddish word-by-word rote translation and Rashi's commentaries.

The later elements of the Russian migration brought changes and refinements to the institutions which had just gotten under way. Thus, for example, the Talmud Torah was influenced curriculum-wise by the arrival of groups imbued with the spirit of Haskalah, the European Enlightenment Movement, and with the Love of Zion Movement, introducing a Zionist orientation to Jewish study. This wave of immigration brought with it a large number of learned Jews who served not only as learned leaven but also as the nucleus for a dedicated and spirited teaching corps, yearning and working for the restoration of Hebrew as a living, spoken language. Their zeal added new, classical texts to the Talmud Torah curriculum. Unfortunately, the economic and social status of the Hebrew teacher was not sufficiently attractive to hold many of these teachers, who began to use Hebrew teaching as a stepping stone to more secure and rewarding callings.

III

The year 1910 marked a turning point in Jewish education, a sort of transition from what had been, up to that point, a more-or-less well-developed system. In 1910, the Bureau of Jewish Education came into being in New York, with Dr. Samson Benderly, whose successful Baltimore experiments had earned national repute for him, serving as its administrator. While names are scrupulously avoided in this essay-survey, it seems logically impossible to omit that of Dr. Benderly, whose imprint still rests heavily on the history of Jewish education in this land.

Dr. Benderly systematically began to introduce the science of general education into Jewish education, without sacrificing Jewish content. A pattern was set for central co-ordinating agencies in Jewish education, agencies which have changed the face of the educational process in the past five decades. Some of the major areas in which outstanding progress has been achieved include: educational research, investigation and survey, curriculum evaluation and reconstruction, personnel training and supervision, preparation of texts and materials, propaganda and public relations in the interest of education, standardization within and among communities, professionalization of teachers, building security for educational workers, and educational experimentation. Central agencies, resulting primarily from Dr. Benderly's stimulus, are largely responsible for the extension of Jewish education beyond the elementary level. By gathering together the graduates of various Talmud Torahs and organizing Hebrew high schools, Bureaus influenced impressionable boys and girls to pursue their studies further. These high school departments have been utilized as the source from which Hebrew Teachers' Colleges and Training Schools have drawn many students.

IV

Many significant developments have occurred in Jewish education during the past generation, however dissatisfied many may rightfully be with lack of achievement and genuine progress. With ideal goals yet beyond the horizon, Jewish schooling is much healthier than it was prior to World War I. Today, for example, perhaps through the chance of curtailed immigration and the devastation of European centers rather than by choice or planning, our school staffs are manned for the most part by college-trained, American-produced personnel, instead of the untrained *melamed* described above. Instruction takes place in modern, light, airy, functionally adequate quarters, in contrast to the woefully substandard facilities of the early twentieth century. In our day (for the first time in America) adolescents are beginning to be exposed to Jewish cultural activity. Girls receive instruction in greater and greater numbers. Most gratifying of the many signs of progress witnessed on these shores is the consistency of improvement in Jewish education on all major religious fronts. Each branch or religious denomination has selected its own content and methods and is contributing its share toward the general pool of educational development.

The contemporary Jewish educational scene offers a wide variety of school organization, with sponsoring elements of different denominational types overlapping and resembling one another. Since, among others, there are major differences in curriculum, religious orientation, standards and financial involvement, perhaps we might consider the dominant classifications on the basis of their hours of instruction, which, proceeding from the least to the maximum, include the one-day-a-week school, the weekday afternoon Hebrew School and the private all-day school.

More than fifty per cent of the pupils enrolled in Jewish elementary schools attend one session per week, averaging two hours, either on Saturday or Sunday. These schools are conducted for the most part by Reform and Conservative congregations, with the tendency among the latter group to eliminate the one-day school above the primary department in favor of more intensive study. While not characteristic, some Yiddish labor groups and Orthodox congregations also maintain Sunday School organizations. The curriculum of the one-day school, generally conducted in English, includes elementary approaches to general Jewish history, American Jewish history, selections from the Bible, customs and ceremonies, religious orientation in accordance with the spirit of the sponsoring synagogue, current events, simple demography, usually a little Hebrew sufficient for participation in the more important prayers of the particular group's services, some Hebrew or liturgical singing and some philanthropic activity. Incidentally, it should be noted that in recent years a concerted effort has been made to introduce an additional session or two weekly for the study of Hebrew in the Reform one-day institutions. Since Hebrew plays a minor role in this type of school, teachers usually are recruited from among the current or past public school teaching ranks.

The one-day school is clearly a product of the American scene

and is evidence of the general environment's tendency to influence minority elements, this time borrowing a technique from
Protestant Christianity. Contrary to common opinion, the one-day
school was not an ideological development identified historically
with the Reform movement; it arose in response to the general
dissatisfaction with the accomplishments of Hebrew educational
efforts here in the late nineteenth century. It became a popular
instrument when, to the unperceiving eye, it seemed to transmit
superficially Jewish emphases and background within a schedule
that provided a minimum of conflict with the other activities that
were demanding children's time. Although affording fewer hours
per week, this type of school partially compensates by a higher
degree of retention of its pupils generally until a much later
chronological age than other forms of school organization. In
many quarters sponsoring groups are today concentrating on improvement of methods, expanding curricula, introducing more
qualified personnel technically and Jewishly prepared; also they
are tending to add to the hours of teaching by adding Hebrew
sessions and so-called extra-curricular activities.

Approximately another forty per cent of the Jewish elementary school population receives its training in the weekday afternoon school. Within this category, there is reflected a wide dispar-
ity in the hours of attendance, ranging from two to five sessions,
or from four to ten hours per week. These schools, conducted generally under Orthodox or Conservative congregational or communal auspices, offer courses of study averaging six years, with
some recently having extended their programs to cover eight
years. Unfortunately, the experience of retention of pupils in this
type of school is discouraging. Too frequently pupils enter several
years prior to Bar Mitzvah and leave upon attaining the "sanctity"
of this "all important milestone" in American Jewish ritual
usage. In many cases boys are withdrawn even prior to their thir-
teenth birthday and subjected to a special program of preparation for their performance. The emphasis upon the importance of
Bar Mitzvah has held down the registration of girls in the weekday Hebrew School, although some improvement has been shown
in this connection during the last generation.

The afternoon school or Talmud Torah, as it is often called, provides a curriculum which varies in intensity with each sponsoring group and the weekly hours of instruction. The most common elements of this general type of school include fluency in mechanical Hebrew reading, practice in prayers and their interpretation, some selected passages from or abridgment of the Pentateuch and early Prophets, customs and ceremonies, some current events, philanthropy projects, slight exposure to outstanding Jewish personalities and simple Jewish history, with an added offering of a group of supplementary activities. It has adapted itself to the American scene, salvaging as many hours of instruction as possible, and transmitting to its pupils a sense of close identification with historic Judaism. The constant reduction in hours brought with it obviously a resultant shrinkage in the scope of the traditional curriculum. The weekday afternoon school, rather than devising and developing a program native to the American scene, has for decades been engaged in an unloading operation, with but the skeleton of the original remaining.

This program has been acceptable to a large segment of the Jewish people interested in what they term "intensive" education, as compared with the offerings of the one-day school. However, a nucleus of American Jews has not permitted this meagre fare to sate its cultural appetites. This devoted and enthusiastic group somehow senses the impossibility of honestly transmitting to their young the vast literary heritage, the very soul, of their people, in so few hours. At the same time, anxious that their children be able to take advantage of many general and cultural and recreational activities available on the American scene without restraining them day and night, these parents are interested in better balancing their children's "work" day. They are willing to make the additional economic sacrifice required by the support of the private all-day school. This type of institution conducts sessions during the morning and afternoon and combines the secular and Jewish educational programs. The growth of this form has been unpredictably rapid and sustained not only among its logical supporters, the Orthodox, but among Conservative, Yiddishist and Hebraist elements as well; until now the pupils registered in the all-day schools comprise almost ten per cent of the elementary school population.

Naturally there are many variations as to curriculum, emphases, schedule. Most recently, a new development has been the combination, in such programs as that of the Foundation School, of the all-day school and the public school. In this arrangement, children attend the all-day school from the nursery level up to and through the primary grades and thereafter continue in the public school. This results in a more basic preparation and facilitates subsequent progress in the afternoon Hebrew school. While valid observations are difficult at this point, because of the newness of the venture, first indications are that the harvest to date more than justifies the investment of energy and finances so necessary to maintain this costliest of all educational forms. These schools are already laying the foundations for secondary school studies.

A heartening development in recent years, particularly with the support of central agencies, has been the secondary school systems. Pupils are encouraged to continue their studies beyond the point of elementary school graduation, naturally paralleling the level of intensity of their previous studies. Upon reaching high school, boys and girls begin the serious study of the classical texts of their heritage, the Bible, the Talmud and its commentaries, medieval and modern Hebrew literature, Jewish philosophy and religion, Jewish history, Zionist literature, as well as Jewish music and sources of current happenings. From their ranks there seem to be emerging Jewish literates who are assuming positions of leadership on the lay and professional levels. Indeed, following completion of these high school courses, more and more pursue Jewish scholarship further in teacher training institutes, in rabbinical seminaries, in schools preparing for Jewish social work, in cantor training schools, and in general graduate schools for Jewish studies. These are the spawning points out of which may emerge that American Jewish scholarship, that indigenous torch of learning which promises cultural salvation and spiritual uplift for the Jew in his fourth century on the American continent.

Already, secondary schooling has responded to some of the dire spiritual needs of our times, chief among them the beginning of training the personnel needed to implement the various developing educational programs described in this paper. This phase of preparation began in the nineteenth century with the establishment of Gratz College in Philadelphia, an institution which somehow has managed to average the production of ten graduates per year over a period covering a little more than half a century.

Some twenty years after the founding of Gratz College, the Conservative Movement brought into being the Teachers Institute of the Jewish Theological Seminary, which from its very inception was guided by another of those pioneering educational geniuses whose name must be mentioned even in an article that deliberately omits personalities, Rabbi Mordecai M. Kaplan. This revered educator has reared an entire generation of disciples in whose hands are vested the educational leadership of the major Jewish communities of America. The Teachers Institute was the first to operate on a full-time schedule, offering courses not only to teachers-to-be but to many teachers already in service. Early in its development, this institute tied in organically with Teachers College of Columbia University, bringing the latest findings of modern educational science to bear directly on the Jewish field. In an era which frequently witnessed competition among many of the forces operating in the American community, Teachers Institute offered an example of community cooperation through its close work in collaboration with the Bureau of Jewish Education of New York. Perhaps this mutually helpful joint functioning explains the growing tendency on the part of so many congregational schools to work together through the guiding hands of the central agencies for Jewish education.

The third decade of the twentieth century witnessed the opening of the first teachers training institution under Orthodox auspices, the Mizrachi Teachers Institute, which later merged with the Isaac Elchanan Theological Seminary. This school naturally stressed classical texts rather than methods, techniques and philosophies, and its graduates have greatly intensified Hebraic education. Additional teacher training schools came into being in metropolitan areas, including Baltimore, Boston, Chicago, Cleveland,

Detroit, and Minneapolis. Basically following earlier patterns, these schools, stressing divers ideologies and emphases, all in all offer one of the bright spots in an educational picture that carries many gloomy areas.

Jewish education in recent years has been meeting its challenges with newer responses. Admittedly the trend toward curtailing the Jewish school year from approximately a fifty to a thirty-five week span, and the less frequent classroom visits even during this shortened season, stimulated the exploitation of the increased free-time of the summer period. A chain of successful experiments led to the development of a number of summer camps which combine study and play in pleasurable experiences to the delight and growth of the student-campers. Sponsored by all-day schools, teachers training colleges, national and regional educational bodies, central agencies, ideological groups and others, a constantly growing number of day and resident camps has been established under the direction of educators, rabbis, social workers and enlightened lay leaders. Programs of varying intensity are maintained, ranging from formal classes under natural and desirable conditions on the one hand, to competely informal recreational activity immersed in and colored by a completely Jewish atmosphere and pattern of living on the other. In some programs, Hebrew is featured as the spoken language; in others, the creative arts play a leading role in exposing the young camper and the teachers and group-leaders-in-training to Jewish living marked by aesthetically and spiritually elevating experiences. Each fall, therefore, campers return home elated, inspired, hearty and fresh in body and in spirit, ready to continue in their home environment that which was experienced at camp. Maintaining this enthusiasm and heightened spirit then becomes the challenging responsibility of the home, the school and the community.

v

For the past thirty years and more, Jewish educators and communal leaders in the United States, in spite of the significant progress already indicated, have been keenly aware of the general inadequacy of the school program in most of our educational efforts. It has been apparent that ours is predominantly a literary curriculum, transplanted from Eastern Europe without proper adjustment to the American scene; hence its patent ineffectiveness. Undoubtedly, the Jewish school did originally reflect Jewish life; but on these shores this becomes increasingly difficult. For, since Jewish life is relatively limited in its scope by the non-Jewish environment, the premise that the school be a reflection of life can at best have but a limited application in the Jewish school. The curriculum of the Jewish school, it has long been advocated, should, therefore, be adapted to the conditions of life in this country. This, of course, means the adaptation of Jewish values to the social, economic and cultural conditions under which American Jews live.

In response to this desperate challenge, then, our educational philosophers have been hard at work attempting to crystallize the manifold ramifications of the complex problems into simple rules of operation. First, tentative aims and objectives were articulated. These defined the goals of American Jewish education as the development within our educands of the following desires and capacities: to participate actively and meaningfully in Jewish life; to understand and appreciate, where possible, the Hebrew language and literature; to put into practice Jewish religious and ethical patterns of conduct; to appreciate and adopt Jewish aspirations; and, to express Jewish values through artistic creativity. As noted, the emphasis in this cataloguing of objectives was upon the perpetuation of Jewish life and culture. Early in the twentieth century, pioneering Jewish educators began to come under the influence of leading American educators of the John Dewey school, and soon clearly realized that the foregoing aims had also to reckon with the general well-being and growth of the individual child. With "child centeredness" as a new criterion, the feeling grew that the Jewish educative process should start with the actual experiences of the child as he lives them in the present, and lead him constantly to reorganize and reinterpret his experiences so that he comes to identify his own good with the good of society in general, in a manner indicative of growth in mind and character.

Thus, the objectives of Jewish education, restated from the standpoint of the child, began to be formulated by early Jewish educational philosophers, as follows: To give insight into the meaning of spiritual values and their application to different types of experience; to foster an attitude of respect toward human personality as such; to train appreciation of individual and group creativity in the values of civilization; to inculcate ideals of justice and kindness in our social and economic relationships; to condition habits of reflective thinking and purposive experiencing; to impart the knowledge of the Hebrew language, Jewish history, Bible, Talmudic literature, and similar subject matter as instruments of the preceding objectives.

Lists of aims of this type were received skeptically by many. How, it was asked, could such an utopian program be implemented? First, of course, it was pointed out that goals of this nature could not rest solely upon the school but required the cooperation of many social elements. This led to our being reminded by modern educationists that the latest concepts in the field insisted that education is definitely not a process distinct from life itself; nor should it, as only too often it is, be confined to the four walls of the classroom. We were admonished to forsake the growing notion that the Jewish school is the almost exclusive conveyor of Jewish education. Formal classroom instruction is to be regarded as only one link in a chain of factors instrumental in transmitting Jewish culture and values to our children. Above all, we were told to bear in mind at all times that if an activity is to develop a child's interest in Jewish life, he must be made to feel that he is a necessary part of the Jewish community.

Philosophical aims such as these, for example, coincided with later developments in Jewish life. One of them illustrates the ap-

plication of some of the new principles in evolving survival patterns. Early Jewish settlement, for many historical and sociological reasons, had centered around the larger metropolitan
communities in this country. Within these communities, in turn,
the tendency was for the development of compact, closely-knit,
centralized Jewish groupings. The pattern has been changing
within recent times; and now a trend toward urban decentraliza-
tion is in full swing. This movement outward has highlighted the
emergence of the Synagogue-Center as a dominant organizational unit. Catering to many of the religious, cultural, and social
needs of its affiliates, this new type of congregation has brought
about a familial group set-up, in which the coordinating organization exerts a greater influence than in the past. Thus, to illustrate, almost every newly-developing congregation has from its
very inception developed a Jewish school, a type of school which
seems to be replacing the large and prosperous Talmud Torahs of
the immediate past. It is true that many congregational schools
have experienced serious problems in curtailed hours of instruction, improperly graded and classified groupings, inadequate
personnel, and, therefore, lower standards when measured by the
yardstick of the literary curriculum. Offsetting these disadvan-
tages, however, the congregational school has had a greater holding and influencing power because of the institution's catering
to and serving the entire family unit, as well as the totality of the
child's felt needs through all sorts of activities that aid and supplement the formal instruction of the classroom, and through the
greater home-school cooperation and complementary activities
made possible by the concept of the expanded family approach.

The fascinating question remains, of course, as to whether it is
the educational philosophy that guides and sustains new approaches and methods, or whether the philosophy merely reflects
the changes that inexorable time has a knack of introducing. An
illustration of this point is a type of Jewish educational institution
that we have but scarcely mentioned thus far: the Yiddish culture
school. With the tremendous influx to the United States early in
the twentieth century of large masses of working classes whose
mother tongue was Yiddish, a cultural movement arose revolving

around this language. Yiddish schools were subsequently developed which, while functioning physically on schedules comparable to the Talmud Torahs and one-day schools, were notably different in content and emphasis. Their curricula usually included such subjects as Jewish history, Yiddish literature, Yiddish folk music, folk dances, Jewish art, and current events. Generally these schools were unrelated to synagogues and followed that portion of Jewish customs that bordered upon the folk mores, rather than that based on supernatural aspects of religion. There were ideological and cultural differences even within the Yiddishist movement. Groups similar to those sponsored by the Poale Zion naturally included the study of Hebrew and Zionism; whereas most of the other elements chose to ignore these facets of Jewish background. During the height of the dominance of Yiddish as a language of communication and cultural satisfaction, there were quite a few schools of this type, most of them having relatively small pupil-population. But here relentless time has been at work. With Yiddish-speaking immigration cut off almost completely, the second and third generation in this land more and more find themselves unable to understand and use what, to them, has become an insignificant foreign language; so that, from our educational perspective, it would appear that the Yiddish culture school has been a passing phenomenon in the Jewish readjustment to the American cultural scene.

## VI

A number of problems that will undoubtedly engage the planners of Jewish education in the coming decades may be briefly described.

The first is that of recruitment of effective, adequately trained personnel. Jewish education faces a situation in which the percentage of enrollment in Jewish schools is on the increase while the number of available teachers is diminishing. Neither the economic returns involved nor the status of the Jewish teaching profession are presently attractive enough to draw a sufficient number of high calibre, dedicated people into the field. While the problem has been subject to considerable discussion in professional circles, little of a constructive nature, pointing towards a remedy for the critical situation, has as yet emerged.

Again, means must be found whereby the trend which virtually limits Jewish education to juveniles is arrested and reversed. True, some progress has been made in recent years in attempts to include adolescents and adults within the orbit of Jewish education. But to date the results have been on the meagre side. The problem calls for bold, imaginative programs, new devices and techniques, with the ultimate goal of an all-year-round educational program that offers learning on various levels for the entire age range of the Jewish community. We must be prepared to counsel Jews on how to utilize some of their increasing leisure time for the purpose of Jewish self-enhancement.

Finally, Jewish education confronts the problem of providing a learning that will at once reach the masses and provide the background for the future spiritual and intellectual elite of American Jewry—its scholars, writers, rabbis and thinkers—and, at the same time, set up lines of communication between the two groups. A vital indigenous American Judaism presupposes both "consumers" and producers of Jewish culture, and the latter presupposes the former. The development of an audience receptive to and concerned for creative Jewish expression in its various aspects, is no mean task in the American cultural climate. Indeed, it is formidable enough to discourage the boldest spirit. But seen against the background of the long, upward climb of Jewish education in America, this problem, like those described above, may well find its solution at the hands of the educators who, undaunted by conditions of chaos and decay, have brought Jewish learning to its present growing, improving status.

# Jewish
# Music in
# America

## HUGO D. WEISGALL

A survey of Jewish music in America can easily
be bogged down at the outset by ever-recurring
semantic difficulties. It would seem that every
time the subject of Jewish music is broached, these selfsame problems intrude. Does Jewish music exist? And if so, what makes it
Jewish?

Certainly it is not the chief purpose of this essay to resolve
these questions. Let us, however, posit the existence of Jewish
music for purposes of argument; and, for the sake of clarity, propose a definition.

It appears that the most fruitful approach to such a definition is
provided by the concept of functionalism which maintains that
the nature of a work of art is determined by its function. If this
concept is applied to the problem at hand we may conclude first
of all, that Jewish music is that music which is used by Jews *qua*
Jews in their various activities, and also that it includes that music
which, from its very inception as music, functions Jewishly. As
illustrations of these two categories we cite: ( 1 ) the familiar Han-
nukah melody *Mooz Tzur* (which may or may not be a variant

of a German folk song), and (2) Darius Milhaud's Purim opera
*Esther de Carpentras.* Further to spell out the implications of this
definition, it is contended that there are no specific, objective musical qualities which make a piece Jewish or not. On the other
hand, a composer's intentions (frequently expressed, but often to
be assumed) are considered primary determining factors in the
classification of a work.

Perhaps this definition may be an arbitrary one, but its positive
advantages are numerous. It readily enables one to categorize
Jewish music within the general field of music; similarly we can
identify French music or Catholic music. Thus established, Jewish
music can be subjected to rigorous aesthetic judgment, and if
desired, the additional criterion of "suitability for Jewish purposes" also can be applied. A telling argument in favor of functionalism is that extraneous problems are easily avoided. Metaphysical considerations such as: what are the Jewish qualities in
Gershwin's *Porgy and Bess,* or in Schönberg's *Opus* 11, fascinating though they may be, do not have to be considered within the
scope of this definition. With these considerations in mind let us
consider our main theme.


I


Jewish music in America before the first World
War has little to recommend it. Its recorded material does not
antedate the third quarter of the nineteenth century, and does
not become sizable before its close. The circumstances in which
this music was produced and developed easily explain its lack
of distinction. The historian concerned with American Jewish
thought will do well to examine these nineteenth century music
collections, these hymnals and songsters, for they are not insignificant sociological documents. To the musician, however, this music is the pitifully weak record of a pioneer community uncertain
of its musical past, and fearful for its future. There can be no
question of comparison between this music and the Negro spiritual which was growing up at the same time. Moreover, this Jew-

ish music lacks both the virility sensed in the best of the New
England hymn books, and the occasional primitive charm found
in the "shape note" music further South.

Though most of this material has been summarized in some detail by Idelsohn, in his still indispensable volume *Jewish Music*,
certain principal facts must be restated here. Above all, it must be
noted that during the first two and a half centuries of American
Jewish life, Jewish music is synonymous with synagogue music.
The same situation prevailed in Europe, with the notable exception of the Jewish folk song which was sprouting in different
places. It is regrettable that we have no precise records of the
music used by Sephardic congregations in this country in the
eighteenth and early nineteenth centuries. Thus, the early Jewish
music that survives stems from one chief source. It is the music
of early American Reform. One part of it is indistinguishable
from contemporaneous German and Anglo-American Protestant
church music. Indeed, the consistency with which traditional
Jewish materials were avoided makes it abundantly clear that
conscious efforts were being made to approximate these non-
Jewish models as closely as possible. In contrast with this music,
nerveless, trite (but adequately constructed and grammatically
correct), there are at least two native literary figures who worked
with this music and whose names deserve mention. In the earlier
part of the century there is the Charleston poetess Penina Moise
(1797-1880), several of whose hymn texts became current in the
Reform ritual, and later there appears the work of the gifted
Emma Lazarus (1849-1887), who contributed some excellent
translations from the Hebrew to the Hymnal issued in 1886 by
Dr. Gustav Gottheil. How consistently the Jewish creative spirit
prefers the ideating disciplines of literature to all the other arts!

Side by side with these dreary Jewish hymnals and songsters,
which so faithfully reflect their equally moribund non-Jewish
counterparts, there was another important musical influence at
work in Jewish music. The vast appeal of nineteenth century Italian opera is nowhere more apparent than in its ultimate fusion
into the music of the American Reform Temple. Unhappily, this
union was not consummated directly. Italian opera had first to

pass through the "refining fire" of what we today identify as "salon music" to emerge transfigured as Temple music. The lilting valse-like tune of *Father Hear Thy Suppliant Children*, still used as the chief Confirmation hymn in scores of musically unenlightened Temples, the thinly disguised, completely platitudinous versions of the *Miserere* from *Il Trovatore* or the *Sollenne quest' Ora* from *La Forza del Destino* sung to the text of *Shiviti* in the Yom Kippur memorial service—these are grim survivals of a taste which became fashionable almost a century ago. Lest it be thought that this sin is peculiarly one of Reform, let us hasten to add that to-day's Orthodox and Conservative synagogues frequently continue not only to employ this type of "operatic" music, but feature a kind of military music in their numerous march-like settings of liturgical texts, which is musically and ideologically much more suspect.

The name of Sigmund Schlesinger (1835-1906) is mentioned for historical purposes only, as the most typical and best known composer of this kind of music. He came from Württemberg via Munich to settle in Mobile, Alabama, where he served as choir-master and organist of Temple Shaarey Shomayim for forty years. He enshrines in his music the absurd combination of an Italian romanticism (which, when debased and debauched, becomes German sentimentalism) with a quasi-virile Anglo-German oratorio style. All is direct, easy to sing, easy to listen to, unproblematic and above all, completely extroverted. Obviously, his music became immensely popular.

To fill out the record, passing note must be made of a few other men who actively participated in the music of Reform. None attained Schlesinger's renown; none was as bad. There were Alois Kaiser (1840-1908), Morris Goldstein (1840-1906), Samuel Welsh (1835-1901), indifferent composers each, whose joint effort, a four volume collection of synagogue music entitled *Zimrath Yah*, never rises above a futile mediocrity. A more curious combination is the work of Max Spicker (1856-1912) and William Sparger (1860-?). Unlike Schlesinger, their operatic locale shifted from Italy to France and Germany. Their *Seu Sheorim* is adapted from Gounod, and when inspiration flags they turn unabashedly to invoke the solemnities of Wagner's *Rienzi*. Both Gounod and Wagner are given due credit as a sign of pride, one feels, rather than as an acknowledgment of just debts properly paid. Finally, there was Edward Stark (1863-1918), somewhat different from his contemporaries. His music has more substance, though at the same time he finds it immensely difficult to sustain the level. As a welcome change there is some identification with a Jewish past. This was a good omen of things to come.

## II

The music of Orthodoxy and what today is the Conservative movement can be considered together, though this music is more difficult to describe owing to the lack of historical records. It is fairly safe to assume that, in the German congregations which grew up in the second half of the nineteenth century and remained traditional congregations, the various customary *nushaot* were employed, plus the standard European synagogue repertoire. The works of Sulzer, Naumbourg, Lewandowski, and Weintraub comprised the chief fare, in addition to whatever other composers a particular *hazzan* may have been acquainted with.

Frequently this music was performed in arrangements made for existing local conditions. Many times during the process of transcription or copying the name of the rightful composer disappeared to be superseded by the name of the local transcriber, arranger or copyist. Sometimes in the case of a long text, such as the *Min Hametzar*, or one of the Yom Kippur *piyutim*, particularly adventurous "composers" might even attempt to combine compositions, culling the most melodious and the most effective parts from each to be combined in one great overwhelming potpourri.

With the gradual disappearance of the German element and the influx of East European Jews, both the *nusah* (traditional mode) and choral music underwent great changes. Omitting the occasional pieces by such composers as Novakowsky, Schorr,

Shestapol or Gerovich, most of the choral music again derived
from the theatre. This time the influence was not an operatic one
but came by way of Second Avenue and the Yiddish theatre.
Nostalgically, this music may seem to have some value. It certainly elicited and continues to evoke an active and fervent response from those people who heard it in their childhood. To
those who did not it can only be a source of wonder, amusement
or perhaps even mild desperation.

The story of East European *nusah* in America is not to be dis-
sociated from the figures of the "star" *hazzanim*. The problem of
the "star" *hazzan* and his influence on American Jewish music is a
subtle one not easily disposed of in a brief survey. Most writers
on Jewish music tread lightly when this treacherous ground is
approached. Again there can be no question of the great effect
these *hazzanim* had and continue to have on the minds and
hearts of their devoted listeners. The objective musician tends to
be more critical. Exhibitionism without content, no matter how
great the virtuosity, soon palls. It is certainly not a healthy creative influence and becomes vulgarized quickly. Idelsohn writes
delicately of Rosenblatt, Hershman and Kvartin. Of their phono-
graph records he says "By the latter means they have popularized
(and at times vulgarized) the Synagogue song." Later on, "none
have thus far created music of any originality." This writer, if
sufficiently goaded, might be tempted to use stronger language.

III

In summarizing the foregoing it may be helpful
to consider these facts from several viewpoints. Judged aesthetically, we may conclude that up to 1914 Jewish music in America
did not show much promise of developing into a significant cultural movement. Neither in the Reform temples nor in the Orthodox and Conservative synagogues was the traditional material
revitalized in any way. And what was new was second rate. Nowhere could one distinguish an authentic voice.

Viewed against the specific background of American music

these facts remain gloomy, but somehow manage to fit into the picture. American music at the turn of the century was just beginning to find itself and assume its place in the mainstream of Western culture. It is perhaps entirely unreasonable to have expected more from American Jewry, whose communities were still small and, for the most part, not yet stabilized.

It is only when we examine the over-all condition of Jewish music as part of general music history at the end of the nineteenth and beginning of the twentieth century, that the true significance of the foregoing facts emerges. Certainly week to week performance standards in European synagogues were higher than they were here. The *nushaot* were also better known and probably more intimately appreciated and preserved. Creatively, however, the differences between Europe and America tend to become obliterated. For if the truth must be told, European Jewish music had not fulfilled the splendid hopes of the first half of the century. We had long known that Sulzer was no Schubert, Weintraub no Glinka, Lewandowski no Mendelssohn, nor was Naumbourg a Meyerbeer. Yet all these men wrote music that was stylistically valid, and on the basis of what they had accomplished there was a reasonable hope that some major musical figure active in Jewish music would arise. This did not happen. And the swarm of minor Jewish composers who wrote and published from about 1880 to 1910 did very little that had not been done before and done better. They neither developed new methods of expression within traditional Jewish idioms, nor did they absorb the new vocabularies and techniques which were springing up around them. For the most part those were sterile years.

During the past four decades these conditions have changed. To examine these changes in our country comprises the second part of our task.

IV

The ideas, the movements, the personal influences which have brought about a flowering of Jewish music in

America during the past forty years are for the most part still operative today. Jewish nationalism (with all that the term implies), the maturing of the American Jewish community, and the gradual decay of Jewish life in Europe are the factors which have shaped our musical life since 1914. The same forces which fashioned our music have affected all other phases of American Jewish life.

It is not always easy to distinguish one of these factors from another in any given situation. Nor is it intended to force all the facts into a preconceived framework bounded by these ideas. When dealing with manifestations of the human spirit one must frequently accept what one finds; often there are no explanations. However, in an attempt to give a somewhat unified account of a mass of complex and unrelated data we will again forsake chronology and deal generally with our material in terms of the forces or movements referred to in the preceding paragraph.

The factor chiefly responsible for the rise of Jewish music in America has been the continued presence in this country of many of the world's leading Jewish composers, performers, and musical scholars. Although native American Jews are becoming increasingly active in Jewish music, the great impetus (at least creatively) has come and continues to come from a group of men who came here from Europe with reputations already firmly established. These men did much to widen the horizons of Jewish music in this country. Their work frequently caused the public to alter its own circumscribed notions of what Jewish music is or should be. Their general recognition as significant contemporary composers largely removed the stigma of parochialism from Jewish music. Their work made it possible to apply to Jewish music that "rigorous aesthetic judgment" to which reference is made in the opening paragraphs of this paper. People concerned with these matters had long been applying a double standard when thinking of Jewish music—music on the one hand—Jewish music on the other. Now there was no further need for apologies.

Ernest Bloch, the first major composer to write consciously as a Jew since Salamone Rossi (fl. 1600-1628), came here during the first World War. Though one may wish to quarrel with many aspects of Bloch's work, it is impossible to overestimate his personal contribution to Jewish music. Nor can one deny that in the eyes of the world he, more than any other single composer, has moulded the image of Jewish music. Of the many works he has written here since 1916 the most important, from our point of view, is the *Sacred Service* (1932). This work is unique because here at last a composer of the first magnitude has given the Hebrew liturgy the large and spacious musical setting it deserves. The Service is distinguished by a dramatic lyricism, a transparency of texture and an elusive simplicity, a combination of qualities which other less gifted composers have since frequently sought to imitate unsuccessfully. It has become a twentieth century classic, but even more surprising is the fact that, despite its avoidance of traditional material (except in the *Tzur Yisroel*), it has already attained a permanent place as an integral part of American synagogue music. It is of particular significance to note that however fortuitous the business of commissioning works of art may be, this Service is a product of the Reform movement. Here it remains but to point out that Bloch has been teacher and mentor to a whole generation of American composers, including such diverse personalities as Douglas Moore and Roger Sessions. He has never been prominently identified with causes or movements, and his Jewishness has always been a personal and musical matter.

Unlike Bloch, who nurtured his Jewish idiom quite alone and ideologically uncommitted, there came to this country within a few years of the Bolshevik Revolution a group of Russian Jewish composers and scholars who had long been identified with Jewish music, and had worked together in the famous Society for Jewish Folk Music. The more prominent members of this group include the late Joseph Achron, Solomon Rosowsky, Lazare Saminsky, Jacob Weinberg, and Joseph Yasser. Since their arrival in this country, each of these men in his own way has made important contributions to the advancement of Jewish music.

Most important has been the work of Lazare Saminsky. Unfortunately, a searching critical appraisal of his music has not yet appeared, and his accomplishments as a composer are not gen-

erally as well known in this country as they deserve to be. Even
in the most cursory review of Jewish music in America, his name
looms so large that the chief facts must be rehearsed once more.

Saminsky's outstanding achievement in American Jewish music
(leaving aside his creative work for the moment) has been his
one-man fight for decent standards. At Temple Emanu-El, New
York, where he has been musical director since 1924, he has
attained them. There is probably no other temple or synagogue
in the country where similar standards prevail. In view of the
scores of magnificent choruses scattered all over the country in
American churches, it seems pathetic to be forced to single out
this one Jewish congregation. Of perhaps equal importance has
been Saminsky's sponsorship of young composers and his ability
to attract good new talent into the synagogue. No doubt it was
owing directly to his inspiration that the Choir Committee of
Temple Emanu-El commissioned the Services by Frederick
Jacobi (1931), Joseph Achron (1932), Isadore Freed (1939),
not to mention the many new and old scores Saminsky has performed at his annual Three Choir Festival. If we add to these
activities a not inconsiderable body of critical writing, a tireless
enthusiasm, a brain packed with new schemes and ideas, and a
fondness for the direct and incisive phrase, it may be possible to
imagine what Saminsky, the non-composer, is like.

It serves little purpose to describe Saminsky's music in general
terms. To do so is to crouch behind a few of the hundred and one
phrases available alike to every reader and writer of workaday
music criticism. Perhaps it may be said that the best of Saminsky's
music, typified by such a work as *By the Rivers of Babylon,* has
qualities of sweetness, joyous ecstasy, a gentle and a turbulent
lyricism, combined with a virile sense of sound and movement.
We have in Saminsky one of the most sensitive composers of our
time.

Obviously in an article of these proportions it is not possible to
mention or consider each personality, let alone do them justice.
Nonetheless we cannot leave this group of composers without a
few words devoted to Joseph Achron. Here again is a formidable
body of work that demands critical attention. More than ten years

have passed since his death, and all we have are a few articles and a chapter in a book. Worse than this is the fact that so many of his major works remain in manuscript. Under existing conditions it is virtually impossible to form a proper estimate of the man and his work. There is, however, no doubt that Achron was one of the most gifted of the Russian-Jewish composers. Of particular interest was his constant concern with Jewish materials which he used as the basis of his music. In his best work he succeeds, like Janacek and Bartók, in making the idiom of the particular serve as the language of the universal.

Without in any way presuming to assign relative values to individual lives, American Jewry cannot help but be grateful that so many first rate creative minds were spared the Jewish doom which settled upon Europe from 1933 to 1945. Many gifted leaders perished, many fortunately escaped to enrich Jewish life here, in Great Britain, and of course in Israel. It is still too soon to estimate accurately the effect of this large influx of competent and talented individuals on American Jewry, though obviously their impact has been very great. In no phase of general American life has the influence of these immigrants, Jewish and non-Jewish, been more apparent than in music. American music has been made infinitely richer by the few years Bela Bartók lived and wrote here, by Paul Hindemith's having trained half a generation of composers, by Arnold Schönberg's austere vision of beauty, by Darius Milhaud's infectious personality and his direct approach to the problems of creation. Jewish music too has benefited greatly. The contributions of composers such as Schönberg and Milhaud, the scholarship of a man like Eric Werner, and the work of many other composers and performers, who in one way or another have been drawn into the field of Jewish music, will figure very significantly in the final and definitive evaluation of the Jewish music of our time. A partial list of the better known composers in this grouping includes the names of Kurt Weill, Mario Castelnuovo-Tedesco, Ernst Toch, Karel Rathaus, Herbert Fromm, Herman Berlinski, Julius Chayes, Stefan Wolpe, and Heinrich Schalit.

Particularly challenging to the future of Jewish music has been

the work of Arnold Schönberg and Darius Milhaud. It is fitting
that among the last works of Schönberg there should have been
at least three that must be classified as Jewish. Schönberg's road
back to Judaism was long and hard, travelled perhaps only as a
sign of protest not conviction, though the *Kol Nidre,* the cantata,
*A Survivor from Warsaw,* and his setting the *Min Hametzar*
might belie the latter half of this statement. Here is Jewish music
which many would fail to recognize as Jewish; it has been in-
dignantly spurned. Yet here, perhaps the most seminal musical
mind of the twentieth century has chosen to write as a Jew. For
the sake of the future the challenge cannot be ignored.

Equally challenging though musically not so problematic are
the Jewish works of Darius Milhaud. How different his approach
to Judaism! *"Je suis musicien français d'origine Israélite,"* reads
the first sentence of his autobiography. The consequences follow
naturally. Milhaud's chief Jewish work written in America has
been a setting of the Sabbath morning Reform liturgy (with additional numbers for Friday evening). How French, how "un-
Jewish" this music sounds to the worshipper accustomed to
Ashkenazic *nusah* intoned with Germanic, Magyar or Slavic variations. Yet can one conceivably deny the Jewishness of this service when we can point out page and line showing Milhaud's use
of material from the *Minhag Carpentras?* Apart from its unmistakable Jewish stamp, the musical qualities of this piece are such
that many would place it on a par with that of Bloch's, and still
others would place it higher. The Service is constructed section-
ally as is Bloch's, though unlike Bloch's, it contains many long instrumental passages intended to be played while certain prayers
are being read. The chief impressions are of serenity, light, joy
and ease, and a species of Gallo-Hasidic intimacy with the Deity.

Surely the contributions of former Europeans to Jewish music
in America have been great. Without estimating the role that
America has played in this it is safe to say that Jewish music has
never flourished any place in the world as it has here in our time.
The American locale has by no means been an insignificant factor.

V

To isolate the elements of nationalism in Jewish music in America is a complex task. The semantic problems pile up very quickly and the predispositions of any writer do not remain hidden for long. Even if one adopts a most limited and conservative position with regard to nationalism it is difficult to deny the potency of this force and the direct and indirect influence it has had on our music.

The area of Jewish music in America most intimately connected with nationalism is the Jewish folk song. Here is another field which could very well be illumined by a series of monographic studies. During the years of mass immigration from Europe the Yiddish folk song must have been an important cohesive factor in Jewish life. For first generation Americans it provided the chief linguistic and musical link with their European backgrounds. Strangely enough, there seems little evidence of any Yiddish folk songs having originated here, despite the fact that the music of the Yiddish theatre was "folksy," immensely popular, and could reasonably have provided a fertile breeding ground.

With the growth of the Zionist movement and the gradual decline in the use of Yiddish, the Hebrew folk song slowly replaced the Yiddish folk song. That is about how matters stand today. If there is any genuine folk music now extant among the Jews of America it consists largely of the folk songs imported from Palestine and subsequently from Israel for a period of over thirty years. It might not be superfluous to indicate that on the whole, the musical trappings in which these folk songs have been attired have not been of very high calibre. The best arrangements smack of an easy sophistication and a slick use of "contemporary" techniques. No composer in America, with the exception of Milhaud, has provided settings of Jewish folk songs comparable in quality with those produced by Bela Bartók, Maurice Ravel or Benjamin Britten. Unfortunately, the same negative judgment must be made of all the "original" music written here in a Jewish "folk" style or employing folk motives. True, much of this music is intended as *gebrauchsmusik,* but these utilitarian motives, frequently belied by pompous, deceptive sub-titles such as "symphonic cantata," do little to justify piddling arrangements of folk material. No one in America has yet done with the Jewish folk song what Copland or Cowell have been able to do with the American folk song.

VI

The future of Jewish music in America depends largely on the increasing maturity of the American Jewish community. Such maturity is essential for the development of composers and performers who will be able to continue and consolidate that which has been accomplished during the past forty years. It alone can provide a musically intelligent audience prepared to appreciate and support the work that is being done. Signs of growth are to be found everywhere, but unfortunately, concomitant with this growth is a pervading atmosphere of the second-rate which makes it very difficult for the uncompromising musician to remain active in Jewish music. Fixing the blame for this is a complex problem. In the first instance, the responsibility must be borne by the people who direct Jewish music activities. Even among professional groups where normal professional competition might be expected to force proceedings to a high level, one is frequently subjected to "concerts" of the worst possible music executed in the worst possible taste. The difficult task of training a popular audience which can appreciate something more in Jewish music than *Rozhinkes und Mandlen,* or Lewandowski's *Hallelujah,* or a facile "modernistic" version of the latest Israeli *hora* has, in large measure, been shamefully neglected by our professional Jewish musicians. Frequently this is caused by the lack of adequate training among the people charged with the task of purveying Jewish music. This can be and is being overcome. Fortunately, in the overall battle for standards where the aesthetic problems become more subtle, there are a few men like Lazare Saminsky to lead the fight. More recruits are needed.

One happily notes, on the positive side, that the past two decades have given birth to numerous groups such as the National Jewish Music Council and the Jewish Music Forum which have done much to promote the cause of good Jewish music. The National Jewish Music Council under the sponsorship of the Jewish Welfare Board has been especially active in spreading Jewish music throughout the entire country by publishing bibliographical lists, making musical material available, and assisting in the arrangement of concerts.

On the creative side, particularly in the field of synagogue music, it must be reëmphasized that the Reform movement has thus far achieved the most permanent results. The *Services* by Bloch, Milhaud, Achron, Saminsky and Jacobi are impressive achievements; they redound to the credit of the various individuals who were foresighted enough to enlist the talents of these composers. The Conservative movement has also recognized the need for fresh music in the synagogue and has thus far produced the very useful, but stylistically inchoate, four volume *Cantorial Anthology,* edited by Gershon Ephros. The volume of music commissioned and published by the Park Avenue Synagogue at the instance of its *Hazzan,* David Putterman, is also most welcome in that it brings to the synagogue a whole group of composers whose individual contributions, if continued in subsequent works, might prove of lasting value.

To those who believe that Jewish music is a valid means of expression and a valuable source of inspiration, it is heartening to realize how many excellent American composers have contributed to the body of Jewish music in recent years. Composers who come to mind immediately include Jacob Avshalomoff, Arthur Berger, Leonard Bernstein, Henry Brant, David Diamond, Lukas Foss, Isadore Freed, Irving Fine, Miriam Gideon, Frederick Jacobi, Ellis Kohs, George Rochberg, and Leo Smit. This list of names becomes doubly meaningful when it is realized how representative it is of contemporary American music, and how much Jewish music is enriched by the variety of styles and tastes represented by these individual composers. In the cases of most of these composers it would be premature to discuss their contributions to Jewish music because they have been so few. This statement, however, does not apply to Frederick Jacobi, David Diamond, Isadore Freed and Leonard Bernstein, all of whom are well known in this field.

This brief survey of Jewish music in America cannot omit some mention of Jewish musicology. American Jewish music scholarship was begun very tentatively with the publication of Alois Kaiser and William Sparger of *A Collection of the Principal Melodies of the Synagogue* (Chicago, 1893), in which the two editors, in a prefatory article, summarized the state of research in Jewish music up to their time. When Abraham Z. Idelsohn became Professor of Jewish music at the Hebrew Union College thirty-one years later, American Jewish music scholarship suddenly matured. His ten volume *Thesaurus of Hebrew-Oriental Melodies* (1914-1932), and one volume *Jewish Music* (1929), despite their shortcomings, remain imposing monuments to his scholarship. Upon Idelsohn's death he was succeeded by Eric Werner, who stands out as one of America's foremost musicologists. Of equal stature are Solomon Rosowsky, whose long awaited book on Biblical cantillation is now in press, and Joseph Yasser, the noted theoretician and authority on Jewish and medieval modality. The field of Jewish musicology is an important one, and it is hoped that an increasing number of talented men and women will devote themselves to it. So much of Jewish music is in flux and on the verge of extinction in Europe and the Near East that vigorous action must be taken immediately to preserve it for future study.

Jewish music in America is today a strong, living cultural force, capable of offering much of value not only to the Jewish community but to the common life of America. It is rich, above all, in creative talent. Fostering this talent and absorbing its achievements present a challenge and imposes a responsibility on the American Jew.

# Visual

# Arts in

# American

# Jewish

# Life

## STEPHEN S. KAYSER

American Jewry has become intensely aware of the importance of the visual arts. Building committees of synagogues struggle with architects and interior decorators to give their houses of worship meaning and significance. Women's organizations strenuously seek to impress upon their members the necessity of making the Jewish home beautiful. Art work occupies a significant place in the curricula of Hebrew schools and in the program of summer camps. Arts and crafts coming from Israel are eagerly absorbed. Congregations everywhere are establishing small museums of ceremonial objects on their own premises and auctions of Jewish ritualistic items are widely publicized events. Public museums include showings of Jewish art objects in their programs. All in all, a new and increasing emphasis on art in Jewish life is to be observed on the Jewish scene in America.

To be sure, one misses, in all these efforts, a central guiding theme or leading principles. Yet the inner tendency of all these endeavors seems to point in the direction of a new integration of the visual arts into the over-all structure of Jewish life. A look into the past can well serve to illustrate that tendency.

Wherever art is applied to Judaism, the result is Jewish art. The fact that the synagogues of the past had to be built in the styles of the surrounding world does not make those buildings anything else but Jewish houses of worship. Synagogue architecture is, by necessity, a part of Jewish art. In each country in which Jews have lived there is at least one significant monument of synagogue architecture. In Eastern Europe there was an abundance of them, most of which are now in ruins. It was, therefore, an event of no mean significance that when, in the immediate post-war years, American Jewry was trying to bring order out of the chaos left by the destruction of Nazi tyranny, the venerable Touro Synagogue of Newport, Rhode Island, was dedicated as a national shrine in 1947. Fiske Kimball, the director of the Philadelphia Museum of Art and one of our foremost experts on the history of architecture, has called this building "one of the most perfect works of colonial architecture." It was created by the amateur architect, Peter Harrison (1716-1775), who in designing the interior, selected the various motifs from all kinds of sources. Yet, because of the power of integration still alive at that time, he was able to combine them in a harmony which resulted in one of the finest achievements in the history of architecture of all times.

Thus, the Touro Synagogue, dedicated on the first day of Hanukkah, 1763, is as important an architectural monument as the synagogues of Worms, Prague, Toledo, Cracow, Amsterdam, and London. This position was never challenged by any other synagogue structure in this country during the entire 19th century. Its graceful use of the elements of colonial architecture, particularly in the structural arrangements of the Torah ark, was an important innovation compared to other Sephardic synagogues. In its utter simplicity it was the first successful attempt to overcome what had been, up to that time, the dominant impulse of the Baroque style.

How daring this attempt was, can best be seen from the fact that when, towards the end of the 18th century, the synagogue of Charleston, South Carolina, was built, its Torah ark was still fashioned in the late Baroque manner. This shape of the ark, rather elaborate with the drapery on top, did not entirely harmonize with the otherwise very simple colonial structure of the building itself.

These two buildings proved that in the short period between the erection of the first synagogue in this country, Shearith Israel, on Mill Street in New York (dedicated in 1730), and the refined and noble edifices of Newport and Charleston, American Jewry had developed a great sensitivity towards the aesthetic requirements of a synagogue structure. This change was made possible by improved economic conditions. Already in the simple brick building on Mill Street, one could notice the tendency to impart beauty to an otherwise very small, crowded, and for many reasons not too practical building.

The synagogues of Newport and Charleston still belonged to an age which was dominated by organic principles in architecture. All too soon, however, the revivals of the 19th century were to uncover the lack of a central stylistic force in art. Instead of the Baroque or the Colonial styles, various imitations of the past shaped the architectural scene everywhere. Rachel Wischnitzer, stressing the Egyptian revival in the synagogue architecture of this country, has pointed out that it lasted longer here than in any other part of western civilization.[1]

The 19th century revivals reveal the paradox in the architectural thinking of that period. In the same house of worship in which Jews thank the Lord for having redeemed them from Egyptian bondage, they visually perpetuated Egyptian forms! This strange relationship between form and content persisted until our own age. The architects of B'nai Jeshurun Synagogue in New York City (finished in 1918) proudly proclaimed that in their structure they had brought out the glory and splendor of "Roman and Byzantine" times. The slight mistake of confusing

---

[1] See *Publications of the American Jewish Historical Society*, Vol. XLI, No. 1, 1951.)

Roman with Romanesque is not as serious as the unawareness of
the fact that neither Rome nor Byzantium furnishes any historic
reason for the continuation of any of its features in a Jewish house
of worship.

While today we look with contempt at these revivals of the
past, we should also be aware of the fact that until modern
times there was no organic style available which could furnish
the forms for building a synagogue. It seems only just, therefore,
to emphasize that in some cases the revivals led to the construction of buildings which in themselves displayed a great amount
of skill in their graceful appearance. It was sound to preserve
them to this very day. One such example is the Plum Street Synagogue in Cincinnati, Ohio, which was built in the 1860's. The
Moorish overtones of its charming interior remind us of the times
when our forbears thought they had to express themselves archi-
tecturally in terms of the Moslems.

The Romanesque and the Byzantine proved to be the most
time-resisting styles of the past in the building of Jewish houses
of worship. This is illustrated by the still impressive structures of
Temple Emanuel in New York or San Francisco, and of The
Temple in Cleveland, Ohio. It will take great efforts on the part
of our contemporary architects to outdo the impressive interiors
of these buildings. One must point out, however, that the revival
of these styles is achieved by means which cannot be called
quite legitimate. The renewal of a style pertaining to the past is
in itself not objectionable. It only becomes so when the structural
methods through which that particular style came into existence are falsified by methods which are not in line with the
original stylistic principles. For instance, a Gothic structure that
uses steel frame supports is no longer an organic creation.

All synagogue buildings based on revivals of the past are, therefore, superficial in the true sense of the word, for they reflect the
stylistic principles of by-gone centuries only on the surface and
not in the inner structural composition. The true character of this
superficiality came to be recognized as modern building techniques gradually developed throughout the Western world. Contemporary architecture has not yet arrived at a new style, but it

has brought about new technical methods which enable us to create spatial arrangements unimaginable before. Aside from this, the possibilities of using various kinds of electric lighting have increased a hundredfold during the last twenty years.

On the Continent, this new approach led to the creation of modern synagogues in Vienna and Amsterdam during the 1920's. By far the most outstanding building of that kind was the synagogue of the liberal congregation in Hamburg, finished in 1932 and destroyed in 1938. It proved that the Jewish house of worship was very well suited to the application of modern architectural means.

American Jewry became aware of the new possibilities mainly in the period after the Second World War. The principal reason for this was the important change in the American scene, which can be characterized as the suburbanization of life. Since 1941, more people have moved from the city to the country than from the country to the city. Jewish communities have been affected by this development. New residential areas arise sometimes overnight, and can change quickly. In one instance, a congregation in Baltimore recently had to abandon its community center built only three years ago, because of shifts in the population trends of that particular neighborhood. While this is an unusual case, the change in downtown surroundings can be seen everywhere. The outskirts of the city and the country neighborhood are becoming the primary scene of Jewish communal and congregational activities.

While it is not at all strange to erect a building in traditional styles in a downtown district where forms of the past meet, not always in perfect harmony, a building reminiscent of Byzantine or Romanesque structures would look very much out of place in the suburban or country surroundings of today.

Other factors have also favored the choice of modern architectural means for the creation of synagogue structures. Only a generation ago the main emphasis was placed on the hall of worship, while the parts of the synagogue dedicated to educational and social functions were more or less neglected. The assembly hall was placed in a basement and the classrooms, in most instances, were highly inadequate. Now the pendulum has swung to the other extreme, and the assembly halls as well as the classrooms have become the most important building problem. In too many cases this part of the synagogue structure is now so much over-rated that by necessity the hall of worship has to suffer. Be that as it may, the more utilitarian aspects of the building have come to the fore and with that, the desire to utilize the functionalism of modern architectural methods.

An enormous building activity, such as Jewish history never witnessed before, has now started. In every Jewish community in this country one or more synagogues were constructed during the past decade. Many more are still under construction or on blueprints. It seems characteristic that only a small proportion of these buildings does not employ the contemporary architectural forms and principles. In particular, the flexibility of modern architecture, its most characteristic feature, has proved to be the force which has out-moded the styles of the past. The main problem of the synagogue, the enlargement of the hall of worship for the period of the High Holy Days, has called upon the inventiveness of the modern architect. Vanishing walls, movable Torah arks, and adjustable classroom arrangements have created an entirely new type of structure—a genuine American creation which has opened another chapter in the history of the synagogue.

The funds raised for these buildings are enormous. Projects which were estimated to cost $600,000 finally amounted to two and one-half million. While many of these buildings are still unfinished, in a few years they will have changed the American Jewish scene completely.

In connection with this extensive building activity, an important new factor has emerged, namely, the Jewish architect, who only in our time has come into prominence. The outstanding architects in this country who are Jewish participate in the building of synagogues. All of them have made important contributions to this cause. That should not mean that the Gentile architect does not have his proper place in the building of synagogues where he is needed for local and artistic reasons. Whenever the necessity arises to employ him, he should be welcomed

in the same spirit in which he was received in centuries past, as a
builder of Jewish houses of worship. In this connection it is
gratifying to note that the internationally famous architect, Frank
Lloyd Wright, has recently designed a synagogue for a congregation in Philadelphia.

The modern synagogue presents more than an architectural
problem. The shaping of its interior includes many other artistic
aspects. Particularly, the ritualistic objects necessary for the
service call for serious consideration. Only a few architects realize the importance of the questions involved here and try to employ artisans and artists for the shaping of these details and objects.

The history of American synagogues from the mid-eighteenth
century until our time shows an uninterrupted development from
the organic creations of the colonial period, through the manifold and not always successful revivals of the 19th into the 20th
century, and finally the triumph of modern architectural thinking.
In comparison, the history of Jewish ritualistic art in this country
is rather fragmentary. A few venerable objects by anonymous
artists are preserved by Congregation Shearith Israel in New
York. However, these simple and graceful pieces do not give any
substantial account of what Jewish ceremonial objects were like
at the time when the foundations of the American synagogues
were laid.

The only exception is to be found in the small amount preserved of silver-work by the American-Jewish silversmith Myer
Myers (1723-1792). Five pairs of Torah headpieces made by
him have come down to us. They are connected with the names
of Congregation Shearith Israel in New York, the Touro Synagogue in Newport, and Congregation Mikveh Israel in Philadelphia. These items belong to the important Jewish treasures of
all times. Above all, they were made by a Jewish silversmith
who lived at a time when the Jews in Western European countries were still excluded from the craftmen's guilds. Aside from
this fact, the *Rimonim* by Myer Myers, with their intricate work-
manship and iconographic significance, belong to the finest Jewish silver objects of the eighteenth century period. In a careful

study, Dr. Guido Schoenberger has shown how their form developed, and in what way they represent an important phase in
the history of Torah ornaments.[2]

Myer Myers' works were all made for Sephardic congregations,
or rather (since these synagogues had many Ashkenazic members) for congregations that observed the Sephardic rite. For this
reasons, Myers did not shape any Torah breastplates, as they were
not used in the Sephardic observance. It would have been most
interesting to see how such an item by Myer Myers would have
looked. At any rate, the search for Myer Myers' pieces of Jewish
relevance is still on. If the rumor in collectors' circles is true, a
Hanukkah lamp by him must be preserved somewhere in Holland. A genuinely American type of ritualistic objects was created
by this artisan. It vanished only too soon.

The 19th century created practically no ritualistic art, and it
was not until the Russian immigration that Jewish silversmiths
came to America in greater numbers. Here they supplied the
ever-growing number of synagogues, as well as homes, with ritualistic silver. Their creations were anything but original, while
the demand for their work was by no means governed by the
quest for taste and quality. Forms which were brought over from
Eastern Europe were repeated time and again, and there is
hardly a Torah crown created on these shores which would not
reveal its Russian ancestry. The Torah breastplates likewise display the Eastern European origin of their design—a design un-
improved by transplantation, if one compares them to the outstanding production of old Jewish craftsmen in Eastern Europe.
Torah curtains and mantles also adopted standardized designs
which were perpetuated for decades. The objects made for the
home did not fare much better. They were at their best when
they preserved the genuine form of the Russian and Polish items.

[2] See *Publications of the American Jewish Historical Society*, Vol. XLIII,
No. 1, 1953. It is to be regretted that the historic significance of the *Rimonim*
created by Myers is dealt with in a very superficial way in the monograph
published about this important artisan by Jeanette W. Rosenbaum (Phila-
delphia, 1954). And it is more than astonishing that the investigations of Dr.
Schoenberger, which were presented in Boston at a meeting of the American
Jewish Historical Society in February 1953, are completely ignored in Mrs.
Rosenbaum's book.

But all too soon, they deteriorated into a commercialized production which dominates the market to this very day.

At the New York World's Fair of 1939, American Jewry for the first time realized the change that had taken place in Jewish ritualistic art. In the Palestine Pavilion of that fair a small but impressive selection of objects done by craftsmen in the Holy Land proved that new avenues had been opened across the seas in the field of Torah ornaments and candle holders, plates and textiles, for Jewish religious practice. Yet no serious attempts were made to create something similar in spirit for the American synagogue and home.

Not until the State of Israel came into existence was the interest in these creations renewed. While synagogue after synagogue in this country is being built in the forms and techniques of today, the Torah ornaments to be found in them are those of yesterday. Only a half dozen sets of modern Torah ornaments done in Israel today can be found in American synagogues all over the country.

Fortunately, there are signs that a change in this respect is about to take place. To give one example, the Joslyn Art Museum of Omaha, Nebraska, recently asked the Jewish community to donate a selection of Jewish ritualistic objects for permanent display. The local committee decided to present to the museum a selection of contemporary ritualistic objects, not only because valuable old pieces are very difficult to obtain, but also to demonstrate that the shaping of those items did not stop with the end of the last century.

An exhibit of creations by the modern Israeli silversmith, Yehuda Ludwig Wolpert, in the Jewish Museum of New York and in The Museum of the Hebrew Union College in Cincinnati, Ohio, arranged in 1953, created an enormous interest in ritualistic art of this kind, and efforts have been made to organize the production of these objects in this country. In the meantime, the Jewish public is eagerly absorbing the various arts and crafts objects imported from Israel.

The American output in this respect is very small. There is

among us at least one outstanding craftsman who works in silver and creates pieces of a highly personal style, characterized by intricate details of great significance. Yet this cannot possibly satisfy the enormous demand from all over the country. Another silversmith of very dubious aesthetic merits can certainly not be taken seriously when he claims to have created a unique form of the *Kiddush* Cup, one with a lid on top. Cups with lids were to be found hundreds of years ago, and such claims, channeled through television and radio, prove that the time has come to inform the public properly regarding the artistic aspects of Jewish life.

There are already indications of an ever-increasing active interest in Jewish art as needed in our worship and the religious practices of our homes. During the first decade of Mill Street Synagogue of Shearith Israel, the oldest congregation in the country, a special blessing was said for women on the eve of the Day of Atonement. It was not quite clear where this custom originated until congregational records revealed that the blessing was for the pious duty which the women of the congregation had fulfilled in presenting to the synagogue the white Torah curtain and the Torah mantles for use on the High Holy Days.[3]

Although it is not recorded that these items were made by the same women who donated them, it is safe to assume that such was the case. It was customary in many congregations of the past for women to provide the textiles used in the synagogues. In Poland and Russia they used their own wedding dresses as fabric for the Torah curtains.

It is a good sign that in American synagogues today, this active participation of the women in the beautification of the hall of worship has been revived. The Sisterhood of the B'nai Israel Synagogue of Millburn, New Jersey, produced the Torah curtain for the ark in the new building, which was finished in 1952. This structure, because of its bold designs, became widely known in the American art world. The Baltimore Hebrew Congregation displays an impressive Ark covering designed and woven by

[3] See David de Sola Pool, *The Mill Street Synagogue*, 1930, p. 37.

women of the Sisterhood. In a similar way, the Sisterhood of
Temple Beth El in Rochester, New York, furnished the Torah
mantles for use on Sabbaths and Festivals.

The main problem in all instances of this kind is to provide
proper designs for the various objects. In the case of the Millburn
Synagogue, the curtain was executed on the basis of a painting
by one of the leading abstract artists in this country.

This brings us finally to the question of the contemporary Jewish artist and his possible integration in the reshaping of the Jewish scene in its esthetic dimension.

The 19th century brought the Jewish artist to the fore in the
wake of the Emancipation. In the second half of the century,
there were Jews who were prominent artists in practically all of
the European countries, among them: Joseph Israels in Holland,
Camille Pissarro in France, Max Liebermann and Lesser Uri in
Germany, Isaac Levitan in Russia, Maurice Gottlieb in Poland
and Ernst Josephson in Sweden, masters who were born Jews
and remained Jews throughout their lives. It is an acknowledged
fact that during the last century there were no Jewish artists of
equal stature in this country. A number of Jewish artists lived in
the United States during that period and their history is still to be
written, but their role was in no way prominent or significant.

This situation changed completely with the beginning of this
century, particularly with the immigration from Eastern Europe.
The listing of Jewish artists who found public recognition in this
country would fill many pages. Like their prominent colleagues
in Europe, most of them belonged and still belong to the van-
guard of the arts in our time. Coming from countries of persecution and oppression, they breathed the invigorating air of freedom and responded gratefully to the many opportunities offered
to them.

Events like the Armory Show of 1913, which opened the door
to modern art in this country, would have been greatly diminished in influence without the participation of these prominent
Jewish artists. Their contribution to American culture has been
widely recognized. Theirs has been a contribution by Jews, not a
Jewish contribution. By the same token, the realm of the Jewish

artist does not necessarily have to be Jewish. As we understand Jewish art, it is every kind of art applied to Judaism. It can be produced by both Jews and Gentiles as is proved by the majority of the ceremonial objects that were made prior to the 19th century. In painting and sculpture, the Jewish content has to be taken into consideration, and it is in this respect that the Jewish artists, hailing from Eastern Europe and educated in a Yiddish-speaking surrounding, are of unquestionable competence and importance. In their work, Jewish subjects become a natural outgrowth of their own lives and early environment. The majority of them came from Russia. They had seen the world of the ghetto as a basic form of Jewish existence. It was a fulfilled world. When they arrived in this country, many of them at an early age, they brought with them impressions which they could never forget or overcome. Time and again they depicted the main motifs of their childhood and adolescence. The Jewish surroundings of the metropolis, where they grew up, only helped to deepen this relation to the past, and institutions like the Educational Alliance Art School, where they received their training, retained the atmosphere of their upbringing.

Their biographies show an amazing outer similarity whether they worked as painters, etchers, or sculptors. The freedom of their artistic development resulted in a strong and uncontrolled individualism. Their Jewishness was but a natural part of their lives, and in a good many cases of their work. Their productions were generally intended for the art galleries and from there their works found their way into the homes of art lovers and collectors, Jewish and Gentile alike.

In this pattern, the specific Jewish contents and values inherent in their work were deepened by the two events which changed world Jewry in our times: the Hitler destruction of Central and Eastern European Jewry, and the establishment of the State of Israel. It was most impressive to witness how the Jewish artist of this country reacted to these events. His self-identification with the fate of his Jewish brethren became clearly visible in his work. At the same time, it became more and more apparent that the Jewish public needed him more than ever before. The bare walls of the new synagogues, community centers and schools called for the work of sculptors and painters to give them significance.

Responding to this call of the community, the Jewish artist changed from an individualist into the creator of those works which are not dependent on the mere coincidence of purchase but are destined to become an organic part of a greater unit.

More and more the Jewish public has come to feel that it has to draw upon the vast resources of inspiration possessed by the Jewish artists living in this country. The second generation of these artists, those born after 1900, has in the meantime come to the front. Now one sees young and daring painters and sculptors who no longer struggle for recognition, which they already have received from the art-loving public of this country, but for employment by the Jewish community as a whole. This second generation of artists, born in this country of a parentage that preserved the Jewish traditions of the past, has experienced an important emancipation which must be stressed if we want to understand their particular situation. The older generation of Jewish artists, who emigrated to this country, came via Paris. The impress of that birthplace of modern art on their work is unmistakably dominant. The representatives of the younger generation may occasionally visit Paris. They, however, have received not only their basic schooling but also their most important artistic experiences in this country, which from the 1920's onward established one important art center after another. If the Jewish public will learn how to integrate the work of these artists where it is urgently needed, they will produce a Jewish art which can contribute decisively to the renaissance of Jewish life in this country.

From the viewpoint of this survey—with a broadening tide of interest in the visual arts, a heightened esthetic sensibility, increased opportunities, the availability of gifted artists—it appears as though at the beginning of the fourth century of Jewish life in this country, forces are at work which, if united, will help us bring about a more beautiful, which is to say, a more meaningful future.

# THE COMMUNITY

# Interfaith Relations in the United States

## MORRIS N. KERTZER

*Historical Background*

Recently, at an informal meeting of religious leaders, a prominent Protestant church official declared: "I wonder if the Jews of this country realize that, despite their comparatively small numbers, *psychologically* they represent a third of the nation. Since we are in the habit of dividing all Americans into neat religious categories, there is also a tendency to regard the Jewish group as one-third of the total, and in all public occasions, they are assigned, symbolically, one-third of the representation."

If the observation is accurate, it is a far cry from the story of America's beginnings. As late as 1776, a century and a quarter after the Jewish landing at New Amsterdam, the nation was as Protestant as Saudi Arabia is Moslem. Less than one out of every 125 residents was Catholic; less than one out of a thousand was

Jewish. The Catholic and Jewish communities did not impinge upon the consciousness of the average Protestant American until well into the 19th century.

Normal interfaith relations, that is, the free association of different religious groups on a basis of parity, and without fear of assimilation, did not appear until late in the 19th century. The Jewish and Catholic communities had not yet developed their own resources for self-perpetuation. They had no theological seminaries, practically no American-born religious leaders, no native cultural institutions, until well after the Civil War. The Catholic population passed the million mark in the 1840's, but in 1855, the Irish religious press continued a campaign against immigration for fear of assimilation. As late as 1864, the *Brooklyn Tablet* bewailed the fact that 60 per cent of Catholics were lost in America: "Catholicism puts 500 daily into the grave for one it wins over to its communion."

According to Professor Sperry, the pre-Revolutionary Catholics were largely lost to the Church. It was virtually impossible to persuade priests to emigrate to America, and only a few hardy Jesuits risked settling in the New World. As a result, according to Sperry, a quarter of a million Catholics were assimilated, and there were fewer than 100,000 in the United States by 1800.

What is true of the early Catholic community certainly applies to the minute Jewish settlement in colonial America. The rise of a self-conscious Jewish group, aware of the heterogeneity of American life, was not manifest until the later decades of the 19th century.

The culture pattern of the United States is, of course, still predominantly Protestant. The Jewish population remains below 4 per cent, and the Catholic population, while it has increased proportionately (12.1 per cent in 1870; 12.8 per cent in 1880; 16 per cent in 1900; 16 per cent in 1926; 16.1 per cent in 1940) was below a fifth of the population in 1952 (19.3 per cent).

The basic institutions of American life—the public schools, the institutions of higher learning, the principle of separation of church and state, and many others—are colored by Protestant tradition.

## *Separation of Church and State and its Effect on Interfaith Relations*

The provision of the First Amendment against an established Church was the first historic attempt by any nation to provide constitutional guarantees for interreligious amity. The common notion that the separation of Church and State was an effort to right the evils of the European experience is misleading. Actually, it was the American experience of interfaith tensions in New England, in Maryland, and in other States, which gave birth to the conviction that "separation" was the only road to interreligious peace. While the principle was Protestant, it was the Catholics, and later the Jews, who had most to gain by the First Amendment.

This fact is dramatically brought out by the state of affairs in the years immediately following the Revolution. Several State constitutional drafts, such as that of Vermont in 1777, required office-holders to profess the Protestant religion. Massachusetts, New Jersey, Connecticut and Georgia followed suit. South Carolina, in 1778, proclaimed Protestantism as the State religion, and it was not until 1818 that the Congregational Church was disestablished in Connecticut.

The public schools were Protestant in character, even though, under the influence of Horace Mann, the principle of secularism was adopted. This was especially true during periods of religious revivalism. A wave of Protestant fundamentalism swept the nation in the 1820's and 1830's, which, according to Ray A. Billington (*The Protestant Crusade,* Macmillan 1938), "aided immeasurably the anti-Catholic movement . . . and a crusade against Rome."

The driving force in maintaining the secular character of the public schools in mid-19th century was Roman Catholic. The Protestant reaction to this pressure is seen in the bias of the above-mentioned author, who states: "Thousands of middle-class Protestants were jarred from their complacency by Catholic meddling in politics and *especially by the attempt to eject the Word of God from the school room.*" (Italics mine.) In 1842, the New York State Superintendent of Education recommended a daily reading of the Bible by teachers. The Catholic Church strove in vain to resist what it regarded as sectarian invasion of the classroom, but "the public school Bible was firmly entrenched . . . and Bishop Hughes, in despair, concentrated his efforts in building parochial schools for the education of Catholic children." (op. cit.)

A grim picture of Protestant pressure on the public school is given by Leo Pfeffer's *Church, State and Freedom* (Beacon, 1953), in an account of a Boston Catholic youngster, eleven-year-old Tom Wall, who refused to recite the Ten Commandments, as required by the school regulations. Following the advice of his priest, Tom Wall resisted the school requirement. After a ten-minute paddling by his teacher, the boy relented, and the Ten Commandments once more reigned supreme in the public schools of Boston.

### The Current Interreligious Scene

The religious population of the United States, or the total number of religious affiliates, was 94,900,000 (1953), close to three-fifths of the total population. The accuracy of these statistics, furnished by the Year Book of American Churches, is a perennial source of discussion. Protestants claim that their figure (over 54 million), includes only those with formal membership in church bodies, and not merely those baptized, as in the Catholic Church. Others declare that some of the Protestant figures are based on over-optimistic estimates. At all events, the Jewish statistics, 5 million, are predicated on a unique formula, viz., the total number of Jews resident in those communities which have synagogues. The author has long questioned this method of reporting Jewish religious statistics, not only because it is misleading, but because, among other things, it conceals the facts of synagogue growth in recent decades. Professor Kenneth S. Latourette, in his definitive *History of Christianity* (1953), contrasts the phenomenal growth of Christian church life in the 20th century with the modest increase in synagogue life, a conclusion drawn from the inaccurate figures that are based, not on synagogue reports, but on the unpleasant realities of recent American immigration laws.

## The American Catholic Community

Numbering over 30 million adherents, Roman Catholicism has come into its own within the last two decades as a tremendous force in American life. Though the scars of anti-Catholic discrimination remain, and a considerable residue of anti-Roman sentiment exists, overt acts of bigotry are generally a thing of the past. Less than a century ago, following the assassination of Lincoln, America saw anti-Catholic riots. Rumors were spread that the President died as a result of a Jesuit plot, and Catholics in Hartford, Connecticut, and Newark, New Jersey, were almost lynched. The fantastic charges of the inventor, Samuel Morse, that Irish-Catholic leaders were plotting against America, found their way into Protestant Sunday School textbooks.

Leading the so-called Know Nothing Movement, the Grand Council of the Supreme Star Spangled Banner boasted that (in 1852) it had 635 lodges in Pennsylvania, with a membership of 110,000 (among whose leaders was a prominent Jew); it elected Governors in nine states; won a majority in Massachusetts, and exactly a century ago elected 104 out of 234 Congressmen in the national elections.

Today, the Catholics of America are, without question, the strongest bulwark of the Roman Church in the world. On the defensive everywhere in Europe, driven underground in the Iron Curtain countries, its missions destroyed in most of the Far East, weakened by the inroads of Communism in Italy and France, and ruling supreme only in two politically insignificant countries, Spain and the Irish Free State, Catholicism finds its centrifugal core moving to Latin America and the United States.

There are several important factors at work in the American Catholic community, in its relation to non-Catholics. It has been pointed out that for the first time in over a thousand years there is not a major political power in the world that is Catholic. Among the great world powers, Great Britain, Soviet Russia, China, the United States (and perhaps, because of its numbers and strategic position, India), only in America have Catholics the opportunity to make their influence felt on the course of human history.

Within the past few decades, American Catholics have seen a tremendous improvement in their economic status. While continuing to provide the bulk of the labor class, they have outgrown the inferior status they once occupied as an immigrant group. The so-called "growing power of American Catholicism" is, most frequently, simply the rise of a hitherto socially inferior group to a position of parity in our society.

With economic advancement has come political maturity and assertiveness. Concentrated in the large cities (40.8 per cent of the Chicago population; 42.9 per cent in Baltimore; 52 per cent in Buffalo; 74.3 per cent in Boston), Catholics have risen to prominence in the nerve centers of American economic, social and intellectual life at a time when there has been a marked trend away from rural America, and when the focal points of mass communication have been concentrated in the great metropolitan areas of the nation. It might also be observed here that since the vast majority of American Jews—over 85 per cent—live in these areas, the problem of Jewish-Christian relations in the United States is becoming more and more a matter of Catholic-Jewish relations.

Within the last decade, American Catholicism has become aware of the serious inroads which assimilation has made into its ranks. Gone is the acquiescent attitude towards depletion of its ranks through intermarriage, and falling away from the Church. In Catholic journals, a great deal of soul-searching is found whenever the annual report of conversions to the Roman Church is released. Estimates of a 30 per cent intermarriage rate are most prevalent, with some regions reporting as much as 50 per cent.

Catholic authorities are by no means convinced that intermarriages produce accretions to the Church. John D. Smith, writing in the *Catholic World* (October 1952), in an article called "Why They Marry Others," quotes a Father Thomas to the effect that, "In our survey we found that post-marriage conversions amounted to only 3 per cent." Among the factors leading to intermarriage, Mr. Smith blames separation of the sexes in education, which leads to social life with non-Catholics. Typical of the narrowness produced by such separation is a plea which the author heard from a rather excitable German educator: "Boys—I beg you—stay away from girls of the opposite sex!" Even in French Canada, intermarriage statistics show a 16.4 per cent rate among Catholics, compared to 11.2 per cent for Protestants and 5.06 per cent for Jews.[1]

Resistance to assimilation has taken on several forms. Prominent among those are the building of more social barriers for Catholic youth, encouraging Catholic Boy Scout troops, Catholic Youth Organization, etc., and the construction of hundreds of parochial high schools throughout the nation, in order to avoid social contact of young people as they approach the marriageable age. Likewise, there has been a steady withdrawal of Catholic participation in interfaith movements in the YWCA, and others. (The very phrase "interfaith" is no longer acceptable to Catholic circles.) This trend was dramatized a few years ago, when Catholics were urged to resign from such service groups as the Rotary International. Similarly motivated has been the creation and development of Catholic lay organizations within the frame-work of the Church; Holy Name Societies; Catholic War Veterans; and scores of other professional and vocational groups such as Catholic Teachers and Nurses associations. Symptomatic, too, was the ban issued by Cardinal Stritch, of Chicago, against Catholics visiting the World Council of Churches Assembly, in August 1954.

Another interesting phenomenon within American Catholicism is a marked revision of its strategy concerning religion in

[1] Louis Rosenberg studies, "The Jewish Population of Canada—A Statistical Summary 1840-1943," *American Jewish Year Book*, Vol. 48, 1946-1947.

the public schools. We shall deal with the problem below, but it is significant that the strong resistance which the hierarchy traditionally offered to sectarian invasions of the public school has all but vanished. Far from rushing into litigation on such issues as Bible reading and common prayer, the Catholic Church apparently is willing to compromise on principle in order to strengthen what it regards as the spiritual basis of public education. It is hard to explain this shift in strategy except in terms of the long-range objectives of the Church in America.

### The American Protestant Community

The sociological and psychological forces at work within American Protestantism are equally significant. Its sense of security by virtue of numbers has yielded to a grudging feeling that it must assert itself in order to survive. When the National Council of Churches was organized in December, 1950, and decided to establish temporary national headquarters in New York, the leading Protestant journal, the *Christian Century*, echoed the sentiments of many in the ranks when it deplored the move to "that Catholic-Jewish canyon that is New York." In January, 1954, the Minister of a distinguished Park Avenue church resigned his pulpit, asserting that Protestantism in his city had become "a struggling minority." Protestantism sees itself as a majority weakened by internal divisiveness, and displaced by the growing impact of Catholics and Jews upon the American scene.

Within the past decade, Protestants have met this "challenge" in several ways: The National Council of Churches of Christ, embracing most of the trinitarian Churches (including the Eastern Orthodox groups), has been formed to coordinate the efforts of Protestantism in such broad areas as religious education, social action and the mission field. They have embarked upon a bolder program of public relations, pouring increased resources into the mass media, radio, television, and publications. Protestants have adopted a more militant attitude toward what they regard as

Catholic political pressure. On both the national and local level, organized Protestantism has entered into political debate on such issues as the proposed appointment of a U.S. ambassador to the Vatican, and Federal support for parochial education. The National Council of Churches went so far as to appoint a strategy committee to devise means of rousing public support in favor of their position. It is altogether likely that this massive array of resistance to President Truman's proposal in 1951 was the major factor in having the nomination shelved.

On the community level, there is growing evidence that Protestants are becoming more outspoken on what they regard as unwarranted Catholic preponderance in political and judicial positions. Following a statement by a New York Protestant Council official that "the disproportionately few Protestant judges in the courts of New York" can be blamed on "lack of proper cooperation among Protestants of various denominations," a formal committee was established in February, 1954, to seek adequate Protestant representation. Critics of the movement pointed out, with a good deal of cogency, that the Protestant counter-attack was misguided. The principal effort should have stressed that appointment to political or judicial office should be determined on merit alone, without regard to religious affiliation. At all events, Protestants are concerned that in such sensitive matters as family, adoption, divorce and censorship, a good deal of law is made by Catholic jurists.

Protestants have shared in a general trend toward conservatism in faith. The liberal groups, Unitarians and Universalists, have not expanded their ranks, while the fundamentalist groups, such as the Southern Baptists, have reported extensive gains. Billy Graham, and revivalists of his type, have been embraced by the more representative Protestant bodies as an asset to their cause. Political leaders now find it necessary to conform, at least externally, to conservative religious patterns.

The by-products of religious conservatism in Protestantism, as they affect Jewish-Christian relations, are considerable. The "social gospel" which formed the heart of Protestantism in the

1920's and the 1930's, with its emphasis on greater intergroup
cooperation in social action, notably in the field of discrimination, has given way to a more cautious willingness to cooperate
with non-Protestants only within a narrower frame of reference.
Christian-Jewish exchange of pulpits, popular in the 1940's, is
now frowned upon in official church circles.

The fundamentalist trend has also left its mark on the religious educational demands of Protestants. At its annual meeting
in Denver, early in 1953, the National Council of Churches issued a call to infuse moral and spiritual values in public education. Protestant educators interpreted this as a mandate to introduce as much religion as was feasible in the face of opposition
by those who wished to maintain the traditional "secular" character of the public schools.

Another serious consequence for Christian-Jewish relations lies
in the more fundamentalist interpretation of the Jew in Christian history. Professor Walter M. Horton, speaking at the 1947
Conference on Science, Philosophy and Religion, on "Chasms
and Bridges Between Christianity and Judaism," pointed out
that "to eliminate everything in religion which had ever created
strife would reduce religion to a mere shadow of itself, incapable
of exerting influence for either good or evil." Dr. Horton went
on to say that the "Jews' situation in Christendom is indeed difficult, sociologically as well as theologically. Cultures are fundamentally determined by their supreme values. The culture of
Christendom finds its supreme values embodied in and around
the person of Jesus Christ. Jews, to whom this figure does not
represent supreme value, cannot be fully at home in the culture
of Christendom. They cannot make the social adjustment which
would reconcile them to their environment, without ceasing to
be Jews. That is the deepest root of the Christian-Jewish tragedy."

The greatest stumbling-block to Jewish-Christian understanding lies not in the stereotype of the Jew as Christ-killer, but as
Christ-rejector. The basis for cooperation between liberal Christians and Jews is one of mutual respect for differences. The
foundation-stone for amity between Fundamentalist Christians

and the Jews can hardly be other than a willingness of the latter
to see the "true light"!

### The American Jew and His Christian Neighbor

The last decade has been marked by new attitudes of the American Jews toward their Christian neighbors.
The tide has not been in one direction, because of the peculiar
nature of the Jewish minority. Despite the growing impatience of
Jews in the matter of intergroup cooperation and the avowed
belief that "anti-Semitism is after all, not a Jewish question, but
a Christian one," there is a grim recognition that the truth of the
aphorism is much more apparent to Jews than it is to the majority, and that the initiative in intergroup education must remain, for the time at least, with minority groups.

On the other hand, the following factors are clearly discernible. American Jews have achieved a degree of self-assurance,
born partially out of economic and political well-being, and in
some measure, out of firmer organizational structures. A community capable of raising a billion dollars or more since the end of
World War II for its religious, cultural and philanthropic needs,
inevitably develops a sense of self-esteem. In such issues as
"Christmas in the public schools," the Jewish community has overcome the timidity of a decade ago, and speaks out with vigor
and forthrightness. This sense of security has been enhanced immeasurably by the creation of the State of Israel. The dramatic
victory of fellow-Jews in defense of their homeland, and in the
face of colossal odds, has given American Jewry a mood of pride
and self-confidence. The sombre realization, however, that two-
fifths of world Jewry was destroyed in countries ruled by so-
called Christians, and with only the feeblest kind of protests
from the Church; and the spectacle of Christian lament over the
plight of Arab refugees on the part of those churchmen whose
silence was spectacular during the days of Buchenwald and Da-
chau, have naturally chilled the enthusiasm of Jews for cooperation with Christian groups. The marked resistance of Catholics,

and more recently of Protestants, to interfaith activities, has produced a counter-feeling of impatience and disquiet about the value of interreligious cooperation. Julius Rosenthal writes:[2] "Jewish spokesmen and writers are increasingly given to voicing their thoughtful misgivings concerning the entire interfaith enterprise . . . The change in attitude has profound roots in the temper of the times. The optimistic premises of liberalism are succumbing to the travail of our years, and our age cries out, 'Herbert Spencer is dead! Long exist Kierkegaard'!"

Rabbis who have followed the annual practice of inviting Christian clergymen to their pulpits are now waiting for their Protestant colleagues to take the initiative. A curious by-product of this impasse has been the growing custom of celebrating Brotherhood Week by bringing together Orthodox, Conservative and Reform Jews—a far cry from the original purpose of the architects of American Brotherhood.

In a smaller measure, the trend toward fundamentalism within the Jewish community must be noted. The proliferation of Yeshivoth, particularly those which discourage secular education and resist the forces of integration, is not unusual in the larger Jewish centers. The remarkable increase in Jewish all-day schools during the past decade, some of which remain open on the "Gentile Thanksgiving," gives us a further clue to the separatist tendency in a segment of American Jewry.

## Sources of Tension and Conflict

The observer of intergroup relations in America is struck by the fact that tensions stemming from racial differences have been clearly mitigated during the past decade, while interreligious conflict has been intensified and aggravated. Open hostility, and overt discrimination, are more of a rarity. Laws protecting the rights of employment, as well as the general mores of our times, have stripped the mantle of respectability from the overt bigot. On the other hand, the restraint which characterized

[2] *Reconstructionist,* March 6, 1953.

the 1920's and the 1930's has given way to much more candid speech and writing, especially in conflicts involving Protestants and Catholics.

The following factors in interreligious tensions may be noted: As the various communions turn more *ad fontes,* to traditional modes of religious teachings, the ideological considerations which divided Protestants from Catholics have taken on more substance. The genesis of Congregationalism, according to Roland H. Bainton, Church historian, was "anti-Romanism." The Congregationalists desired to strip from the Church of England all "the rags of anti-Christ." A reversion to historical roots inevitably revives quarrels long dormant.

Increased emphasis on traditional areas of theological dispute have been widely broadcast by mass media. Witness, for example, the production of the film, *Martin Luther,* ostensibly for commercial theatres, but financially underwritten by American Lutheran church groups; the publication of such pamphlets as *If I Marry a Catholic,* calling attention to the pitfalls involved in intermarriage, and the popular acclaim within Protestant circles of Paul Blanshard's indictment of "Catholic Power."

In Jewish-Christian relations, the pattern repeats itself. A resurgence toward evangelism, as in the attempts of various Protestant laymen's groups to "make better Christians out of citizens, and better citizens out of Christians," has received the blessing of high government authorities. The introduction of a bill in the United States Senate by a liberal legislator, Mr. Humphrey of Minnesota, to mark Mother's Day, 1954, by printing the picture of the Virgin Mary on a postage stamp, was another indication of the lack of sensitivity to Jewish feelings on the part of Christians motivated by a new zeal for the faith.

The renewed emphasis given within Protestant and Catholic circles to a "mission to the Jews," and their declaration that the millions of Jews formally unaffiliated with the synagogue offer a legitimate target for such endeavors, is another symptom of the sharpening of theological lines.

The division in social outlook is largely between Catholics and non-Catholics. John Cogley, executive editor of *Commonweal,* took cognizance of the fact that "some of the Church's basic moral teachings have direct consequence on the political behavior of Catholics" (June 12, 1953). The solid alignment of Catholic forces in opposition to a study of the divorce laws of New York State, and the concentrated fire of the Protestant Council and the New York Board of Rabbis in support of changes in the law; the political debate in New Jersey on the merits of bingo playing, with the Protestant State Council of Churches calling on candidates to declare their intentions in this issue, while the Catholic chanceries endorse the opposing view; the acrimonious debate on censorship of films, books and plays, especially in the case of "The Miracle," in which theological considerations were involved; the perennial battle over birth-control information in Massachusetts and Connecticut—all of these issues tended to irritate relations between the contending religious groups, and perpetuate the tensions between them.

### The Impact of Tension Situations Outside the United States

American Protestantism recently organized a Department of Religious Liberty within its National Council of Churches. Primary targets of its attacks have been the Roman Churches in Spain, Italy and Latin America. The Protestant mission field, severely affected by the political upheaval in China and other parts of the Far East, has naturally shifted the focus of its activities to other parts of the world. In addition to its historic concentration on the African missions, this movement has allocated more of its forces to Catholic countries. American Catholicism has frequently voiced its concern over Protestant "intrusion" into Catholic Argentina and Colombia. Protestants have vigorously critized what they regard as the partisanship of the U. S. State Department in withholding visas from their missionaries on the pretext that their activities would create tensions abroad.

The pronouncements of Cardinal Segura of Spain, reflecting

an intolerant attitude toward non-Catholics reminiscent of the Inquisition, have had a disturbing effect on Catholic-Protestant relations in the United States. On December 6, 1953, Pope Pius XII issued a statement on religious toleration that was obviously meant to allay the fears of non-Catholics living in non-Catholic countries. He declared that "the duty of repressing moral and religious error cannot . . . be an ultimate norm of action. It must be subordinate to higher and more general norms, which in some circumstances permit, and perhaps seem to indicate as the better policy, toleration of error in order to promote a greater good."

The recent papal pronouncement is not likely to assuage the feelings of non-Catholics in the United States. The normal inter-action of groups based on a broader principle than expedient "toleration of error" is still remote.

## Differences in Political Outlooks

The religious voting bloc has changed its charac-ter in the last decade. Richard L. Stokes, in the *Catholic World* (July, 1952), observed: "Twenty years ago, when Tammany was in full flower, it was a matter of losing job and home if a registered Democrat (Catholic) should fail . . . to vote the straight ticket. Officially, in 1952, the churchman is a Democrat. Catholics . . . are now joining the band of independent electors who hold the nation's balance of power." The formula, Protestant-rural-Republi-can versus Catholic-urban-Democrat, has all but vanished. Daniel Cleary, writing in *Commonweal* (July 24, 1953), ascribes this trend to the improved financial status of many Catholics. But there are other variables of greater force in the situation. The Republican party has been more aggressively anti-Communist in the eyes of the Catholic Church, and less enthusiastic about in-volvement in the "secularist" United Nations. Protestants and Jews have been concerned with the infringements upon civil lib-erties in the anti-Communist program.

Typical of this new area of conflict was the alignment of forces

in the controversy regarding Communist infiltration into the
clergy, which raged throughout 1953. The diocesan press was
generally pro-McCarthy; the Protestant press almost universally
anti-McCarthy. Cardinal Spellman's implicit endorsement of the
Senator in his Brussels speech in the fall of 1953 lent added fuel
to the political debate in its religious aspects.

Peter Viereck's statement, quoted in the *Catholic World*
(April, 1953), that "Catholic-baiting is the anti-Semitism of the
liberals," is an oversimplification of the facts. Liberals, finding
themselves the objects of consistent pillorying in the diocesan
press, seem justified in drawing inferences about the Catholic position.

In international affairs, a breach has appeared in recent years
between Catholics on the one hand, and Protestants and Jews on
the other, in supporting the U. N. and UNESCO. Papal declara-
tions endorsing the U. N. as "the fond and holy hope of mothers
and wives and sisters, and of all men of good will" (1947) have
been modified some, in American Catholic circles, by criticism
of the United Nations' deficiencies in promoting disarmament, its
lack of success in dealing with atomic weapons, and elimination
of the veto. UNESCO has been a particular object of attack because of its so-called secular, humanistic emphasis.

The *Catholic Messenger* (December 3, 1953), organ of the
Davenport, Iowa, diocese, took the Catholic press to task for
what it called "*Tribune* journalism," in preventing readers from
learning the truth about Church support for international unity.
The *Messenger* reported that only 12 out of 37 diocesan papers
carried an important story of the Catholic Association for International Peace, in which several bishops and priests endorsed
the U. N.

Protestant and Jewish religious leaders have embarked on an
ambitious educational campaign to acquaint church people with
the importance of U. N. and UNESCO. Communities such as
Los Angeles have been the scenes of conflict over U. N. teachings in the public schools, with Roman Catholic authorities leading the opposition, and Jews and Protestants pitted against them.

## Religious Freedom

The historic fact that by the middle of the twentieth century, two out of three Jews in the free world had made a permanent residence in the United States is more than the result of a fortuitous set of circumstances. It can rather be traced to the guarantees of religious freedom incorporated not only into law but into the social and political fabric of American life.

A few years ago, the Federal Council of Churches gave the following definition of religious liberty: "Religious liberty shall be interpreted to include freedom to worship according to the conscience and to bring up children in the faith of their parents; freedom for the individual to change his religion; freedom to preach, educate, publish, and carry on missionary activities; and freedom to organize with others, and to acquire and hold property for these purposes."

The security of Jewish rights in the United States is intimately bound up with deep-rooted Protestant traditions. The Puritan character of Colonial America, despite many evidences of obscurantism and lapses into intolerance, laid the groundwork for religious liberty. There were two motivating forces involved, both the outgrowth of basic theology. Roger Williams expressed the fear that state control of the church would corrupt religion. Power led to sin, no matter how loftily motivated. "It is necessary," said John Cotton, "that all power that is on earth be limited, church power or others."

The other element in early Protestantism was its emphasis on voluntarism. A congregation was to consist of those whose consciences dictated that they worship God in a certain way. Nor was there any fear that lack of sanctions or coerciveness would lead to godlessness. Since the teachings of God were true and His word expressed in Holy Writ was infallible, free and untrammeled discussion, and ample opportunities for persuasion were the safest guarantors that the people would be led to God's kingdom.

The Founding Fathers, notably Jefferson and Madison, gave
little indication of any special or specific concern for the religious rights of Jews, but the language of the Virginia Declaration of Rights, "The religion then of every man must be left to
the conviction and conscience of every man . . . We maintain
therefore that in matters of religion, no man's right is abridged
by the institution of Civil Society . . . ," laid the groundwork
for the unique development of Jewish religious and cultural life
in the New World. It was Madison who pointed out that the
same "authority used to establish Christianity in exclusion of all
other Religions, may establish with the same ease any particular
sect of Christians, in exclusion of all others."

Religious freedom, of course, was limited by larger considerations of public welfare. The Mormon principle of polygamy was
made to yield to considerations of general welfare. Similarly, Je-
hovah's Witnesses and the Christian Scientists were constrained
in some matters of conscience. For observant Jews, the Sunday
Blue Laws also imposed economic penalties on those constrained
to keep their business establishments closed two days a week.

But generally, freedom of Jewish worship has been unim-
paired. Litigation involving the right of a synagogue to build in
any part of a community, a right challenged with greater fre-
quency during the past decade in a score of city suburbs, has invariably brought victory to the Jewish congregation. The privilege of establishing all-day schools, comparable to Catholic
parochial schools, has also been reinforced by the 1925 Oregon
decision (Pierce vs. Society of Sisters).

The only area in which the principle of religious freedom has
been threatened is in the arena of public education. In such
matters as federal aid to non-public education, the principle has
not been impaired. To a lesser extent, in the distribution of
Gideon Bibles, the courts, when called upon, as in New Jersey,
have also stood firm. In the issue of released time, the McCol-
lum decision of 1948 prohibited religious teaching on school
premises, but the Zorach decision of 1952 sanctioned off-the-
premises teaching, utilizing the machinery of the public school
in the enforcement of attendance.

And in a number of other areas, such as sectarian observance of religious festivals, and the reading of the New Testament, the weight of public opinion has been so strong that litigation on the basis of a strict interpretation of the First Amendment would not be practical.

The pressures on the school for introducing religion, with all the attendant dangers of insinuating sectarianism, are not likely to abate in our time. It is only hoped that the original spirit which animated the Protestant founders of the nation will be renewed. Already, there are voices like that of Professor Winthrop Hudson, of Colage-Rochester Divinity School, who declares that religion "cannot be legislated or coerced. It must be a free expression of the mind of the community which will take substance, not in formal courses of religious instruction, but in the basic assumptions of the teachers and the writers of textbooks." (*The Great Tradition of the American Churches,* Harpers, 1953.)

### Church-State Issues

In this complex area, we limit ourselves to a few generalizations. Each of the three religious groups in America has declared its support of the principle of separation of Church and State. Most notable of Catholic pronouncements has been that of Cardinal James Gibbons, in 1927: "I believe in the absolute separation of Church and State and in the strict enforcement of the provisions of the Constitution that Congress shall make no law respecting the establishment of religion . . . I believe in the support of the public school as one of the cornerstones of American liberty. I believe in the right of every parent to choose whether his child shall be educated in a public school or in a religious school supported by his own faith."

But beyond assent to the basic principle there has arisen, particularly in the past two decades, a variety of interpretations of the separation doctrine that has led to serious conflict.

The Baptists, most zealous in defending separation, have applied the principle in such issues as tax support for parochial education and church hospitals; one Lutheran group has inferred from the doctrine that the military chaplaincy represents an infringement; all of the Protestant groups are united in applying it to the issue of sending a United States envoy to the Vatican. Jewish groups have generally placed their emphasis on another area —that of the public schools, where a number of sectarian intrusions have become more pronounced in recent years.

As a community relations problem, the question of religion in the public school has been most explosive. The Catholic hierarchy has long maintained that the public schools are godless— that by maintaining neutrality in religious matters, they have bred an indifference which has led to antagonism. To the defense made by Professor Conrad Moehlman and others that the schools are indoctrinating children with moral and spiritual values by teaching "fair play, breadth of mind, humanity, and kindness," J. S. Sheerin answers (Catholic World, June, 1952): "This may be a preparation for life in a democracy, but we Catholics do not feel it is sufficient education for living the life of Heaven."

In recent years, the anti-public school ranks have been reinforced by Protestant educators, who share the Catholic concern about secular teachings. The official Protestant position was stated by the National Council of Churches in December, 1952: "A way must be found to make the pupils of American schools aware of the heritage of faith upon which this nation was established, and which has been the most transforming influence in western culture. This we believe can be done in complete loyalty to the basic principle involved in the separation of Church and State."

Christian educators make two basic demands of public education. The schools have a responsibility for overcoming "religious illiteracy," and teaching the historical facts about the role of religious institutions in our culture; and secondly, the schools have an obligation to inculcate a general religious "commitment"—a positive attitude toward God's existence and Providence.

Jewish groups see several serious hazards in this program. Granting that religious literacy is desirable, they question whether enough safeguards can be established to permit objective teaching about religion. Even with well trained teachers and adequate lesson materials, it would seem impossible to present religious "facts" without emotional involvement. To the claim that other subject matter, such as politics and economics, also involve controversy, Jews counter that religious teaching is much more volatile, and likely to transform the classroom into a veritable battleground of sectarian debate. On the matter of commitment, Jewish groups have consistently maintained that the home and the religious school must bear the burden of religious education, and that parents should neither assign nor permit responsibility to be shifted to the public school teacher. So heated has public discussion in this area been that opponents of public school religious education have been labelled as atheists and believers in totalitarian education, while on the other extreme, supporters of religion in the schools have been branded as destroyers of democratic institutions. It is probable that during the next decade further tension will be manifest in this sensitive area.

## The Impact of Events in Israel

Editorial comment on Israel in the Jesuit weekly, *America,* for the past five years, has had one consistent theme. There is a tremendous Christian stake, as well as Jewish and Moslem, in the land of Palestine. It is by no means limited to the Holy places. As one writer observed in the official New York Chancery weekly, the *Catholic News,* all of the soil upon which Jesus trod is precious to the faithful Christian. In April, 1949, the National Catholic Welfare Conference called on American Catholics to obtain from our government and the U. N. continued assurances that the original commitments as to Christian rights in Palestine would be carried out. Generally, debate among religious groups on Israel has been restrained, with occasional flareups on such issues as the internationalization of Jerusalem and the plight of the Arab refugees.

Pro-Israel sentiment among Christians has various philosophic roots. Among liberals a persistent guilt feeling reminds Christians of their apathy in the face of Nazi mass extermination of Jews. They see in the development of the new state a democratic force which can help raise the standard of living in the Near East, and lay the groundwork for peace. Some fundamentalists discover in the miracle of Israel's rebirth fulfillment of Biblical prophecy.

Anti-Israel sentiment in the churches stems from two sources. Some American missionary groups who have worked successfully in the Arab world have a natural kinship with Arab Christians. Many others find it difficult to reconcile the end of homelessness for the Jews with the theological doctrine that Israel's sin of rejecting Christian dogma was to be expiated only by eternal wandering.

### Future Outlook

The complexity of the factors affecting interreligious cooperation in the United States makes it difficult to offer, with any degree of meaningfulness, a prognosis for the future. Faced with the threat of Communism, dramatically revealed by persecution of Lutherans in Eastern Germany, by the steady onslaught against the Roman Catholic church in every Iron Curtain country, and by recent manifestations of Soviet anti-Semitism (documented in *The Jews in the Soviet Union* and *The Jews in the Satellite Countries*), the religious forces in the free world have underscored the need for a spiritual front to turn back the tide of godlessness. On the other hand, the factors of separatism and parochialism have been pervasive enough to prevent the implementation of a genuine program of Protestant-Catholic-Jewish interaction.

Healthy and harmonious relations between the three religious groups will, it seems to me, be determined in the first instance by the degree of religious liberalism in our society. Religious liberty is possible only in an atmosphere in which there is less emphasis on monopoly of truth, on aggressive evangelism, on a turning back to the past, with its heritage of mutual distrust and accent on dogma. Latourette, in his *History of Christianity,* reflects the conservatism of our times when he declares that, in addition to the threat of militant atheism, "the less obviously hostile humanism represented by such men as John Dewey is probably more dangerous" (p. 1230).

The temper of mid-century America is one of political intolerance, suspicion of unorthodox economic theories, and general xenophobia. Religious intolerance, a natural by-product of such a mood, may be intensified if the current wave of hysteria does not subside in the next few years.

Our basic American institutions, the public schools, voluntary civic associations, sports and entertainment, as well as the various media, radio, television, and the press, are all arrayed in a solid mass of public opinion supporting interfaith cooperation. Religious groups are constrained to give lipservice, at least, to the cause of religious amity. If church and synagogue spokesmen insist on building walls instead of bridges, they may find a considerable chasm growing between themselves and their lay following. In the field of race relations, many church leaders, during the past decade, have ruefully pointed to the fact that the churches have been the last to abjure "Jim Crowism." In interfaith cooperation, we shall see the story repeated. Strange indeed, that the brotherhood of man should grow, not out of the Fatherhood of God, as is most logical, but from the secular soil of American democracy.

An important contributory factor in the improvement of interfaith relations is the increased heterogeneity of American life, particularly in the nerve centers of the country, where public opinion is fashioned. The more diverse the religious composition of a city, the more evenly distributed its church and synagogue groups, the greater is the likelihood of relaxed attitudes in Christian-Jewish and Protestant-Catholic relationships.

There are a number of almost irreducible areas of tension, as outlined above—church-state problems, religion in the public schools, evangelism, the problems of divorce, birth control, and censorship. The most we can now aspire to is a reduction of friction, a minimizing of conflict, and a greater amount of mutual forbearance in the face of differences. We can achieve these objectives only by creating the opportunities, on community and national levels, for discussing these problems on a face-to-face basis. It is my firm conviction that this kind of common endeavor, carried out by mature men and women with candor as well as good will, is the *sine qua non* for interfaith peace.

# The Impact of

# Zionism on

# American

# Jewry

## ABRAHAM G. DUKER

The emergence of Israel was a sudden—and to a large extent forced—realization of the Zionist idea of a Jewish national home. Though the idea itself, in various mutations of its original messianic form, had long been entertained and vigorously fostered through Zionist activities, actually, Jewish statehood is the answer to the massive irresistible pressure of world events on the situation of the Jews. Confronted by the horrible reality of physical genocide, followed by a belated tentative awakening on the part of the "civilized" nations, after years of indifference, to the fearful plight of the Jewish survivors of World War II, the Zionist leaders of the Jewish community of Palestine found their hand forced, and, with a courage born of desperation, proclaimed the establishment of the State of Israel. Psychologically, Zionist leaders—and they alone—had long since rid themselves of the vacuous illusory optimism spawned by the Emancipation. Among the Jewish bourgeoisie, this optimism took the form of a faith that progress and enlightenment would secure complete social equality for Jews within the nations that had begun the process, some time before, by granting citizenship to their Jewish residents. Among Jewish intellectuals, pseudo-intellectuals and semi-educated proletarians, that optimism based itself on faith in a social revolution that would, among other things, automatically solve the Jewish question. In either case, these emancipationist delusions constituted a major obstacle to the acceptance of the Zionist idea by the broad mass of the American Jewish community. The relentless logic of events, however, pointed to but one road out of the ever-narrowing impasse in which Jewry found itself on the morrow of the conclusion of the war. The solution of the Jewish question, in its physical aspects at least, could be found only in statehood.

Slowly, but with mounting intensity and with the force of trip-hammer blows, the inexorable march of anti-Semitism in the 30's dissolved the emancipationist mirage of permanent legal equality for Jews and their gradual acculturation or assimilation to the culture of the Christian world. (Recent writers, embarrassed by the negative connotations of the term assimilation, prefer the positive-sounding term "integration." The intent remains the same and offers evidence that the process of disenchantment with emancipationist philosophy is yet to be completed in certain Jewish circles.)

The more drastic of the events referred to may be briefly chronicled here. The closed-door immigration policy of the United States of 1924 was the signal for the adoption of similar policies throughout the world. In Palestine, immigration restrictions culminated in the racist brutality of the White Paper of 1939. The mass murder of Jews by Hitler, and its tacit acceptance by the German people; the host of willing accomplices the Nazis readily found in almost all occupied countries; the general indifference of the leadership of the Western World and of the Soviet Union; the active hostility of Islamic leaders—taken together, these constituted an irrefragable case for the Zionist contention that the Jewish people, if it were to survive, needed control over at least one door open to Jewish immigration. Thus,

the vast majority of American Jews, educated by the unforgettable lesson taught by unforgettable events, came to enthusiastic
espousal of the statehood (Zionist) solution. This espousal,
strikingly expressed in enormous financial and political support
of Zionism and Israel, has tended to obscure the spiritual, psychological and cultural contributions of Zionism to the welfare
of American Jewry. In the absence of an authoritative cultural
and social history of American Jewry, let alone a history of Zionism, the present essay will be perforce in the form of a tentative
sketch of the theme. The author trusts that in time the details
will be filled in and documented.


II


            The Hitler holocaust has naturally served to ac-
centuate the physical achievements of Zionism; namely, rescue,
refugee absorption and statehood. In its advocacy of a Jewish
renaissance, however, Zionism had also set for itself the task of
rescuing Jewry from the assimilation and self-deprecation that
followed in the wake of the emancipationist ideologies. Arthur
Ruppin concluded his classic sociological treatise *Die Juden der
Gegenwart* (written before World War I) with a presentation
of Zionism as the prime movement capable of checking the cor-
roding influence of assimilation and spiritual deterioration. Ruppin's analysis and thesis were essentially correct. Ever since the
rise of the Emancipation, Zionism has been the chief factor in
raising Jewish morale. It has served as the basis for the continuity of Jewish life in both its spiritual and physical dimensions.
Up to the Emancipation, Judaism—a synthesis of religious faith
and peoplehood—effectively sustained Jewish morale. But with
the advance of Emancipation, it could no longer adequately
perform this task among most Westernized Jews. Like the overwhelming majority of American Jews today, Ruppin, as a Westernized Jew, sensed that Zionism would succeed where the
Jewish religion by itself had failed. Thus, Zionist ideals were a
potent factor in raising the morale of every type of Jewish com-

munity, whether Western, Eastern or Oriental. To each, Zionism
was able to bring that which it needed most: into Eastern European Jewry, it brought Western civilization without assimilation; into the West, it brought renewed Jewish vigor and the
basis for a return to Judaism as a religion; and to the Jews of the
Orient, it gave an introduction to Westernization without de-
Judaisation.

The generalization may be allowed that Zionism, a democratic, nationalist movement, functioned differently among Westernized and relatively non-Westernized communities. In such
Westernized communities as Germany, France and the Nether-
lands, Zionism meant a return to Judaism of the assimilated. One
thinks, in this connection, of figures like André Spire in France,
Hannah Senes in Hungary and Enzio Sereni in Italy, and the
thousands to whom Zionism spelled a return to Judaism. Sym-
bolic of its morale-sustaining power is the dignity with which
Zionist leaders and their press met the Hitler onslaught in Germany. "The yellow badge—wear it with pride."

We are apt to view Zionism among East European Jews as a
predominantly secular nationalist movement. However, the character of Zionist secularism can be gauged only by comparison
with other secularist movements in Eastern Europe: Bundism,
Yiddishism (in the main), Assimilationism, both of the right and
left. By studying these movements we observe that even "secular" Zionism enjoyed much more intimate relationship with Jewish religio-cultural tradition, and therefore with Judaism, than
the other secular movements. Unlike the Yiddishist secularist
schools, the Zionist Hebrew schools observed *kashrut*, Jewish
holidays, paraded their children through the streets to the synagogue on holidays and celebrations with a nationalist tinge such
as Hanukkah, Balfour Day, Herzl Day. This spelled less of a
break with tradition. Even the Hashomer Hatzair, with all its
secularism and deadly combination of primitive Leninism and
Freudianism, guarded the Bible, at least under the pretense of
teaching literature, just as it had retained circumcision. The
attempt to "capture" the *kehillot* (communities), the folk-
character of the Zionist movement, its closeness to the masses—

all these factors reduced Zionism's anti-religionist tension. Just as Zionism rescued the Russianized Jews (e.g. Pinsker) from assimilation, it did so for Polonized, Rumanianized, Magyarized, and even Czechized and Slovakized Jews.

Since the turn of the century, the inroads of liberalism and socialism in the environing cultures, the hedonistic bourgeois and capitalistic acculturation, and the rigidity of Orthodoxy, made a revolt against religion in East Europe communities inevitable. The break with tradition on the part of Jewish youth meeting Western culture face to face was drastic. Its motivation must be sought in the spread of rationalism, in intoxication with a seemingly open "everyman's culture," utopianism, material rewards, and the very slow development of a vital Westernized Orthodoxy or Conservative Judaism.

To East European Jews who no longer could accept their religious life, Zionism supplied a way of life with substantial Jewish cultural background in which the religious elements were often concealed under nationalism to suit the taste of the times and the escapists from religion. Zionism also helped to develop Westernized forms of Jewish culture, and thus made it possible for the latter to compete on a psychological level with the local culture. This is seen most strikingly in the rise of modern Yiddish and Hebrew literature, press and other media, and the fashioning of a new type of Jewishly Westernized individual. While Zionism cannot claim full credit for the renaissance of Yiddish, it can make such claim for the thriving revival of Hebrew. To a large extent, the growth of a Jewish scholarship that is no longer motivated by apologetics as was its earlier precursor, *Juedische Wissenschaft,* can be ascribed to Zionist influence. The significance for spiritual Jewish continuity of a Jewish cultural home for intellectuals and semi-intellectuals was profound. It lent them stamina to face a milieu where not only was Judaism sneered at as an inferior religion but Jews were uniformly labeled as second-rate human beings. In such climate, Westernized Jewish intellectuals called Yiddish a jargon, Hebrew a dead language attached to a dead culture, Zionism a chimera and Judaism a barbaric relic. Persons whose Western culture is derived solely or predominantly from the "general" culture—a combination of Christian and secular elements—and who have little background in Jewish history and Jewish social development, find it difficult to understand that there can be a Western culture in a Jewish medium. However, to the student of the history of Jewish culture, the function of Zionism as a dike that stemmed the drift of Westernized Jews from Jewish belonging-ness is quite clear. Zionism saved millions of Jews from assimilation and Communist nihilism, by offering them an outlet for living within the Jewish community, outside of, or in addition to, the *Shulhan Arukh* (orthodox code of Jewish law) way, which they could no longer accept. Those who accepted the logic of Zionism and had the opportunity to emigrate to the Holy Land were saved from Hitlerism, physical genocide and Communist spiritual genocide, and were thus preserved for the Jewish people and ultimately, we hope, also for Judaism.

My emphasis on the importance of Zionism for Judaism as a religion should not be misinterpreted as an effort to limit Jewish cultural expression to its religious form only. For myself, I cannot visualize a creative Jewish life in or outside of Israel without religious forms. At the same time, however, as a believer in cultural pluralism and cultural democracy I fully recognize the right of a fully secularized Jewish culture to exist anywhere. This is a democratic right of all cultures, and to condemn a culture to one channel of expression—the religious—is as totalitarian and spiritually genocidal as it is to restrict a culture to its secular expression. Jewish culture in the Soviet Union is a case in point. The religious and Hebraic expressions of Jewish culture were severely restricted and later even its secular forms were virtually outlawed. I shall discuss the religionist onslaught on Zionism elsewhere in this essay. At this stage, I merely want to register my view of at least the tolerability of different forms of Jewish culture as a democratic group right.

To evaluate the course of Zionist influence on American Jewry, we must first analyze the cultural character of the community. American Jewry began as a culturally emancipated community. Its mixed origin and small numbers made English the

daily language and did not permit the continuity of Portuguese or
Yiddish in the Colonial Period. Similarly, German and Yiddish
culture did not last beyond the immigrant generations in the
later periods. Until the present generation, American Jewry has
been composed predominantly of immigrants, in various stages of
adjustment to Western culture, mainly through the process of
acculturation or Americanization. This process has generally
been accompanied by Jewish deculturation, depending on the
length of stay, background and social adjustment.

American Zionism performed in this country the same functions that characterized it among both Westernized and non-
Westernized Jews. For the immigrant, upon his first stage of
contact with Western culture, Zionism performed here the function of a *maskilic* (enlightening) and Westernizing influence,
without the excesses of the vulgar acculturation particularly
typical of the *allrightnick* and pre-*allrightnick*. The latter was
to be found even in the proletarian stage of Jewish social development and was not even lacking in the refined assimilation
of the "better elements" that too often passed for true Americanization. To the assimilated descendants of the earlier immigrants, Zionism brought here, as it had done to their European
counterparts, the vigor and will to continue as Jews. It laid the
basis for Westernized Jewish culture in English. Zionism was the
major factor in continuing here the concept of *Klal Yisroel*—one
Jewish people—in a community driven apart by differences in
religious outlook, class, ethnic origin, ideology and the continued escapism from Jewish life and affiliation.

Unlike the cosmopolite type of laborite enlightenment of the
1890's and its Yiddishist laborite versions, American Zionism was
never anti-religious. The early *Hoveve Zion*—East European
*maskilim* and the few rabbis of German and even Sephardic origin who joined them—never separated themselves from religious
life. This tradition was continued even by the "secular" Zionist,
few of whom were really consistent secularists. Even Labor
Zionists never ran Yom Kippur balls, although they were non-
religious and some even anti-religious. In its revival of Jewish
education through the *hedarim metukanim* (modern Talmud

Torahs) and other institutions, Zionism emphasized Hebrew, the Jewish national home and the national renaissance, but not in opposition to religious life.

As was the case in Eastern Europe, many Jews who came face to face with Westernization in this country and could no longer find their place in any synagogue, found expression for their Jewish life in the Zionist movement. Like the *landsmanschaft* and the lodge, Zionism, too, performed functions of Americanization, such as inducing, though less consciously perhaps than other institutions and movements, the linguistic change from Yiddish to English and acquainting the newcomers with American parliamentary procedure and political action.

Zionism played an important role in destroying some negative residues of the East European experience. It rejected the now romanticized *shtetl* (small town) atmosphere whose quietist stagnancy served to alienate children from their immigrant parents. It would seem to me—to judge by the relatively larger participation of the American-born or trained youth in the Zionist movement than in other movements with a cultural or ideological rather than purely social or institutional basis—that Zionism succeeded in stamping a Jewish pattern of cultural continuity more effectively than other movements. Unlike the *landsmanschaft,* the lodge, and even the trade union, Zionism brought to its participants a broader perspective, Jewishly speaking. It fostered a point of view that embraced the world Jewish people and world political developments, with some awareness of Jewish literature and even scholarship on a popular level. The Zionists waged ideological battles with the assimilationists, both Reform and laborite, without the resources of wealth of the former and the mass appeal and mass pressure of the latter. The Labor Zionists, in particular, carried on a difficult struggle as a small and unpopular minority against the strong appeals of naive cosmopolitanism, the Bundist Marxist utopianism and the anti-Jewish complex of the Anarchist. Anti-Zionist proletarian movements controlled the trade unions for a long time. The latter were slow in even accepting Yiddish secularism. Their failure to think in terms of an American Jewish community was reflected

in their version of Jewish education. The latter's anti-religious
and anti-Zionist emphasis (these have changed, of course) may
have been as costly in cultural survivalist terms as the bourgeois
type of assimilationism through hedonism (known in the immigrant milieu as *allrightnickism*). Its dire effects paralleled the
less vulgar acclamation of Judaism as a religion only, and the
drastic reduction of its cultural contents that followed such definition.

"We are one people"—Herzl's summary of the essence of Zionism—constituted its chief distinction from the other turn-of-the-
century ideologies in an era of cosmopolite optimism and belief
in progress on the right and center, and revolutionary expecta-
tion on the left. This call for Jewish peoplehood negated the
laborites' unrealistic division of the Jewish people into classes
that supposedly had nothing in common with each other and the
Marxist decree of doom for the Jewish people by proletarian assimilation following the revolution. Peoplehood also implied dis-
agreement with the *Protestrabbiner* (German rabbis opposed to
Herzl), with the Frankfort *Trennungsorthodoxie* (separatist Orthodoxy) and its more primitive offspring, the Agudist movement
of Eastern Europe. Most of the adherents of these movements
came to the United States in large numbers following the Hitler onslaught. But by that time, the culture patterns of American
Jewry had been stamped as distinctly pro-Zionist for at least a
generation to come. These Orthodox separationists presented a
scant problem for Zionism here, just as the pro-*Neturai Karta*
(extreme Orthodox anti-Zionist) elements of today constitute an
annoying but harmless group in contrast to the American Council for Judaism, their counterpart, if not partner, from the
"integrationist" side of the fence. The intellectual and spiritual
antecedent of the Council movement, the *Trennungsreform* (separatist Reform), followed a less primitive and even less escapist
line in the assertion of its emancipationist ideology and its ex-
clusivist religionist Jewish group definition than its present per-
verse offspring. Its view of Judaism, moreover, was combined
with the ethnic culture of the German Jews.

Zionism in America also furnished the chief bridge between

the self-appointed yet generally recognized leadership élite of German provenance and the East European newcomers. Remnants of the tradition of cleavage between the two groups are still with us. The 19th century "German" Jews left relatively few descendants, because of their lower marriage and birth rates and probably also because of their high intermarriage and assimilation rates. Those descendants who have remained Jews and their offspring who want to remain Jews are becoming or will become a part of the American Jewish melting pot, a community that is predominantly East European in descent and whose Jewish cultural ingredients of the more intellectual type are basically East European- and Israel-influenced. The newcomers of the Hitler era find few difficulties in being absorbed into the American Jewish melting pot. The exodus from the Jewish community has by this time become, numerically speaking, the problem of descendants of East European Jews, and this is the basic problem of Jewish survival in America. We have no knowledge of the extent to which the desire for separation from the East European newcomers had been a factor in the exodus from the Jewish community on the part of the descendants of the earlier arrivals, although I suspect that it is not to be underestimated. (Perhaps a similar course may be followed by the descendants of the present initiators of the American Council for Judaism in their hopeless struggle to read themselves out of the Jewish peoplehood collectivity.) Our children are but little cognizant of the old hostility between the "Bayers" and the "Pollacks." They are more aware of the strife between the "Yiddin" and the "Yahudim" or "Deitchen." But they have little notion of the extent of this hostility and are apt to view it in the light of the relatively minor *Litvak-Galitsianer* family quarrel. In contrast, the German–East European feud was bitter and enduring. Of course, the abandonment of the peoplehood concept was honored more in theology and ideology than in defense and philanthropy, and the German Jewish leadership was conscious of its responsibility to the newcomers. However, this group, well entrenched in the middle and upper classes and painfully conscious of the snobbery of the Gentile *nouveau riche,* was in dreadful fear of being compromised by indentification with the bearded, radical and poor newcomers. Attempts were made in the seventies and eighties to "regulate"—really check—Jewish immigration. European organizations were asked to stop passage payments for the poor and some even sent immigrants back to Russia. Editors of Anglo-Jewish papers advised that the newcomers be sent to Alaska or that Russian Jewry fight the Tsar to gain freedom as Americans had fought for freedom in 1776. When the Germans realized that they could not turn the tide back they concentrated on Americanization efforts, characterized all too often by de-Judaisation and religious-cultural uprooting. Relief to newcomers involved the strained relationship of donor and recipient. The common interest in European relief during World War I could not overcome the social separation that was widely practiced even against the American-born children of East European Jews. Religion could no more function as the molder of communal unity than it can today. In this cleavage, Zionism became the bridge between some intellectual descendants of the earlier arrivals and the newcomers. Prominent among these intellectuals of Western European provenance were Mendes, Friedenwald, Felsenthal, Gottheil, Wise and Magnes (half-Russian, but acculturated in the German group). Brandeis, Mack, Szold and others shared the struggle of the small group that attempted to revolutionize the Zionist movement. At the time, the Zionist movement was despised and ignored by "better class" Jews. Its leaders were portrayed as an odd assortment of *schlemiels,* and upstart trouble-makers given to abstract theories who did not know their place in American society. However, it was this movement that paved the way for other efforts of understanding and unity between the "Up Town" and "Down Town" Jews.

Zionism, as I have stated, maintained the idea of *Klal Yisroel,* a concept that overrides parochial denominational or class lines whether on the trade union or country club level. To a generation still troubled by Jewish intellectual problems, Zionism brought a countermeasure to the rising tide of smugness and hedonism and served as a meeting ground on an equal level between Jewish intellectuals and the masses, living in all kinds of cultures. How much of this ideology is still with us to offset the impact of the new *allrightnick* hedonism is unknown. That fact, that Zionist youth is still the most idealistic and even dreams of *halutziyut* (pioneering in Israel), is evidence of some degree of idealism. Moreover, it would indicate that we still live to a large extent by the ideas diffused by Zionism in its heyday.

III

In the field of Jewish education, Zionism's contribution has been signal. Before its emergence on the American scene, Jewish education consisted of old-fashioned *hedarim* (Jewish schools) and Sunday Schools. During the period of East European immigration, Zionism furnished one of the main motives of Jewish education. The *hedarim metukanim*—improved *hedarim*—out of which grew the modern communal Talmud Torahs that were adequate for a generation in many communities, were pioneered by Zionist *maskilim* and intellectuals. Zionists were in the forefront of the efforts to preserve the Hebrew language in American life. Zionists constituted the rank and file of Hebrew teachers and of the newer modern experimenters in Jewish education. Religious Zionist groups have spearheaded the new and more modern Yeshiva type of education. The directors of the bureaus of Jewish education, the principals of schools, and the young people who were willing to enter upon Jewish education as a career found their initial stimulation in the Zionist movement.

There is a tendency in some quarters today to limit Jewish education to its purely religious aspects. This type of education characterized 19th century Reform Judaism. It is doubtful whether it will be more successful in perpetuating Judaism here in the 20th century than it was in the 19th. The indispensable folk element of peoplehood is lacking. Zionism supplied that ingredient. It supplied the folk song, the dance, the costume, the element of modern Jewish heroism.

A word must also be said about Jewish scholarship. American Zionism is guilty of not having created any scholarly institutions or traditions. The reasons for this failure are complex. The fact that it had been and continues to be pressed for funds may furnish it with a legitimate excuse. But with persons like Schechter and Neumark and Tchernowitz on faculties of rabbinical institutions there was evidently no thought of the need for stimulating and subsidizing scholarship. Most scholars in the Jewish field have been Zionist or stem from Zionist background. Zionism supplied a rationale for scholarship among non-religious scholars just as all national renaissance movements served to inspire research into their respective pasts.

Hardly less pervasive than Zionism's influence on Jewish education has been its impress on religious life. Paradoxically, this has been most obvious in Reform Judaism, precisely because the latter movement stood farthest removed from the concept of Jewish peoplehood in the national rather than the strictly religious sense. The reintroduction of Jewish cultural patterns into Reform Judaism in recent decades must be ascribed, in the main, to the influence of Zionism. It was the espousal of Zionism by some of the leading spokesmen of Reform, and by the overwhelming majority of Reform rabbis, that prevented the movement from becoming isolated from the rank and file of American Jewry of East European background. Indeed, it was from the latter group that Reform drew its rabbinic leadership in the past forty years. Had it not then been for Zionism, it is quite likely that Reform would have remained a small frozen minority rather than a major wing, in numbers and influence, in American Judaism. Zionism has been a significant factor in the formation of Conservative Judaism. Its role in the growth of Conservatism, though owing much to the personal Zionist commitments of Schechter, Friedlander and other Conservative leaders, had another important origin. The Westernized Zionists among the immigrants who wanted to retain their connection with the synagogue very often found Conservative Judaism most attractive, and that largely because of its Zionist position. In turn, Conservative Judaism was identified as an out-and-out Zionist wing in American Jewry. Conservative Judaism's Zionism gave the erstwhile Orthodox a feeling of at-homeness and democracy in that branch of Judaism.

With the exception of some of the Hasidic and Agudath Israel groups of today, American Orthodoxy has always been militantly Zionist. Orthodox Zionist sentiment was not confined to the rather limited membership of Mizrachi. In fact, there were more members of Orthodox synagogues in the general Zionist movement than in its religious wings. The Orthodox *shul* was the place where the itinerant Zionist *maggid* (preacher) or his modern counterpart would deliver his message in the era before the ornate synagogue or community center. It was the locale of the Zionist appeals, the telegrams, the elections, the Jewish National Fund box collection, the Talmud Torah Hebrew recitals, the Young Judea clubs, and even the earliest Hadassah chapters. As in Europe, Zionism was the chief influence that kept the would-be *Trennungsorthodoxie* within the fold of *Klal Yisroel* (the Jewish collectivity).

Zionism became the chief factor in maintaining Jewish morale during the nightmare of the Hitler period and the years that followed it. The 1930's constituted a tragic period in American Jewish life. Both the depression and the rise of the New Deal numbed the sense of reality of the community. The established Jewish leadership was unable to face the fact that Germany, the home of its ancestors, could relapse into barbarism and that something could be done to save European Jewry. In 1935, a prominent Jewish defense organization actually dispatched a good-will rabbi to try to talk sense to Hitler. So much for the "official" leadership. The situation was worse when it came to the intellectuals and would-be-intellectuals. To the Stalinoid fellow travellers, Communism with its united fronts and people's fronts brought the delusion that the Red Messiah would save European Jewry by saving the entire world. The actual party members, like their comrades everywhere, were willing to grease the wheels of the revolution with Jewish blood. Fellow travelling was particularly rampant among the communal functionaries ruled by the established leadership. Coughlinism and

America First served to frighten American Jewry further, and its established leadership was even afraid to commit itself openly to the support of the war against Nazism. Some escapism was found in the 1940's in the war activities which turned out to be another outlet for non-sectarianism.

At that stage, Zionism provided the major outlet for maintaining Jewish morale and the avenue for Jewish re-identification of the youthful and the estranged. First, it resisted Communism and indifference. Secondly, it offered a practical program and a rallying ground. Zionism was not popular in government quarters where it was viewed as a delusion that Jews would be well rid of. That notion continued to sway some influential segments of Jewish public opinion. The Hitler slaughter and the resistance of the *Yishuv* (Jewish community of Palestine) and the D.P.'s, together with the determined activities of American Zionism, just about dispelled this notion even among "respectable" Jewish elements, including important religious spokesmen.

American Jewry relived in the 1940's some of the exhilarating experiences of World War I, when Zionism was successful in establishing the American Jewish Congress, an overall representation of almost the entire community. The Congress proved helpful in the initial realization of Zionism through the Balfour Declaration and the establishment of the British Mandate over the Holy Land. There was a difference, however. During World War I the rank and file in this mass drama was composed of European-born Jews. In contrast, the moving force behind the realization of Zionism during World War II consisted of American-born Jews. Zionist sentiment found expression not only through the phenomenal growth of the Zionist movement, but also through the non-sectariam "Hebrew National" front organizations sponsored by Revisionist groups. Only a high degree of group morale made it possible for the Zionist movement to defy government regulations and, on occasion, the highest officials when they proved unwilling to cut red tape in the desperate efforts to save the remnants of European Jewry. Indeed, the 1940's marked a period of commitment of Jewishness and identification with it through Zionism that required greater cour-

age than, say, the act of joining a synagogue center in the suburbs. (I suspect that many of these joiners once marched in
veterans' parades against government policy.)

Much of this Jewish reidentification through synagogue institutions in the 1950's has been a result of the earlier Zionist impact. During this period, many American-born Jews were
touched by the morale of the ghetto Jew and achieved proud
Jewish commitment. This identification with Zionism was a
most important factor in Jewish community life. It was fund
raising for Israel that helped to maintain communal unity and
successful campaigns for local Jewish causes. The impact of
Zionism as the solution to the physical problems of persecuted
Jewry, propounded theoretically before statehood and practically
achieved after it, was the major factor in building Jewish morale.
Even allowing for the trend to the suburbs and the subsequent
broad movement towards Jewish reidentification, Jewish morale
in America does not stand at the high level it reached in the
1940's.

The expression of Jewish identification through Zionism has
many facets, all of them worthy of study. They range from the
introduction of regular prayers for Israel in the Orthodox synagogue to the normalcy of the appearance of the Zionist or Israeli
flag at Jewish gatherings whose participants cannot imagine that
their Americanism thereby becomes suspect. They are seen in
the little synagogue art shops, in the Israeli Seder plates and pic-
tures in homes committed to Judaism, in the substitution of the
*hora* (Israeli dance) for the *sher* (East European dance) at
weddings and other *simhot* (celebrations) where notions of
middle-class dignity do not inhibit Jews from expressing joy in
Jewish dance forms. It is to be noted in the Yeshiva youth that
does not hide its *yarmulke* (skull cap) in the subways.

The impact of Zionism is also seen in the change of the status
of the Jew among non-Jewish Americans. Until very recently,
community relations experts have generally operated on the notion that the security of the Jews in America rests upon the reas-
sertion of the concept of religious tolerance and the democratic
way of life. Its negative pole is the avoidance of any impression

of international Jewish contact or of Jewish group definition that
goes beyond the mono-religionist view. It is only of late that
people engaged in the field have begun to realize that Arab hostility against Israel must have repercussions in world Jewry and
therefore in American Jewry. In considering this problem, it is
essential to remember how many non-Jews became actively interested in the Zionist solution in the 1940's and continue to
maintain their interest in it. This type of non-Jewish co-operation
in concrete pro-Jewish projects that requires actual commitment and not merely vapid expressions of good will is a signal
achievement in community relations. Another achievement is
the popularization of the image of the fighting Jew—not only the
Jew fighting for America—all Americans are expected to fight
for America—but the Jew who fights for his own people, a creature of flesh and blood. This image has largely displaced the mysterious, self-effacing, behind-the-scenes figure widely diffused by
the deadly myth of the Protocols of the Elders of Zion. The fact
that Jewish East Sides, or whatever is left of them, are nowadays
called Little Israel, like Little Italy, and not ghettos, is a sign of
normalcy of status. Zionism has also made and continues to make
a significant contribution to democracy in America by insisting
on a culturally pluralistic America. As I have pointed out, it has
been fashionable in some Jewish quarters to exclude non-
religious persons from genuinely Jewish as well as American
identification. It is maintained that only religious differences are
to be tolerated in American life and that the fostering of ethnic
culture is un-American. This has been a potent argument for
rallying Jews to the synagogue. However, I deem it un-
American since there can be no religious qualifications for
Americanism. Furthermore, once we establish that only religious
persons can be good Americans, other persons will define what
religious persons are. Conceivably, they may exclude Jews from
that category, just as, according to some theologies, Judaism is
really not a religion. Zionism, by continuing to assert the principle of cultural pluralism, performs a useful service to American
society; by insisting that Jews maintain their own Hebraic culture and language it contributes to a culturally symphonic rather

than a totalitarian America. It is quite possible that in due time
other ethnic cultures will vanish through assimilation in the various racial-religious melting pots: the White Protestant, the
White Catholic, the Negro Protestant and the Negro Latin-
American Catholic. This putative assimilation, however, has no
bearing on the status and future of American Jews. We are an
international people connected by ties of peoplehood and religion. To sunder any of these ties is to bring an end to our existence in the Diaspora, and perhaps also in Israel. Jewish historical experience since Emancipation provides sufficient warrant
for this conclusion.

We must face the fact that Zionism as a movement and as an
effective influence faces many difficulties in Jewish life today. I
am not referring in this connection to the dilemmas that
Diaspora Zionism has been facing since the establishment of
Israel and that revolve around the attitude toward *kibutz galuyot*
(the ingathering of the exiles) and the future of the Diaspora.
Nor do I intend the disqualification of American Zionists as
Zionists by Israeli ideologues and political leaders. I refer rather
to the tendency in some American quarters not only to liquidate
Zionism as a movement but also to erase the awareness of its
past role from the consciousness of American Jewry.

We are now witnessing a return to emancipationist attempts
to divest Jewishness of its elements of peoplehood, a process not
unlike similar efforts by Reform Judaism in the 19th century. Such
attempts are being made not only by public relations tacticians
and the secular and de-Judaised inheritors of emancipationist
assimilation—the followers of the American Council for Judaism—in search of protective coloring, but also by some religionist elements who ought to know better. Thus, the group nature
of American Jewry is represented as predominantly if not exclusively religious, and deliberate efforts are made to present Judaism as a purely religious development. In contrast, Israeli Jewry
is presented as an overwhelmingly secularist and nationalist
community, with whom this presumably pious and religious-
centered American Jewish community has little in common. This
confrontation ignores the obvious parallels of the non-religious

American

bi:

nging

e

NARD J. BAMBERGER

merican rabbi is a novel and unique phe-
on in Jewish experience. His office is re-
o the earlier forms of Jewish leadership by
nity; yet the modern rabbinate presents so
in function and temper as to constitute a
n.

ies to orthodox, conservative, and reform
ent of their message may differ substan-
r, methods, and problems of their profes-
ne same. An effort is now being made to
l journal for the three rabbinical groups
of the Synagogue Council of America.
tempt is successful, it strikingly illustrates
merican rabbinate has new and distinctive
are eager to learn more about the tech-

trends in both communities. An American rabbinical thinker has
even stated that there is more religion in his congregation (typical Eastern middle class) than in all Israel. The tendency to
return to the *Protestrabbiner* attitude is also illustrated by the
statement of an English rabbi who equates assimilation with the
waning of the definition of Judaism as a religion. He equates the
diminishing popularity of the definition with a decline of religion. He terms Zionism, because of its nationalist secular character, an assimilationist influence in Jewish life. However, not all
nationalist movements in Judaism have been secularist: Mizrachi,
for example. Moreover, secularization is a world-wide phenomenon, and is not limited to the Jewish people. Despite the present
emphasis on religion in the West, particularly in the United
States, secularization is an ongoing process. Modern society's increasing secular character appears to be accentuated in Israel
because of the relative youthfulness of its Westernized population. It has been aggravated by the failure of the religious elements in world Jewry to participate adequately either in the
Zionist movement or more directly, through *halutziyut* (emigration to Israel).

American Jewry has also been undergoing a similar process of
increasing secularization. This process is less marked among the
remnants of ideological secularists groups, such as Yiddishists,
than it is among native American Jews, as seen in the latter's
continued abandonment of religious observances and the weakening of its culture patterns. However, the current reidentification and affiliation tendency is a promising phenomenon. It has
been termed a miracle. Actually it is a result of a concatenation
of historical events and social tendencies: namely, the Hitler catastrophe, the struggle involved around the establishment of Israel, the impact of the Jewish State, the increasing distance of
the majority of American Jews from the immigrant generation, their growing middle-class character, the movement to the
suburbs and new housing areas, the current emphasis on religious affiliation as a prime factor in respectability and normalcy
in American society (particularly under the impact of the struggle against Communism), the "New Conservatism," and the in-

creasing influence of the Catholic Church. Those who see this process of reidentification as purely American in causation need to be reminded that synagogue affiliation, promising though it is for a thriving Jewish life, does not always strengthen the individual's own Jewish life or the religious expression of the Jewish community. The criteria for these developments in Judaism go beyond congregational membership and occasional synagogue attendance.

The three hundred years of Jewish life in America have been three hundred years of restorationist sentiment among Jews. Research may reveal the existence of Christian restorationist sentiment in North America even before the official arrival of the Jews on this continent. *Meshulachim* (emissaries from the Holy Land) from Israel appeared here in Colonial times. Proposals of political Zionism date back as far as the beginnings of the 19th century, if not earlier. American Jewry has been a mainstay of world Zionism, but, as we see it, it has also been greatly enriched by the fructifying influence of the Zionist movement. It is not the writer's task to draw up a plan for Zionist activities for the future on the basis of its shortcomings in the past. The failures of American Zionism are readily enumerated. It has failed to create a *halutziyut* movement, to Hebraise Jewish life, to enter more deeply into Jewish education, particularly on the adult level. It has tended to neglect Jewish scholarship and the approach to the intellectuals. It has had surprisingly little impact even on the curricula of the rabbinical seminaries. It has not created media of communications in English, such as a national family magazine, to replace the declining Yiddish press. It has done little to stimulate the academic field into an appreciation of the Jewish point of view in history, humanities and the social sciences. It has shelved its interest in a democratic Jewish community, and has not had sufficient impact on Jewish communal institutions, functionaries and community relations. Finally, it failed to stimulate the establishment of a survivalist intellectual meeting ground or headquarters.

Nevertheless, Zionism has been a chief mainstay of Jewish life here. It is inconceivable to me that American Jewry will con-

niques of their profession; and that these professional tasks are common to all our rabbis, regardless of their denominational philosophy or affiliation. A detailed historical account of the American Rabbinate and its not inconsiderable achievements is a desideratum; since our present purpose, however, is an analysis of the American Rabbi's changing role, we content ourselves with only a brief historical survey. For the evolution of the new profession is not yet complete, and the role and status of the rabbi have not been adequately defined. Neither the American Jewish community nor the Rabbis themselves are ready for far reaching decisions on the subject. The present essay, by assembling some relevant data and stating the chief problems, may contribute something toward a satisfying solution.

For whether American Jews like it or not (and some of them do not), they are heavily dependent on their rabbis. The future character of American Jewish life, in fact its very existence, will be largely determined by its spiritual leaders. It has become ever plainer, above all since the establishment of the State of Israel, that a distinctive Jewish life in America can survive only if that distinctiveness has a religious quality. Jewish life must be centered more and more in the synagogue—and the modern synagogue is to a great extent the lengthened shadow of its rabbi.

Except for a few atypical individuals, the rabbis are our only repositories of solid and authentic Jewish knowledge. Professional Jewish functionaries have multiplied in our generation, but their competence is chiefly in some general field—psychiatric counselling, "group work," public relations, fund raising, etc. With a few notable exceptions, they have only a limited Jewish education; some are not aware of basic Jewish values, or are even hostile to them. Only the rabbi has had a training in which Jewish content was central.

All American Jews must recognize—though the admission may be distasteful to some of them—that their destiny will be decided in no small degree by the caliber of their rabbis. It is to the clear interest of everyone that American rabbis be men of the highest intellectual and spiritual gifts, adequately trained, and working under the best conditions for effective service.

I

Ironically, almost two centuries were to elapse from the date of the Jewish settlement in America before a regular ordained rabbi was to come to the United States. He was Abraham Rice, a traditionalist of the old German School, who arrived in New York in 1840 and shortly thereafter established himself in Baltimore. The ensuing decades saw the coming of a number of European rabbis, many of them university graduates. Max Lilienthal, Isaac M. Wise, David Einhorn, Sabato Morais, Marcus Jastrow, Samuel Hirsch, Benjamin Szold, Kaufmann Kohler, and Alexander Kohut were perhaps the most gifted among them.

But before any of these notables had reached our shores, a new pattern of Jewish spiritual leadership had been set by the Hazzan-ministers already serving in many congregations. The majority of these figures are long since (perhaps happily) forgotten. But Gershom Mendes Seixas, Samuel M. Isaacs, Morris Raphall, and Isaac Leeser were men of stature. It was they who, for good or evil, created the profession of the American rabbi.

True, they had modeled themselves in part on the example of the modernized rabbis of western Europe. But this pattern could not be followed mechanically. The European rabbi was still the head of an organized community, usually recognized by the State. This fact, though it gave him prestige and authority, also restricted his activities in various ways. The American Jewish rabbi, in contrast, was the leader of a voluntary association, sometimes in competition with other synagogues. The techniques of Protestant pastors, which had been adopted to some extent by the European rabbis, were also borrowed directly by the American Hazzan-ministers. But the total pattern they evolved was something new. The American Jewish minister was preacher, pastor, community worker, teacher of the young, and spokesman for the Jewish group. He was often the moving spirit in the establishment of new philanthropic agencies, necessitated by the steady increase of Jewish population.

He also had to create many of the tools needed for his work. In this area Leeser was outstanding. He produced highly serviceable translations of the Bible and prayerbook, and founded one of the earliest American Jewish periodicals. The Bible translation was generally adopted by American Jews; but Leeser's successors vied with him in the production of manuals for worship and instruction, and in the publication of Jewish family magazines.

The American Jewish rabbi was also the representative and ambassador of the community to the non-Jewish world. He defended Judaism against the slanders of the prejudiced and the onslaughts of the missionaries. He explained the beliefs and practices of his religion to Christian audiences that were always curious and sometimes sympathetically receptive. Nineteenth century America saw the emergence of a new and remarkable phenomenon—interfaith activity: and Jewish leaders participated with Christian ministers in joint Thanksgiving services and in offering prayer at patriotic celebrations. Rabbis spoke out boldly on the great issues of American life; the first great dramatic instance, no doubt, was when Einhorn preached against slavery in the slave state of Maryland.

To all these functions inherited from the Hazzan-ministers, the more formally trained rabbis added others. Those who were steeped in the "Science of Judaism" continued their scholarly researches here; some of the most notable monuments of nineteenth century Jewish learning were produced or completed in this country. The controversy over Reform stimulated the creation of important works on theology—and indeed polemical sermons were constantly heard in the nineteenth century American Synagogue.

It was a rabbi who initiated the effort—still unrealized—to weld American Jewry into a coherent, unified organization. Isaac M. Wise, significantly, made this attempt in terms of a union of congregations. His original intent, to unite all synagogues, of whatever ideological tendency, into a single national body, could not be realized. But he did finally create a union, even though it was made up only of reform congregations. Having established this constituency, he was able to found the first viable rabbinical seminary in this hemisphere, and later the Central Conference of American Rabbis.

The influence of these agencies, however, extended far beyond the limits of the reform movement. They served both as stimulus and pattern for the parallel institutions of the conservative and orthodox groups. And they paved the way for later Jewish undertakings on a national scale.

II

As American Jewish life has grown more complex, the functions of the rabbi have become increasingly varied. Some activities have been eliminated or reduced. Many rabbis used to edit (or at least regularly contribute to) Anglo-Jewish weeklies; today few of them engage in journalism outside their own congregational bulletins. In planning the curriculum of his religious school, the rabbi now can draw on a large store of existing materials, as well as on the assistance of local and national educational agencies with trained personnel; he does not have to create program and text books *de novo.*

Preaching is still a major task; but its relative importance seems to have diminished. The silver tongued orator in the pulpit is now a comparative rarity. The rabbi is expected to be a competent preacher, but this alone will no longer suffice. A greater part of the rabbi's task must be accomplished through direct dealings with people—through pastoral service and counselling on the one hand, and on the other by the organization, leadership, and administration of the varied interest groups that have multiplied in almost every synagogue.

The character of his mission to the non-Jewish world has also changed. The rabbi was once an important Jewish community resource simply because he had a college degree and could speak grammatical English. But today we have plenty of "representative Jewish citizens," to say nothing of professional and semi-professional public relations workers, armed with manuals and directives from their national offices. Yet in the long run these functionaries cannot dispense with the help of the rabbis. To most Christians, the Jews are a religious group: cooperation between Jews and Christians means cooperation between "churches." In all such matters, above all in the delicate discussions about religion in public education and related problems, the Christian group is represented by its clergy, who must be met by their "opposite numbers" in the synagogue.

Rarely today need a rabbi go out to collect small sums for a family in distress. Philanthropy has been professionalized; fund raising is conducted on a vaster scale. But the existence of Community Chests and Welfare Funds with paid staffs of their own has not released the rabbi from the task of intensive campaigning. Often, he must also assume personal responsibility for causes which cannot be included in the over-all appeals—notably the support of the national religious agencies, and of various scholarly and cultural enterprises. He must frequently spearhead financial efforts for his own congregation, especially when a building program is under way.

As for participation in the social, political, cultural, and philanthropic affairs of the local community, Jewish and general, and in the regional and national programs of the rabbinical, congregational, Zionist, defense, and fund-raising agencies—there is just no limit except that of the rabbi's time and stamina, and occasionally the demand of the congregation that he give their needs more attention.

No rabbi performs all the functions that conceivably fall within the purview of his office. Each rabbi presents an individual pattern, not only as regards the activities he includes in his schedule, but also as regards the proportion of time and energy devoted to them.

The pattern is determined in part by circumstances: the size, character, and age of the congregation; the physical facilities of the synagogue building and the amount of professional assistance made available to the rabbi; the length of time he has served in the congregation; the size, geographical location, and temper of the general community. But the rabbi's individual tastes, talents, and standards are also an important factor. One man will slave for days over every pulpit address; another will attach greater importance, and therefore devote a larger slice of his time, to visiting in the homes of his congregants; a third will take naturally to community enterprise.

There is a clear, though still not very extensive trend toward specialization. Some rabbis, well past the young assistant stage, are devoting themselves primarily to educational work in the synagogue. Some have fitted themselves to do personal counseling on a relatively expert level. Others are making a career of civilian or military chaplaincy. Some seventy-odd are serving student needs through the Hillel Foundation.

Naturally, a good many rabbis have been drawn from the ministry into teaching and administrative tasks. The seminary faculties include men who, though ordained, have prepared themselves from the start for academic careers, and others who came to their present posts after service in the pulpit. (Of course, a number of active rabbis also teach courses in seminaries, and in universities.) Rabbis hold the major administrative positions in the national religious organizations. Most of the "secular" Jewish agencies also have rabbis on their staffs, in responsible positions, but rarely in the top policy-making echelons.

III

Rabbis do not necessarily work harder than other professional men, but they have to do more different kinds of work than other professionally trained specialists. Though everyone who holds a responsible position in these days is driven by the pressures and the rapid tempo of the age, the Rabbi suffers in particular by the dissipation of his energies into an endless variety of tasks. Some functions, we have seen, tend to fade out; but new challenges constantly arise. There is currently a demand for rabbis who will make effective television personalities.

But perhaps the era of confusion about rabbinical functions is now at its peak, and the process of clarification will soon begin. One reason for the present situation is that we simply do not have enough rabbis—and that, in turn, because we do not have enough congregations. Vast numbers of Jews in the large cities are not affiliated with any synagogue, but they are part of the Rabbi's responsibility. He must marry and bury them, and if he will lend himself to it, "unveil" their tombstones. They do not hesitate to burden him with their personal problems, and they benefit by his service to the Jewish and the general community. If the majority of American Jews were synagogue members, the number of Rabbis could be correspondingly increased; the local and national community tasks could be more widely distributed, and the burden on the individual rabbi reduced. This despite the fact that some rabbis will always be more in demand because of their ability and willingness to serve.

The establishment of many new congregations throughout the country has cheered Jewish leaders for many reasons, and from the special viewpoint of this study, it is likewise an encouraging sign. The rabbis of the young congregations are today preoccupied with the enormous task of pioneering in their respective localities. But as these rapidly burgeoning synagogues attain more stability, their spiritual leaders will be able to devote a larger share of time to other than parochial matters.

In the smaller communities, too, where little numerical expansion can be expected, we may nevertheless hope for a more reasonable setup than prevails at present. The Jewish lay group, now largely college educated, will become increasingly competent to take part in areas of community life other than fund raising and business administration. The rabbi will then perhaps be freer to concentrate on the areas of his special competence, while the laymen will benefit by more significant and creative participation in affairs of cultural and spiritual import. Everywhere young adults are displaying a new interest in Jewish education, especially in preparing themselves to do a better job as Jewish parents. It is not quixotic to expect that in the next generation the rabbi will be less of a surrogate for his people, living a Jewish life on their behalf, and more of a guide and "resource person," helping them to live Jewishly for themselves.


IV


But the rabbi has another problem which is peculiarly his own. Though the present multiplicity of his duties has come about largely through the initiative of rabbis themselves, he is still keenly aware that traditionally the rabbi's business was scholarship. This is the source of an inner conflict.

It begins while he is at the seminary or yeshivah. All these institutions concentrate on the teaching of Jewish sources in the original Hebrew and Aramaic. Such studies as homiletics and public speaking, pedagogy, social service, "human relations," and practical theology receive a lesser amount of time, though it seems to be gradually increasing. Many students, already university graduates, are impatient of the extended academic disciplines, whose value for the work of the ministry is not always apparent, and cry for a more practical training. Some rabbis in the pulpit continue to complain that the seminary curriculum did not prepare them adequately for the job they had to undertake after ordination; and some laymen take the same attitude.

The argument for the traditional course of studies is not difficult to present. In what will the professional distinctiveness and moral authority of the rabbi consist, if he does not have a command of authentic Jewish knowledge? Again it may be doubted whether "human relations" can be adequately learned in the class room or anywhere else except in the school of experience. The rabbi, moreover, is compelled by urgent need to master the practical techniques of his craft; but he is not likely ever to learn "Torah" unless he has acquired a sound foundation in Hebraic studies prior to ordination.

The argument, which continues without showing signs of approaching a resolution, is not just a conflict between practicing rabbis and cloistered professors. The struggle goes on within the hearts of many busy rabbis. The same man who in his seminary days complained that his studies were insufficiently "functional" may later find himself homesick for academic pursuits. A high percentage of rabbis undertake advanced studies while holding full time pulpits. A surprising number possess masters' or doctors' degrees earned (often over a period of many years) in time somehow filched from their professional tasks. There must be an even larger number who enroll for courses but never complete the requirements for a graduate degree. Many others pursue substantial programs of study on their own.

American rabbis are prolific authors. The largest number of their publications fall into three groups: collections of sermons and addresses, doctoral dissertations (sometimes in semi-popularized form), and histories of various Jewish communities and congregations, often written for anniversaries. A different category includes text books and other aids for the practical ministry. But many volumes not so obviously the by-product of other activities appear from the pens of rabbis. They include learned studies, essays in theology, novels, and poetry. These writings are naturally of unequal value, but a substantial proportion of them are highly creditable.

Thus we see the rabbis struggling against severe odds to salvage something of the intellectual tradition of their past. Yet precisely at this point the inner conflict is most plain. Some of the rabbis, in their advanced studies and their publications, have turned back to the study of Jewish history and lore. Others have sought after the new insights and skills of psychology and the social sciences, in order to utilize them for the advancement of Judaism. This division of interest cuts across denominational lines. One can find orthodox rabbis immersed in sociological inquiry, and reform rabbis conducting research in Bible and Midrash.

v

Thus the rabbi may view his own profession with conflicting feelings; but these are far less complicated than the emotional reactions toward the rabbinate displayed by the laymen. Some of the most glamorous personalities in American life have been rabbis. They have been hailed as leading citizens, great orators, and popular authors. Others not so widely acclaimed by the general public receive from their own congregants an adulation little short of idolatry.

There is, however, another side. A few years ago the writer was invited to lead a discussion at a convention of the National Jewish Welfare Board, on the relation between the Synagogue and the Community Center. The subject had hardly been introduced when several individuals rose to deliver violent tirades against "the rabbis." The latter were described as self-seeking time servers, who had failed to inspire their own congregations, and were trying to wreck the Center movement because they were jealous of its success.

The reasons for this outburst were not entirely clear. Perhaps special local situations were responsible, though the emotional laymen came from several different communities. No doubt issues of community leadership were involved, as well as confusion over the proper function of the rabbi. But it is a fact, in any case, that rabbis are the objects of sometimes effusive and often deeply genuine affection—and at the same time, of suspicion and hostility. Of course, individuals react differently to rabbis as human beings; but the case is not that simple. Both the admiration and the hostility attach not only to the rabbi as man, but even more to the rabbi as rabbi. And at least occasionally, both the favorable and the antagonistic attitudes are found concomitantly in the same person.

In our informal American world, the rabbi is often on terms of close personal intimacy with his people. He calls many of them by their first names, and may permit some of them a similar familiarity. They like to feel that the rabbi is their friend, and to invite him and his wife to their homes on a purely social footing. (Incidentally, the rabbi's wife has become a public figure of considerable consequence; this striking change deserves a separate inquiry). The laymen praise a rabbi who is "regular," that is, one who shares their minor vices. But he should not be *too* regular: immoderate indulgence in these vices would shock them. Their respect for the rabbi would be destroyed by conduct they could more readily tolerate in a layman—getting drunk, for example, or appearing frequently at a race track. The rabbi should be "human," but sufficiently different from them that they can look up to him.

Though they pride themselves on their business mentality, and will (for example) try to induce a rabbi to leave another community for their pulpit by the offer of a larger salary, the laymen are bitterly upset if the outlook of the rabbi proves to be commercialistic. They want him to be a leader; yet they are troubled if he is too original and independent and does not accept the advice of "practical people." They are regretful and sometimes even resentful when their rabbi leaves them for a larger congregation; yet if he remains too long in a small or medium sized position, there may be an undercurrent of dissatisfaction despite the ties of personal loyalty and affection. For in a sense the rabbi has let them down by not being more "successful."

Occasionally the security of a rabbi is threatened by factors entirely outside his own control. With our shifting populations, the character and tone of a synagogue may change considerably in a few years. Thus the rabbi may become the symbol of contention between the "old timers" who were originally responsible for his election and the "newcomers" who are struggling for the upper hand in congregational affairs.

It must be added that these ambiguities do not work out invariably to the rabbi's disadvantage. He may be saddened by foolish and unjustified criticisms; but he often encounters touching gratitude for small personal kindnesses, out of all proportion to the service he has rendered. Sometimes it seems to him that he receives greater loyalty and appreciation than he has deserved.


VI


This confusion of emotional attitudes toward the rabbinate has thus far been a handicap in the crucial task of recruiting rabbinical students. Too few of our rabbis have emerged from a background comparable to that of the constituency they serve. Until recently, most students in American yeshivoth have been either foreign born or the sons of immigrants, and the conservative and reform seminaries have drawn a great part of their student bodies from orthodox homes. In their formative years they were influenced by the old tradition of reverence for scholarship, and experienced little of the conflicting emotional reactions we have described. Most of them came from the lower income group. To the congregation likewise they were in a sense "outsiders," however they might be respected and loved.

On the other hand, those families longest established in America and most prominent for wealth, public spirit, and general culture, have produced distinguished attorneys, physicians, authors, artists, and public servants, but few or no rabbis. Rarely has the son of an American synagogue trustee undertaken to fit himself for professional religious leadership. The writer knows of a number of young men from such backgrounds who were attracted to the rabbinic calling; but they were usually discouraged by the apathetic response, if not the overt opposition of their families, from entering a profession in which "you have to please everybody." This, even though the family in question might be the loyal congregants and warm friends of their own rabbi.

Such a situation is not a complete novelty. "Be heedful of the sons of the poor," says the Talmud, "for from them the Torah goes forth." And it is an old story that the poor but brilliant yeshivah *Bachur* might marry into a family of wealth and prominence. No one (least of all the present writer, himself the child of poor folks) wants to impose snobbish restrictions on candidates for the rabbinate. But the present ambiguity in the status of the Rabbi *vis-à-vis* his congregation will not be resolved until a substantial proportion of the future spiritual leadership will emerge from the families of the congregation.

At present, a growing number of young men from conservative and reform backgrounds are entering the seminaries of their respective denominations; and no doubt the Hebrew day-schools, which are predominantly orthodox, will provide a continuing supply of candidates for the traditional institutions. Many sons of rabbis have chosen to follow their fathers' calling. This has little to do with the old custom by which rabbinic dynasties propagated themselves without much concern for the needs or wishes of the individual. It means that young men, who have been able to observe the frustrations and compensations of the rabbinate from the special vantage point of the rabbi's own home, have made a free decision to enter this fascinating, though at times exasperating field.

These encouraging signs, however, are not a guarantee that American Jewry will have adequate spiritual leadership. Our requirements are heavy, as regards both the number of rabbis and their quality. Scientific and technical studies have attracted many of our ablest students; it will be no small task to make the humanities—not to say, the spiritualities—significant and vivid to a sufficient number of our best young men.

VII

It is evident that rabbis will have to continue to labor at the problem of the nature and scope of their profession. Yet they will hardly be able to find a satisfactory solution without help from the members of their congregations. Most American rabbis are able to enter the world of their congregants; they share the interest, activities, and diversions of their people. But the American Jewish layman is wary about entering the rabbi's world. "Inspire me and uplift me," he seems to say, "but don't try to change me." Thus it can come about that a man can qualify as a trustee or officer of a synagogue on the basis of his business ability, though he may have no knowledge or appreciation of the basic facts and values of Jewish religious life.

There are almost always exceptions—laymen who possess the appreciation, and sometimes the knowledge as well—and they are an enormous help and comfort to the rabbi. We have al-

ready shown that there is reason to hope that men and women of
this type will be less of an exception in days to come. A truly
fruitful era can begin when the rabbi no longer has to stimulate
a demand for what he has to offer, and can devote himself
chiefly to satisfying a felt need. Such a situation is still in the
future, though perhaps not an indefinitely remote future.

Our examination of the subject has dealt with only a few of
its aspects, and even these have not been treated thoroughly. Yet
out of the confusion, one may bring together a few solid affirma-
tions.

What are the basic functions of the American Rabbi? He must
be the teacher and interpreter of Judaism to his people. To this
end he must have a comprehensive knowledge of Judaism in all
its historic manifestations, together with an understanding of the
needs and the temper of our time. He must present the message
of the ages in the light of the perplexities and tensions of the
age. Interpretation, however, does not mean accommodation.
Though Judaism has had a remarkable power to adapt itself to
changing social and intellectual circumstances, there are times
when it cannot make peace with prevailing fashions of conduct
and thought. In such situations, the rabbi must maintain the authentic Jewish position with clear-minded courage.

To this function the rabbi must bring the gift of a religious
personality. This has little to do with the engaging externals, the
ready charm, to which in our day the term *personality* is so
often applied. Still less does it mean the adoption of a "clerical"
appearance or style. A religious personality can hardly be cultivated deliberately, yet it is as unmistakable and pervasive as a
perfume. It includes at least three elements—sincerity of purpose,
genuine concern for human beings, and commitment to unseen
realities and values. Moses, we are told, was not aware that his
face shone; but in those days, before "public relations" had been
invented, no one had told him that he must "sell himself" to the
children of Israel. The lack of time and tranquillity for cultivating the devotional life makes the acquisition of religious personality doubly hard today; yet people almost always sense and respond to such a personality when it manifests itself.

They respond, above all, when the rabbi meets the third basic requirement—that he be a friend to his people. He must share in their interests and concerns, so that he can be their companion in joy, their counselor in perplexity, and their support in crisis and sorrow. It is not necessary (and probably not desirable) for him to assume the role of psychological therapist, even though the new insights into human behavior can be very helpful to him. His job is not to correct emotional disturbances any more than it is to cure physical ailments; but both the physically and the emotionally sick can benefit greatly by the warmth of his friendliness and by the faith he seeks to enkindle. At the same time, the rabbi must avoid another pitfall. While making himself available to his people, he cannot afford to dissipate his time and energy in social engagements. He must teach his congregants the difference between a boon companion and a true friend.

These basic functions are easy to state: to perform them requires such a diversity of talents that one may well doubt that any individual will possess them all. Happily, in the Rabbinate as in other professions, we can get along with something less than ideal perfection. Some men will excel in one aspect of the Rabbinic role, some in another. The accomplishments of the present, however fragmentary, are an earnest of far greater possibilities as the American Jewish community matures. Our rabbis, contemporary representatives of a great and distinguished line, face an opportunity both challenging and heartening.

# The Past

# Is

# Prelude

## ROBERT GORDIS

The present volume has sought to analyze the various facets of Jewish life in America with candor, yet with sympathy. This survey was not intended to be all-embracing; many strands in the multicolored pattern of Jewish self-expression, both individual and collective, have not been discussed. One volume cannot treat of Jewish life in its entirety, which runs the gamut from Jewish cooking at one extreme, to the lavish Jewish country clubs at the other—and rarely is the former to be found in the latter!

The solid practical achievements of American Jewry lie largely outside the scope of this volume, yet they are not to be lightly dismissed. American Jewry has given our people and the world a spectacle of philanthropy unparalleled in history. It is not merely that Jews have had a tradition of *Tsedakah* in the past; it is a way of life for them in the present. American Jews, with prodigal generosity, have poured out their substance for their brothers, far beyond any other segment of the American people. They have distributed millions for the emigration, rehabilitation and reëstablishment of the victims of persecution, for the defense of civil rights for Jews the world over, and for the defense and buttressing of the State of Israel, while at the same time creating a magnificent network of social service agencies at home in America.

The basic concern of this volume, however, has been the realm of the Jewish spirit, in the varied American embodiments of the rich cultural and religious heritage of Israel. It is clear that in this area, American Jewry has not yet matured, in spite of the creditable achievements chronicled in these pages.

All the past, however, is prelude. What of the future? A long time ago the Talmud warned that since the destruction of the Temple, prophecy was handed over to fools. The only relatively firm basis for prognosticating the future lies in correctly assessing the past. There has been no dearth of observers who have compared the American Jewish community with other "modern" communities in Western and Central Europe, in which assimilation led to virtual extinction. As they see it, American Jewry is following the same path of retrogression.

What they have failed to note is the unique character of the American Jewish community. It represents something new in Jewish experience. Its structure reproduces neither the inner qualities of East European Jewry, from which most of its human materials have been drawn, nor the characteristic traits of the Western communities, which resemble it externally and with which it is often erroneously compared. Actually, American Jewry is a *novum,* a "mutation," an amalgamation of both types of community, yet different from both. Though all the details cannot be spelled out here, the fundamental distinction may be set forth briefly. While American Jewry resembles the Western communities in its modernity and in the large measure of its assimilation to the majority culture, it differs by being infinitely larger, both absolutely and relatively. The Jews in Germany, the largest Jewish community in the West in modern times, totalled only 1% of the national population, and never exceeded the figure of some 600,000. In the United States, American Jewry, numbering over five million, represents four percent of the general population.

This is only one aspect of the matter. American Jewry possesses a sense of freedom and "at-home-ness" in its country which the

Jews of Western Europe scarcely ever felt. Anti-Semitism is by no means absent in America, but it is a far cry from the organized political Jew-hatred, the unabashed religious bigotry and the shameless academic discrimination practiced in Central and Western Europe for a century and a half. The Damascus Affair, the Mortara Case, the Tisza-Ezlar blood-accusation and the Dreyfus Affair were the acute manifestations of the fatal disease of anti-Semitism. The chronic phases of the malady are represented by the anti-Jewish agitation of Drumont in France and Stöcker in Germany, decades before the rise of Nazism.

The relative weakness of anti-Semitism in America, its total lack of respectability in the American scheme of things, is not a matter of personal benevolence, though the innate decency and the sense of fair play of the American people are undoubtedly tangible assets. In this land, the diversity of the population, ethnically, religiously and culturally, makes possible for the Jew a sense of belonging which he was never able to develop in the far more homogeneous population-structure of Germany, France or Italy. One has only to recall the various religious affiliations and ethnic strains represented in Presidents Hoover, Roosevelt, Truman and Eisenhower, to understand why American Jews find it easy to regard themselves and, in turn, are regarded as free and equal citizens, without being led thereby to deny or undervalue their Jewish relationships. In all these respects, the structure of American Jewry does not resemble that of Western European Jewry and therefore its destiny need not necessarily recapitulate theirs.

The most important trait in which American Jewry differs from these Old World communities lies in the tremendous sense of Jewish vitality, which has created a mass of organizational activity without parallel in Jewish historical experience. With relatively few exceptions, American Jews have a sense of belonging to the Jewish group and take pride in that relationship. Undoubtedly they have not developed the rich pattern of Jewish living which is part of their legacy from East European Jewry, but they have retained much of its warm sense of Jewish identification. The compact masses from Eastern Europe who constitute the base upon which American Jewry has developed, did more than contribute large numbers of men and women to the new community. They transmitted to their American offspring a deep loyalty and a strong desire for Jewish survival, which continues to beat powerfully in the hearts of their descendants. This Jewish pride was tremendously stimulated by the creation of the State of Israel, which revealed unsuspected capacities for courage and creativity among modern Jews.

Another, more general, factor also bears upon our effort to forecast the future. In America, organized religion enjoys a position of confidence, respect and influence which it did not command in Western Europe. Precisely because of the separation of Church and State in America, there is no strong anti-clerical movement in this country, as was the case in Europe. The Jewish community may be plagued by religious indifference and ignorance, but there are few organized groups that are dedicated to fighting religion in general or Judaism in particular. Religion is intellectually respectable in America. As older Jewish neighborhoods have dissolved and new residential areas arisen, it has been a heartening sight to see new Jewish religious and community institutions and organizations come into being, headed by second- and third-generation American Jews.

This Jewish loyalty is the heritage of American Jewry from Eastern Europe; the divergences are, of course, even more palpable. American Jewry is free from the permanent insecurity and sense of terror which characterized the life of European Jews. Moreover, American Jews do not find themselves a "cultural oasis" in a virtual desert of illiteracy and ignorance, as was the lot of the vast majority of East European Jews living in the Russian Pale of Settlement and the adjoining territory. This situation creates a challenge; it may well prove a spur to creative achievement.

In sum, American Jewry is a new experiment, never tried before in the cosmic laboratory which is the history of Israel. Hence anything may happen! Because of the size, strength and loyalty of American Jewry, it may prove possible to build here a rich and enduring Jewish life within an atmosphere of freedom, marked by close integration with the rest of the American nation. No one can tell for certain if American Jewry is moving toward the valley of destruction or to the gateway of hope.

A half century ago, the Hebrew thinker Ahad Ha'am described the Jews of the West as living in a condition of *abduth bethokh heruth*, "spiritual slavery within the context of political and economic freedom." On the other hand, East European Jewry, Ahad Ha'am believed, lived in a state of *heruth bethokh abduth*, "spiritual liberty in a condition of political and economic enslavement." One may venture to believe that for a sizable minority of American Jews at least, it may be possible to achieve a status of *heruth bethokh heruth*, "inner freedom within the context of external liberty."

There are those who condemn American Jewry because it shows little signs of rivalling, in its creative achievements, the Jews of ancient Palestine or Babylonia, medieval Spain, or Eastern Europe in modern times. That it will not be a replica of any of these great communities is self-evident. Whether it will prove a worthy successor lies in the lap of the unborn future. If it does, it will be because of its own unique contribution, not its success in imitating its predecessors.

The only fruitful path for American Jewry lies in adopting a more modest goal. The Hasidic teacher Reb Zisha once said: "When I die and come up before the Heavenly Court, I am not worried lest I be asked, 'Zisha, why weren't you Rabbi Akiba or the Baal Shem Tov? Why didn't you attain their learning and their piety?' Those questions won't worry me. What worries me is another question. What shall I answer when I am asked, 'Zisha, why weren't you Zisha'?"

Similarly, the question facing American Jewry is not whether we have reached the level of the Jewries of the past. What should concern us is whether we shall fulfill the promise which our own great country has afforded us, whether we shall utilize to the full the privileges of America's freedom.

Pose this question and it cannot be denied that there is much cause for concern and honest soul-searching in America. It is not that American Jewry today is worse than its ancestors. It is better educated than were its predecessors fifty years ago. It is much more conscious of its worldwide Jewish obligations. It is far better organized and boasts of scores of valuable institutions, such as did not exist a half century ago. In many respects the present generation has improved upon its progenitors. All this is something, but it is not enough.

If American Jewry today shows too many examples of lack of Jewish self-respect and moral courage, it is no accident. Self-respect does not flourish in a vacuum; courage is not born full-grown, like Athene from the brow of Zeus. Self-respect is the child of knowledge; courage is the offspring of loyalty. Both can be found in the one unfailing elixir of Jewish life, which is Torah, a concept at once untranslatable and measureless.

Therein lies the distinctiveness of the Jewish tradition. It is the essential genius of Judaism that it takes the totality of life for its province. For the Jewish tradition, scholarship and learning, law and literature, music and art, civic defense and public service, social justice and philanthropy, love of country and of humanity, all are part of Torah, because Torah is the lore and the law, the learning and the living of the Jew.

If the Torah comes alive for modern Jews, they will find the source for the loyalty they seek for themselves and their children. Through the Torah they can recapture the self-respect and the courage they need in facing their problems. They will then be worthy of their ancient prophetic tradition and be prepared to speak and act on behalf of justice and liberty, even if there is a price to pay in pain, misunderstanding and sacrifice. Not the life or death of American Jewry lies in our hands, but something more significant, its flowering or degeneracy.

Both those who have faith in the Guardian of Israel and those who put their trust in the limitless resources of the Jewish soul may look to the future with a measure of hope, modest, yet deeply rooted. There are grounds for believing that American Jewry has its future before it and not behind it and that its children can attain a creative and meaningful Jewish life here in America. And what is more, the instruments for translating that faith into reality are at hand.

# Notes on the
# Authors

CHARLES ANGOFF, well-known novelist, teaches literature at Hunter College and New York University. His novel *In the Morning Light* won the Harry and Ethel Daroff Award in Fiction of the Jewish Book Council of America. *The Sun at Noon,* the second installment of a fictional trilogy, appeared in the fall of 1954.

BERNARD J. BAMBERGER is Rabbi of the West End Synagogue of New York and former President of the Synagogue Council of America. He is the author of *Proselytism in the Talmudic Period* and *Fallen Angels.*

SAMUEL S. COHON is Professor of Theology at the Hebrew Union College–Jewish Institute of Religion in Cincinnati. He is the author of *What We Jews Believe, Judaism: A Way of Life,* and other studies in Judaism. He edited the Theology Section of the *Universal Jewish Encyclopedia.*

ABRAHAM G. DUKER is presently at work on a history of American Zionism. He teaches Jewish history at the Hebrew Union School of Education and Columbia University and is the author of *Jewish Community Relations* and other publications.

SOLOMON B. FREEHOF is Rabbi of Congregation Rodef Sholom, Pittsburgh. He is the author of *Reform Jewish Practice* (two volumes), *Preface to Scripture, Commentary on the Book of Psalms,* and other works. His most recent volume is *The Responsa Literature.* He is a former President of the Central

Conference of American Rabbis, and served at one time as a member of the faculty of the Hebrew Union College.

THEODORE FRIEDMAN, formerly Chairman of the Committee on Jewish Law and Standards of the Rabbinical Assembly of America, is editor of an anthology, *What is Conservative Judaism?* He is Rabbi of Congregation Beth El of the Oranges and Maplewood, N. J., and Managing Editor of *Judaism.*

WILLIAM B. FURIE is a member of the National Council of Jewish Education and was formerly associated with the Bureau of Jewish Education in Boston. He is presently serving as Educational Director of Congregation Beth El of Baltimore.

ROBERT GORDIS is Associate Professor of Bible at the Jewish Theological Seminary, Adjunct Professor of Religion at Columbia University, and served as Visiting Professor of Old Testament at the Union Theological Seminary. He is the author of *Koheleth: The Man and His World* and a recent volume, *Judaism for the Modern Age.* He is Rabbi of Temple Beth El, Rockaway Park, N. Y., and Editor of *Judaism.*

JACOB KABAKOFF was ordained by the Jewish Theological Seminary, and is Dean of the Cleveland Institute of Jewish Studies. He was a member of the Editorial Staff of the *Encyclopaedia Hebraica,* currently being published in Jerusalem. Presently, he is Hebrew book editor of *In Jewish Bookland.*

STEPHEN S. KAYSER is Associate Professor of the History of Jewish Art at the Jewish Theological Seminary and Curator and Director of Exhibits of the Jewish Museum. Among his recent papers are "A Polish Torah Crown," "Defining Jewish Art," and "Art in the Synagogue." He is the editor of a recently published (1955) volume entitled *Jewish Ceremonial Art.*

MORRIS N. KERTZER is Director of Interreligious Activities of the American Jewish Committee. He was ordained by the Jewish Theological Seminary. He is the author of *What Is a Jew?*

ABRAHAM MENES, an historian, is co-editor of the Yiddish monthly *Zukunft* and the *General Encyclopaedia* (in Yiddish) and the *Jewish People, Past and Present*. He has written in the field of biblical history, and is a frequent contributor to the Yiddish periodical press.

NOCHUM B. MINKOFF, Yiddish poet and critic, is a member of the faculty of the New School for Social Research, where he teaches Yiddish literature. He is Editor of *Zukunft*.

EMANUEL RACKMAN is Assistant Professor in the Department of Political Science of the Yeshiva University. He is Rabbi of Congregation Shaaray Tefila of Far Rockaway, N. Y. His book *Israel's Emerging Constitution* was published in the spring of 1955.

HAROLD M. SCHULWEIS is Rabbi of Temple Beth Abraham, Oakland, California. Formerly an Instructor of Philosophy at the College of the City of New York, he has contributed to the *Review of Religion, The Personalist,* and the *Reconstructionist*. He is co-author of the volume *Approaches to the Philosophy of Religion*.

C. BEZALEL SHERMAN is a sociologist and Managing Editor of the *History of the Jewish Labor Movement,* to be published soon by YIVO. He is also co-editor of the *Yiddisher Kemfer*.

HUGO D. WEISGALL is a composer and conductor. He is Chairman of the Faculty of the Seminary College of Music and the Cantors Institute of the Jewish Theological Seminary of America. He was recently awarded a grant by the National Institute of Arts and Letters in recognition of his achievements in the field of operatic composition.

# Index

tinue to maintain itself without the concept of peoplehood, or with a concept of Jewish peoplehood so limited as to preclude direct, individual and communal relations with Israel Jewry. Without Jewish culture patterns along folk lines, without a strong ingredient of Hebraic civilization in the face of the continued American and Christian acculturation and Jewish deculturation, Jewish survival in America becomes highly problematical. To such survival, Zionism as an idea and a movement has a great deal to contribute. It will have to change its methods, it will have to re-evaluate and reassess its position. It will have to become a movement of criticism and of protest. It will have to struggle for the equality of Jewish group life, Judaism and Jewish culture in American society against emancipationist delusions much as it has done in other places and other times. It will have to fight for its place in the American Jewish community, even in institutions it helped to create. This is a difficult task. The best we can hope for is that the future of survivalist American Jewry will not belie its Zionist past.

# The American
# Rabbi:
# His
# Changing
# Role

BERNARD J. BAMBERGER

The American rabbi is a novel and unique phenomenon in Jewish experience. His office is related to the earlier forms of Jewish leadership by
a tie of historic continuity; yet the modern rabbinate presents so
radical a change both in function and temper as to constitute a
virtually new profession.

This statement applies to orthodox, conservative, and reform
rabbis alike. The content of their message may differ substantially, but the character, methods, and problems of their professional life are much the same. An effort is now being made to
establish a professional journal for the three rabbinical groups
under the sponsorship of the Synagogue Council of America.
Whether or not this attempt is successful, it strikingly illustrates
three facts: that the American rabbinate has new and distinctive
functions; that rabbis are eager to learn more about the tech-

creasing influence of the Catholic Church. Those who see this
process of reidentification as purely American in causation need
to be reminded that synagogue affiliation, promising though it is
for a thriving Jewish life, does not always strengthen the individual's own Jewish life or the religious expression of the Jewish
community. The criteria for these developments in Judaism go
beyond congregational membership and occasional synagogue
attendance.

The three hundred years of Jewish life in America have
been three hundred years of restorationist sentiment among
Jews. Research may reveal the existence of Christian restorationist sentiment in North America even before the official arrival of
the Jews on this continent. *Meshulachim* (emissaries from the
Holy Land) from Israel appeared here in Colonial times. Proposals of political Zionism date back as far as the beginnings of
the 19th century, if not earlier. American Jewry has been a
mainstay of world Zionism, but, as we see it, it has also been
greatly enriched by the fructifying influence of the Zionist movement. It is not the writer's task to draw up a plan for Zionist
activities for the future on the basis of its shortcomings in the
past. The failures of American Zionism are readily enumerated.
It has failed to create a *halutziyut* movement, to Hebraise Jewish life, to enter more deeply into Jewish education, particularly
on the adult level. It has tended to neglect Jewish scholarship
and the approach to the intellectuals. It has had surprisingly little impact even on the curricula of the rabbinical seminaries. It
has not created media of communications in English, such as a
national family magazine, to replace the declining Yiddish press.
It has done little to stimulate the academic field into an appreciation of the Jewish point of view in history, humanities and the
social sciences. It has shelved its interest in a democratic Jewish community, and has not had sufficient impact on Jewish
communal institutions, functionaries and community relations.
Finally, it failed to stimulate the establishment of a survivalist intellectual meeting ground or headquarters.

Nevertheless, Zionism has been a chief mainstay of Jewish life
here. It is inconceivable to me that American Jewry will con-

trends in both communities. An American rabbinical thinker has even stated that there is more religion in his congregation (typical Eastern middle class) than in all Israel. The tendency to return to the *Protestrabbiner* attitude is also illustrated by the statement of an English rabbi who equates assimilation with the waning of the definition of Judaism as a religion. He equates the diminishing popularity of the definition with a decline of religion. He terms Zionism, because of its nationalist secular character, an assimilationist influence in Jewish life. However, not all nationalist movements in Judaism have been secularist: Mizrachi, for example. Moreover, secularization is a world-wide phenomenon, and is not limited to the Jewish people. Despite the present emphasis on religion in the West, particularly in the United States, secularization is an ongoing process. Modern society's increasing secular character appears to be accentuated in Israel because of the relative youthfulness of its Westernized population. It has been aggravated by the failure of the religious elements in world Jewry to participate adequately either in the Zionist movement or more directly, through *halutziyut* (emigration to Israel).

American Jewry has also been undergoing a similar process of increasing secularization. This process is less marked among the remnants of ideological secularists groups, such as Yiddishists, than it is among native American Jews, as seen in the latter's continued abandonment of religious observances and the weakening of its culture patterns. However, the current reidentification and affiliation tendency is a promising phenomenon. It has been termed a miracle. Actually it is a result of a concatenation of historical events and social tendencies: namely, the Hitler catastrophe, the struggle involved around the establishment of Israel, the impact of the Jewish State, the increasing distance of the majority of American Jews from the immigrant generation, their growing middle-class character, the movement to the suburbs and new housing areas, the current emphasis on religious affiliation as a prime factor in respectability and normalcy in American society (particularly under the impact of the struggle against Communism), the "New Conservatism," and the in-